I0128430

TRADITION
and the Deliberative Turn

TRADITION
and the Deliberative Turn

A Critique of Contemporary Democratic Theory

RYAN R. HOLSTON

SUNY
PRESS

Cover image of Gustav Adolph Spangenberg, *Die Schule des Aristotles (Aristotle's School)*, Fresko 1883–1888 (from Wikipedia).

Published by State University of New York Press, Albany

© 2023 State University of New York

All rights reserved

Printed in the United States of America

No part of this book may be used or reproduced in any manner whatsoever without written permission. No part of this book may be stored in a retrieval system or transmitted in any form or by any means including electronic, electrostatic, magnetic tape, mechanical, photocopying, recording, or otherwise without the prior permission in writing of the publisher.

For information, contact State University of New York Press, Albany, NY
www.sunypress.edu

Library of Congress Cataloging-in-Publication Data

Name: Holston, Ryan R., author.
Title: Tradition and the deliberative turn : a critique of contemporary democratic theory / Ryan R. Holston.
Description: Albany : State University of New York Press, [2023] | Includes bibliographical references and index.
Identifiers: ISBN 9781438492094 (hardcover : alk. paper) | ISBN 9781438492100 (ebook) | ISBN 9781438492087 (pbk. : alk. paper)
Further information is available at the Library of Congress.

10 9 8 7 6 5 4 3 2 1

For Amy

Contents

Acknowledgments

This book contributes to an ongoing dialogue within contemporary political theory, but it would not have emerged without a number of smaller, more intimate conversations among interlocutors who helped inform my thinking on its subject matter. Steve Knepper has been a constant source of thoughtful advice and feedback and has been incredibly generous with his time, for which I am grateful. He read every chapter of this manuscript before its publication and provided me with his usual combination of insight, measured criticism, and encouragement. Justin Garrison and Michael Federici have also been steadfast conversation partners on matters that far exceed but certainly relate to those in the book. I am likewise grateful to them for their encouragement and for inspiring me to contemplate important questions, while being available to discuss various others as they arose. Bruce Frohnen has for many years been "on call" to answer numerous questions as well, both substantive and related to numerous professional matters—I am thankful for his unwavering support on this and other research projects. On the subject of deliberative democracy in particular, I have profited from various discussions with Emily Finley, who for several years now has been a valuable conversation partner. I wish to express my deep gratitude to Claes Ryn as well for having piqued my curiosity long ago, during my dissertation work, on the substantive questions addressed in this book. He helped me at the beginning of my intellectual development to see the world—both that which is lived concretely and in dialogue with others—through a more historical lens. My thinking will, thankfully, never be the same.

I would also like to thank Guido Parietti, a scholar whom I only briefly met but who provided me with some especially helpful feedback on chapter 3 at the 2019 annual meeting of the Northeast Political Science Association. The errors that remain here and elsewhere in the book are obviously my own. I would like to express my gratitude as well to the editors of *History of Political Thought* for the permission to republish chapter 4, a version of which appeared as an article entitled "Two Concepts of Prejudice" in that journal. Finally, the Center for the Study of Statesmanship at the Catholic University of America supported the completion of this work through a Faculty Research Fellowship, for which I am extremely appreciative.

Most importantly, my wife, Amy, has been an endless source of love and encouragement in the throes of researching and writing this book. She is my rock, and it goes without saying that this would not have been completed without her faithful support.

Introduction

Deliberation's Wake

Over the last several decades, contemporary democratic theory has found itself in the wake of what political theorist John Dryzek once referred to as a "deliberative turn."[1] Indeed, it would be difficult to identify a single subject or theoretical orientation over the course of this period that has been the focus of greater elaboration or scrutiny than the theory known as "deliberative democracy." Writing nearly two decades after his initial declaration, Dryzek was able to claim even more confidently that "deliberative democracy now stands at the core of democratic theory."[2] On the cusp of what is now its fourth decade, the literature on deliberative democracy had become so voluminous that Dryzek, along with several other scholars, assembled *The Oxford Handbook of Deliberative Democracy*, a reference work cataloguing the explosion of this scholarship in political theory and related fields, such as law and numerous social sciences. Its contributions comprise just under a thousand pages from over ninety scholars at prominent institutions around the world.[3] To be sure, the centrality of deliberation to moral and political decision-making is certainly not a new concept but has ancient roots, most prominently in the thinking of Aristotle, who discusses it in the *Nicomachean Ethics* and in the *Politics*.[4] Still, the exponents of deliberative democracy approach the subject with an altogether different set of concerns, focusing not on the ethical character of citizen and regime, but on the liberal values of freedom and equality that are said to be secured among citizens when mutual appeal or persuasion is required to establish the legitimacy of laws and policies.

In contrast with earlier strains of democratic theory, which had prioritized the aggregation of individual preferences, deliberative democrats have thus asserted the normative import of citizens supporting their policy prefer-ences through a process of public reason-giving. In doing so, the argument goes, democratic societies are capable of achieving legitimacy by virtue of their having secured the consent or authorization of laws and policies by which citizens are to be governed. In other words, these scholars believe it is truer to the spirit of democracy to say that citizens must *justify* their choices to one another, rather than simply relying on institutional devices, such as the franchise, to ensure that individual preferences are given equal weight in the determination of policy outcomes. With this shift in priorities, it is worth noting, democratic theory may be said to have forsaken the intellec-tual inheritance derived from the social contract theory of Thomas Hobbes and aligned itself instead with that of Jean-Jacques Rousseau. That is to say, the utilitarian understanding of democracy as an attempt to maximize the collective interests of citizens has principally been abandoned for one that sees society's members as joining together to preserve their freedom or self-determination, insofar as all are recognized as authors of the laws that govern them. These two sides of social contract theory, one might argue, have since the eighteenth century been at odds with respect to the norma-tive purposes underpinning democracy, and the shift that has taken place over the last three decades marks a decided "turn" in the direction of such thinking toward Rousseau's priority of individual autonomy.

The present work enters the conversation regarding the importance of deliberation for contemporary democratic society, but it does so by looking at this ongoing discussion through a historical lens. That is not to say that it aims to chronicle the various twists and turns that its arguments have taken over this period from the perspective of a neutral or distanced observer.[5] Indeed, one of the first principles of the approach to be adopted is that no such neutral or detached perspective with regard to this scholarly discussion or any other is accessible to human understanding. Rather, the present study aims to offer its own assessment of the nature of political deliberation as a contribution to this ongoing dialogue that, it must be acknowledged, has a history and did not emerge ex nihilo. The approach being adopted is thus "historical," in the first instance, insofar as it views this discussion regarding deliberation itself as taking place over time, such that the various interlocutors may each be seen as responding to those who preceded them, while interpreting what was previously said in light of its application to their own historical circumstances. According to this view, one might say that any written dialogue, no matter how close together the participants are to one another historically speaking, takes place over time, such that each interlocutor inevitably carries forward a conversation that is already under way and never exists in a historical vacuum. While it is impossible to bear in one's mind the entirety of the various contributions to such a discussion, it is nonetheless instructive to read or interpret its participants in the light of the key predecessors or voices to whom they were principally responding.

In the second instance, the approach to be adopted here is "historical" in the sense that it aims to bring to bear on this conversation a sensitivity to the historical nature of deliberation in any society, insofar as citizens and government officials must be seen as flesh and blood human beings for whom the meanings expressed in their moral language are always informed by particular customs, habits, and practices. Consequently, *genuine* deliberation, which is to say, that which entails the normative "pull" or persuasiveness of those whose lives are embedded within shared, concrete ways of living, will be limited by the temporal horizons of communities of interlocutors and the way that they reason and argue. As the dialogue is enlarged beyond such communities, however, the sharing of concrete meanings necessarily diminishes, and with it the common understandings and interpretations, as well as the mutual persuasiveness or resonance of arguments.[6] Additionally, it will be contended, it is not only shared meanings that are furnished, wherever they exist, by such communities but also a willingness or inclination to deliberate the common good. The preparation for deliberation as a *practice* is again something, wherever it exists, that one learns through participation in received patterns of living and is not invented by the solitary individual out of whole cloth. In sum, the approach to be adopted may be seen as historical in both its form and its substance: it brings a historical sensibility or approach to bear vis-à-vis the existing scholarly dialogue, as well as a historical conception, substantively speaking, regarding the deliberation that takes place among citizens and public officials.

Deliberation without Limits

The central concern of what follows is that the arguments among prominent deliberative democrats regarding mutual justification promote a belief in the legitimacy of democratic societies based on an understanding of deliberation that is unrealistic to the point of being utopian. This is not, to be sure, the first time this charge has been leveled at the theory of deliberative democracy. However, the present analysis is unique in its approach for bringing to bear some of the most important insights into the nature of morality and discourse associated with the thinking of one of the twentieth century's most prominent philosophers of history, Hans-Georg Gadamer. While several political theorists and philosophers, often characterized as having a "neo-Aristotelian" orientation, have previously raised important criticisms of deliberative democracy regarding its neglect of social context and collective norms, the contention here is that such critiques have fallen short without the more penetrating insights of Gadamer into the historical nature of human experience, moral phenomena, and the role of language in understanding. Drawing on Gadamer's practical philosophy, together with his theory of interpretation known as philosophical hermeneutics, the present study aims to shed new light on how deliberative democracy first came to these idealized aspirations regarding moral and political deliberation in democratic societies, as well as the way that it has obscured such problems.[7] Furthermore, it aims to call attention to the significant costs associated with such thinking and to propose a more nuanced approach to questions relating to the importance of tradition, or concrete communities that exist over time, and the tradeoffs that we ultimately confront between meaningful or genuine deliberation, on the one hand, and the freedom of the individual subject, on the other.

What is it, more precisely, that Gadamer's historical, hermeneutical approach has to offer this ongoing conversation that previous critics have neglected and that deliberative democrats have failed to take into account in their thinking about moral and political deliberation? The central claim of the theory of deliberative democracy, which says that political legitimacy is achieved when citizens justify their positions to all other members of society, is based on an understanding of morality that fundamentally severs the latter from the historical practices from which it emerges, resulting in exceedingly optimistic assumptions regarding the possible scope or scale of the dialogue that is to take place. In other words, this severance of morality from the concrete historical contexts in which language develops through its repeated use ultimately occludes the temporal limitations that bound shared understanding, thus prompting such theories to posit deliberation on the largest of scales, that is, among hundreds of millions of radically diverse interlocutors. This abstraction or divorce of morality from the concrete human relationships to which it meaningfully refers is a characteristic of thinking about morals belonging to the Enlightenment, upon which Gadamer's philosophy sheds light. Drawing additionally on interpreters of his philosophy who emphasize the primacy of what Aristotle called *ethos* and G. W. F. Hegel called *Sittlichkeit*, the argument here is that Gadamer's thinking essentially collapses the Enlightenment's dualism between morality, right, or the good, on the one hand, and what may be called ethical substance, historical effectedness, or the existential fact, on the other. It is Gadamer's unique, historically informed account of the good, which borrows insights from the early work of Martin Heidegger into our fundamental facticity and—rather than drawing any relativistic conclusions—uses them to renew or recover our ancient metaphysical tradition, thus allowing Gadamer to show how our thinking has come to sever the moral from the historical.[8] I argue that collapsing this "metaphysical dualism" is precisely what is needed if we are to come to terms with the problem of conceiving moral dialogue as taking place among groups of interlocutors that are potentially boundless or unlimited.[9]

Conceiving of deliberation as if it were possible among the millions of individuals who comprise contemporary democratic societies, such theories essentially graft a familiarity with smaller-scale dialogue among rooted interlocutors onto a significantly larger scale, while no longer appreciating or valuing the essential preconditions that made such dialogues possible. In other words, they idealize practices such as mutual respect and forbearance, and take for granted shared understandings of fundamental values, while positing or presupposing their existence for citizens who lack the sort of background that would make sound deliberation possible. In short, such theories rely tacitly and parasitically on the fruits of traditions that acculturate citizens to living in community with one another, while simultaneously denying the latter's normative import. Of course, this problem—the problem of abstraction from the historical life—has not itself emerged from nowhere, but also has a history. On the longest of time horizons, it can be traced back to the rationalism of ancient Greek philosophy, as found in particular writings of Plato and especially the Neoplatonists. However, for the purposes of the present study, I identify a modern moment in which this tendency became explicitly heightened or intensified—that is, the attack on tradition inaugurated by Rousseau, which preceded the idealizing of autonomy found in his theory of the social contract.

What is distinctive about Rousseau's thinking about morality during an age in which not a small number of philosophers and political theorists were similarly succumbing to this old dualism is that unlike many who were contemplating moral precepts in rather abstract or *ahistorical* terms, Rousseau's conception of the just society became explicitly *anti-historical*. In other words, in the thinking of Rousseau and those such as Immanuel Kant who followed him, there was not merely a neglect of the historical nature of morality, but a self-conscious attempt to articulate what is right or just in terms that were specifically not determined by tradition or customary institutions or, in the broadest sense, by historical experience. Whether one subscribed to the elaborate narrative in Rousseau's first two discourses regarding the thoroughgoing malevolence of Western history and the institutions such as private property to which it gave birth, Rousseau's thinking was foundational for a new conceptualization of morality as an escape from determination by concrete experience and the power to exercise one's free or spontaneous will in a manner that evaded all such coercion. When Kant articulated his more systematic and rationalistic rendering of the central moral impulse in Rousseau's general will in the form of the categorical imperative, one also witnessed this hostility toward experience on prominent display. Prioritizing the free, spontaneous will thus became the central moral imperative of this "autonomy tradition," which perceived threats to individual liberty and human dignity in all such determination by the experiential realm, whether those forces were deemed malevolent or simply the accident of arbitrary historical developments.

It is this autonomy tradition and its normative priorities that have most profoundly shaped contemporary democratic theory, particularly the aim of securing a universal consensus or agreement in order to establish the justice of laws and policies. By the 1990s, there was a broad convergence in the thinking of two of the most prominent representatives of Anglo-American and Continental political philosophy. John Rawls and Jürgen Habermas, whose emphasis on "public reason"—in the former case, an existing consensus with which citizens were to justify their political positions to one another, and, in the latter case, an open-ended deliberative process aimed at securing such a consensus—were inspired by these same fundamental priorities or concerns of their Enlightenment predecessors vis-à-vis the freedom or autonomy of individual citizens. Subsequent generations of "constitutional" and "proce-dural" democrats, that is, those who emphasize settled liberal norms as a means of grounding public deliberation, or those who leave such questions open to a widely discursive public sphere, were largely inclined in one of these directions or the other. Central to both sets of concerns has been the problem of moral diversity or "the fact of pluralism," and how citizens might conceive of the laws and policies that govern them as legitimate in light of the disappearance of traditional communities with a shared ethical orientation in "modern" societies. According to this view, our recognition of the latter demands, above all, seeing discourses about just political arrange-ments in distinctively "post-metaphysical" terms, which indicates that any consensus that achieves the legitimacy of laws and policies must transcend metaphysical orientations, instead adopting "the moral point of view," a universal perspective acceptable to all citizens regardless of their particular ethical background.

Gadamer and the Enlightenment

At the center of Gadamer's life's work is a critique of Enlightenment or post-Enlightenment thinking, which he saw as the flawed or epistemologically naive outlook that exhibits what Heidegger once referred to as the "forgetfulness of being," an ideal of understanding that sees the thinking subject as a spectator to an external world, while blind or oblivious to the concrete historical life that facilitates or makes possible such thinking. Gadamer's philosophy shows that this intellectual legacy has contributed to a number of problematic dichotomies that his work seeks to collapse: "subjectivity and objectivity, ought and is, feeling and reason, authority and reason, rhetoric and reason," all of which seem to confound rather than elucidate the reality of human experience and understanding.[10] To be sure, Gadamer's relationship to the Enlightenment is hardly unequivocal, as Robert Dostal has recently made clear, particularly vis-à-vis the thinking of Kant. Yet, with respect to the ideal of "radical" or "complete" Enlightenment, in which Gadamer clearly believes Kant's philosophy participates, he is most critical, and he makes such aspirations the central target of his critique in *Truth and Method* and in much of the rest of his writing.[11] As is suggested by the range of dichotomies mentioned above, the thinkers associated with these divisions are numerous, and the further development of such intellectual frameworks is often more appropriately associated with subsequent generations of thinkers. Certainly, as Gadamer was well aware, participating in dialogue may entail carrying forward ideas that are perhaps not explicitly articulated by a given thinker, but nonetheless may be seen as an understandable application or extension of the thoughts that the individual originally expressed. This is the nature of historically effected consciousness (*Wirkungsgeschichte Bewusstsein*), according to Gadamer, whether the ideas effected by history are those that have "deceived us and held us captive" or have revealed themselves to contain true "insight."[12]

It is with this in mind, and in the spirit of seeing the present project as its own contribution to an ongoing discussion, that this work should be understood as an application or extension of Gadamer's thinking to a particular area of inquiry—the relationship of morality to dialogue—which the latter may be seen as helpfully illuminating. Consequently, this study represents neither Gadamer's comprehensive take on the Enlightenment, nor an attempt to speak for him on some particular aspect of it. Rather, it is an attempt to profit from his insights and bring them to bear vis-à-vis claims that have been made on behalf of the theory of deliberative democracy. With regard to Gadamer's writing and our interpretation of it, there can only ever be what he famously called a "fusion of horizons" of understanding between present interpreter and historical text.[13] Still, as Gadamer was also quite clear, there are good and bad interpretations, which he characterized in terms of an Aristotelian mean and its corresponding extremes. In any encounter with a text, Gadamer believes we must see ourselves in a dialogue, neither imputing heavy-handedly that which we want the text to say, so that only we "speak" and the text is rendered "silent," nor staying entirely "silent" ourselves, as when one aims at positivist exposition, so that only the text is permitted to "speak." Instead, he says, our approach to the written word must always involve an *application* to the interpreter's situation, as one finds paradigmatically with religious and legal texts, in which one asks how what was previously written may be seen as speaking to one's present circumstances.[14] It is therefore in this spirit that the present study aims to make use of Gadamer's philosophy.

Among the various dichotomies that Gadamer's work calls into question, it is the division between history and morality that will be the focus here, since this bears directly on the question of political deliberation and the possibility of consensus in a morally diverse society.[15] Here, the well-known section of *Truth and Method* entitled, "The Rehabilitation of Authority and Tradition," will be particularly relevant, as will his later work on moral reasoning, as found in *The Idea of the Good in Platonic-Aristotelian Philosophy*, along with various essays that serve to develop his practical philosophy.[16] It is in the latter essays, in particular, that Gadamer engages most explicitly and critically with the Kantian idea of practical reason and the contrast that it presents with his more historically informed, Aristotelian conception of *phronesis*. Although Gadamer participated in a famous exchange with Jürgen Habermas, who is deeply indebted to Kant's thinking about morality, this was prior to the publication of Habermas's seminal "Discourse Ethics" and his more overtly political work that followed pertaining to the idea of public reason. Consequently, Gadamer never explicitly addressed this area of Habermas's philosophy, which attained prominence, particularly among political theorists, toward the end of Gadamer's life.[17] Gadamer's articulation of the dependence of the good on *Sittlichkeit*, or the collapse that he undertakes of the dichotomy between the historical and the moral, may nevertheless be said to "speak to," or have implications for, the plausibility of cognitivist theories of morality, such as those belonging to Habermas, Rawls, and their followers.

The principal insight of Gadamer's work that may be brought to bear on such thinking is that we do not stand apart from, "looking at" morality, as if the latter were merely the words or speech that we use when engaged in moral and political deliberation. On the Gadamerian view put forth here, morality is more appropriately understood as *who we are*, which is to say, it is the person that we have become or the character that we have developed over time. What one articulates in moral language is thus deeply informed by the concrete ways of living in which we always already participate. There is never "our" morality, as if the latter were an intellectual or linguistic "thing"—a tool to be reached for when we go to deliberate with others—and thus viewed as separate from our lived, historical being. Certainly, speech is a vitally important *part of* the moral life, as Gadamer himself emphasizes, and its use can provide lucidity regarding our moral intuitions. However, it must always be kept in view that the language of morality is not morality itself. In other words, the meanings within the word (*logos*) are made possible by the concrete ethical life, which shapes and informs our speech in ways that we sometimes are aware of but often are not. Whenever persuasion happens, one calls forth through recollection (*anamnesis*) the meanings embedded in language from time out of mind, since the experience (*Erfahrung*) upon which the latter is based is not ours alone but given over to us by others, a bequest from prior generations. Our language, therefore, invokes a *sensus communis*—moral intuitions derived from historically mediated patterns of experience—whenever we are successful in persuading others or find others to be persuasive. The particularity of our historically effected consciousness, as Gadamer makes clear, must therefore be seen as the condition that at once facilitates and occludes all understanding. That is to say, it makes understanding possible, insofar as it furnishes a vantage point from which one accesses and makes sense of the world, while also precluding us from ever occupying an Archimedean position from which one might see the whole of reality.

This is the fundamental significance of Gadamer's insight into the productive nature of our prejudices (*Vorurteile*).[18] Collapsing the dualism between historical experience and morality, Gadamer thus confronts the epistemological "idol" of modernity, prejudice-free understanding, or what he derisively refers to as the "prejudice against prejudice."[19] Against this view, he argues that tradition is the essential precondition of all real understanding, which he says is not simply generated by the inertia of history but must be "affirmed, embraced, [and] cultivated."[20] Toward what end, then, are we to affirm such traditions? I believe that it is the possibility of truth that demands this affirmation of the concrete ethical life—most fundamentally, the forging of a *sensus communis* upon which we draw and through which we may achieve real understanding with regard to the good that is common between us.[21] Knowing and communicating about the good requires a knowledge thereof that, on Gadamer's account, only becomes possible *within* the ethical life (*ethos, Sittlichkeit*).

Such development of the ethical person must therefore become a normative priority, and to dismiss or neglect the latter, as has been done by contemporary democratic theory, would have significant consequences. That is to say, when the ethical life is attenuated, whether due to its explicit disparagement or simple neglect, among those things we lose is our ability to "speak" to one another. To be sure, as Gadamer makes clear, interpretation and understanding always remain a possibility, to some degree, irrespective of our sharing a particular ethical orientation. But it is undeniable that not all communication is equally successful, and that there are times, such as in contemporary American politics, when we do not really "hear" one another. There are circumstances, in other words, that are more or less conducive to genuine or authentic deliberation, which depends, at least in part, on the presence or absence of the concrete preconditions Gadamer identified as contributing to true understanding. When the normative import of this situation is denied, the prospects for its improvement are substantially diminished—ironically, in the present case, by those who make sound political deliberation the very centerpiece of their political philosophy.

Continuing the Dialogue

It is thus the utopian nature of contemporary democratic theory and the diminished normative import that it ascribes to tradition, or concrete communities that exist over time, that the present work seeks to address. I begin with a diagnosis of the source of this error, which I believe to be found in the eighteenth century thinking of Rousseau and Kant, the principal founders of the modern autonomy tradition, whose metaphysical dualism accentuated the tendency within the Western philosophical tradition to separate morality from historical experience. The first two chapters are dedicated to identifying this tendency in their respective thinking, but with a particular focus on the relationship between their ideas, rather than their demonstration of this characteristic independently of one another. Chapter 1 thus examines Rousseau's anticipations of this metaphysical dualism in Kantian moral philosophy, while chapter 2 looks at the corresponding reception or interpretation of Rousseau along these lines within the thinking of Kant. In chapter 3, I examine the continuing influence of the autonomy tradition on contemporary democratic theory, focusing specifically on the work of Habermas and Rawls. In particular, the aim of the third chapter is to show the continuation of this "divorce" of the good from history inherited from Rousseau and Kant, along with its perpetuation among subsequent generations of deliberative democrats and the utopian implications of thinking about morality in these terms. The first three chapters, therefore, are principally devoted to diagnosing the origins and modern inheritance of this problematic dichotomy among key figures within the democratic tradition of political philosophy.

In chapter 4, I begin using Gadamer's practical philosophy to demonstrate how the aforementioned dualism may be collapsed via his critique of "historical consciousness" (what he sometimes calls "naive historicism") and the way that his analysis applies not merely to the interpretation of texts but, as he says, to "all human experience of the world and human living."[22] Gadamer's "rehabilitation" of tradition, whose focus in *Truth and Method* tends to be more epistemological than practical, is then joined with his theory of moral reasoning articulated in several other key texts. Here, it is Gadamer's engagement with Aristotle and the critique of Kantian ethics that inform his philosophical position, whose insights underpin both the fourth and fifth chapters. In chapter 5, I therefore continue this discussion by presenting an alternative view of deliberation, which uses Gadamer's more historically informed understanding of morality, as derived from his reading of the Platonic-Aristotelian tradition, to reconceptualize our "use" of ethical principles, which we do not find ready-at-hand but more accurately capable of deliberating *through us*.

In the final chapter of the book, chapter 6, I situate these insights drawn from Gadamer's thinking within a somewhat broader discussion regarding philosophical anthropology and the individual's place within the social order. I argue that the autonomy tradition and its deliberative democratic progeny represent, essentially, an Aristotelian "excess" or extreme corresponding to the atomistic individualism of the Enlightenment. Only, instead of contracting the unit of analysis down to the level of the individual, the autonomy tradition expands it to encompass the whole of society. In the final portion of this chapter, I then discuss the reliance of deliberative democracy on an appeal to "modernity" in order to justify what I see as the disproportionate weight that it ascribes to individual liberty via the ideal of autonomy. This, I believe, represents an illegitimate turn in ongoing arguments regarding the competing values of individual and community. And it is here that the question of normative priorities is brought into sharpest relief. For there is ultimately no settling such fundamental questions once and for all, for our society or any other, and to do so would mean putting an end to the conversation regarding the values that are to be promoted within our political order. The latter is a dialogue that—echoing a recurring theme within Gadamer's work—must always be seen as ongoing, and, in the final analysis, I argue that such appeals to the impossibility of cultivating the ethical life in the present age represent, ironically, an undermining of the very freedom that deliberative democrats set out to advance.

Notes

1. John Dryzek, *Deliberative Democracy and Beyond: Liberals, Critics, Contestations* (New York: Oxford University Press, 2000), 1.

2. John Dryzek, "The Forum, the System, and the Polity: Three Varieties of Democratic Theory," *Political Theory* 45, no. 5 (2017), 610.

3. André Bachtiger, John S. Dryzek, Jane Mansbridge, and Mark E. Warren, eds., *The Oxford Handbook of Deliberative Democracy* (New York: Oxford University Press, 2018).

4. See Aristotle, *Nicomachean Ethics*, trans. David Ross (New York: Oxford University Press, 2009), 41–46 (1112–1113) and *Politics*, trans. Carnes Lord (Chicago: University of Chicago Press, 2013), 225, 345–47 (1281b, 1298a). For an analysis that places the idea of deliberation in Aristotle's *Politics* in a conversation with contemporary deliberative democrats see James Lindley Wilson, "Deliberation, Democracy, and the Rule of Reason in Aristotle's *Politics*," *American Political Science Review* 105, no. 2 (2011): 259–74.

5. Or, as several recent commentators have described these developments, as if to underscore this complexity, the "turns within the turn." Marta Poblet, Pompeau Casanovas, and Víctor Rodríguez-Doncel, *Deliberative and Epistemic Approaches to Democracy* (Cham, Switzerland: Palgrave Macmillan, 2020), 29.

6. The emphasis here is on "diminishes." That is to say, as a dialogue is extended beyond one's community and its *sensus communis*, meanings begin to

change, making mutual understanding more difficult, though never so absolutely as to become incomprehensible. According to Hans-Georg Gadamer, whose thinking is central to the current project, mediation or translation between horizons of understanding always remains a possibility. Hans-Georg Gadamer, *Truth and Method*, trans. Joel Weinsheimer and Donald G. Marshall, 2nd rev. ed. (New York: Continuum, 2004), 444. Still, given the dependence of *logos* (word) upon *ergon* (deed), differences in concrete human practices or ways of living would have to be reflected in or correspond to differences in the uses and meanings of language. For the importance of the relationship between *logos* and *ergon* to Gadamer's thinking, see P. Christopher Smith, *Hermeneutics and Human Finitude: Toward a Theory of Ethical Understanding* (New York: Fordham University Press, 1991), 244–57.

7. To be sure, this is not the first occasion on which Gadamer's thinking has been used to address the issues raised by theories of deliberative democracy. See Darren Walhof, *The Democratic Theory of Hans-Georg Gadamer* (Cham, Switzerland: Palgrave Macmillan, 2017), esp. ch. 3. However, Walhof's work is ultimately more sympathetic than the present study to the theory of deliberative democracy. These differences of application regarding Gadamer's thinking arise from different emphases in our interpretations of his philosophical hermeneutics, specifically the extent to which the facticity of embodied interlocutors is seen as shaping their use of language and the meanings that arise among individuals of shared experience. While both of our accounts acknowledge, with Gadamer (and following Heidegger), that particularity is the ground that both limits and facilitates human understanding, Walhof is more optimistic than I am regarding the emergence of the latter, or, to put it otherwise, he places less emphasis on differences that emerge in the use of language between those of shared versus unshared experiential backgrounds. As the concrete experiences (*Erfahrungen*) of interlocutors begin to differ, I see such differences of background as increasingly taxing mutual understanding and the resonance of meanings between interlocutors, even if not to the point of complete incomprehensibility (see note 6 above).

8. I have elaborated my understanding of Gadamer's relationship to the Western metaphysical tradition along these lines in Ryan Holston, "Anti-Rationalism, Relativism, and the Metaphysical Tradition: Situating Gadamer's Philosophical Hermeneutics," in *Critics of Enlightenment Rationalism*, ed. Gene Callahan and Kenneth B. McIntyre (Cham, Switzerland: Palgrave Macmillan, 2020), 193–209.

9. Here, I am not merely referring to the scale of deliberations themselves, but also the composition of society's interlocutors, that is, the refusal to recognize differences among the latter, such that there could ever be a warrant for preferring engagement with and thus inclusion of some over others. Walhof clearly acknowledges the import of the former, and he speaks of the "vital necessity" of "face-to-face dialogue." See Walhof, *The Democratic Theory of Hans-Georg Gadamer*, xi. However, he is uncritical of the tendency among deliberative democrats to complete openness of dialogues to all interlocutors, regardless of experiential qualification or preparation

for deliberation. In chapter 5, I will discuss two dimensions of such experiential preparedness for deliberative engagement: the shared meanings that are essential to genuine persuasion and the preexistence of a willingness among such persons to deliberate the common good.

10. Robert J. Dostal, "Gadamer, Kant, and the Enlightenment," *Research in Phenomenology* 46, no. 3 (2016), 340.

11. Ibid., 339–40.

12. Gadamer, *Truth and Method*, 350.

13. Ibid., 306–10.

14. Ibid., 306.

15. I believe this dichotomy is what Dostal has in mind when he refers to "authority and reason" in the quotation above. Regardless, his list of dichotomies may certainly be extended, as he rightly suggests. Dostal, "Gadamer, Kant, and the Enlightenment," 340.

16. Such essays are found in Hans-Georg Gadamer, *Reason in the Age of Science*, trans. Frederick G. Lawrence (Cambridge, MA: MIT Press, 1982); *Hermeneutics, Religion, and Ethics*, trans. Joel Weinsheimer (New Haven, CT: Yale University Press, 1999); *The Gadamer Reader: A Bouquet of the Later Writings*, ed. and trans. Richard E. Palmer (Evanston, IL: Northwestern University Press, 2007).

17. The famous "debate" between Gadamer and Habermas took place in the late 1960s and early 1970s, whereas the "Discourse Ethics," was not published in German until 1983 or in English until 1990. For the debate itself, see Gayle L. Ormiston and Alan D. Schrift, eds., *The Hermeneutic Tradition: From Ast to Ricoeur* (Albany: State University of New York Press, 1990). For Habermas's theory of law and political institutions informed by the moral theory articulated in the "Discourse Ethics," see *Between Facts and Norms*, trans. William Rehg (Cambridge, MA: MIT Press, 1996). Some proponents of the discourse ethics are clearly aware of the implications of Gadamer's earlier criticisms for Habermas's later work. See, in particular, Klaus Günther, *The Sense of Appropriateness: Application Discourses in Morality and Law*, trans. John Ferrell (Albany: State University of New York Press, 1993), esp. 190–201. Although he cites Günther's defense of the discourse ethics, Habermas's principal response to his critics refers to Gadamer's thinking only once, and, even then, philosophical hermeneutics is actually invoked by Habermas *in support* of his position. Here, Habermas claims that the possibility of fusing horizons of understanding anchors "universalistic concepts of morality and justice," which must be understood, essentially, in terms of an overcoming of what separates different "forms of life." I believe this to be a misinterpretation of philosophical hermeneutics, which unduly suppresses the particularity of different forms of life. This would be inconsistent not only with Gadamer's fundamental indebtedness to Heidegger's emphasis on the facticity in which *logos* is embedded, but it overlooks the linguistic metaphor to which Gadamer frequently adverts, which is the resemblance of this fusion to a "translation" between horizons of understanding, which uses and

thus maintains (rather than overcoming) one's original, particular perspective. Pace Habermas, philosophical hermeneutics implies that we never occupy an epistemological vantage point beyond our particularity, even when we achieve understanding between different forms of life. See Jürgen Habermas, *Justification and Application: Remarks on Discourse Ethics*, trans. Ciaran Cronin (Cambridge, MA: MIT Press, 1993), 36–38, 104–5.

18. Gadamer, *Truth and Method*, 280.

19. Dostal, "Gadamer, Kant, and the Enlightenment," 339; Gadamer, *Truth and Method*, 273.

20. Gadamer, *Truth and Method*, 282.

21. I argue this point in different ways in Holston, "Anti-Rationalism, Relativism and the Metaphysical Tradition," and Ryan Holston, "Two Concepts of Prejudice," *History of Political Thought* 35, no. 1 (2014): 174–203.

22. Gadamer, foreword to the second edition of *Truth and Method*, xxxi, xxvii.

Chapter 1

Rousseau's Divorce of the Good from History

It is worth acknowledging at the outset of this chapter, which deals with the problematic legacy of Rousseau's political philosophy, that no thinker emerges from nowhere, however novel or radical an individual may be vis-à-vis the tradition in which he is writing. For present purposes, the implication is that Rousseau's thinking, transformative though it was for the intellectual development of the Enlightenment, cannot be viewed in isolation from the broader currents of Western philosophy, both of his own time and extending as far back as the ancients. Indeed, it is impossible to imagine Rousseau's ideas regarding individual freedom, morality, and the state outside this broader historical context, which had a powerful effect on his philosophy, whether as a source of inspiration or rebuke. It is worth noting, in this regard, that Rousseau inherited many aspects of his thinking, which will be discussed below, from the tradition of philosophical rationalism that can ultimately be traced to Plato and his early Christian progeny. In light of this, what follows ought not to be seen as an attempt to place the blame for the problematic features of contemporary moral and political thought entirely at the feet of Rousseau, who in many respects may be seen as furthering an intellectual legacy of which he was a recipient.

However, having acknowledged this context and these influences, the present chapter will argue that Rousseau's writings exacerbated and further complicated what was already a problematic view of moral knowledge in this philosophical tradition, which tended to view standards of judgment as abstract ideas, or precepts of the intellect, whose existence is ultimately separate from the concrete world of human affairs. While Rousseau's thinking was not entirely new, he nonetheless deepened existing fault lines between reason and experience to the substantial detriment of subsequent views of morality. For, even among those intellectual forebears of Rousseau who exhibited this tendency via the most radical views of transcendence, there was still a belief in earthly justice, as God's purposes were thought to be realized through concrete institutions that resulted from sinful human behavior. On Rousseau's account, by contrast, justice and the good were not only identified in opposition to the concrete, experiential realm, but they were comprehended in explicitly *anti-historical* terms. For the purposes of moral and political judgment, such standards could never be informed by human experience accumulated over time, which would, ipso facto, render them suspect. By articulating a view of moral knowledge that was, in the most explicit terms, antithetical to historical experience, Rousseau thus exacerbated a tendency toward abstraction that was already present in the Western intellectual tradition.

Metaphysical Dualism

In light of this focus on the legacy of Rousseau's thinking, the aim of what follows should not be seen as uncovering the "real Rousseau," amid the wide variety of interpretations that exist and the internal tensions that may be observed within his philosophy. Rather, the emphasis will be on those aspects or features of his thinking that later emerged in modern democratic theory, whose conception of moral argument has become problematic for contemporary political philosophy.[1] Particular features of Rousseau's philosophy have thus been selected with an eye toward their subsequent appropriation and development, particularly within the strain of social contract theory that bases the legitimacy of democratic government on a conception of freedom understood as individual autonomy. What is argued here is that Rousseau and Kant, the principal exponents of the autonomy tradition, establish a problematic framework for thinking about morality within which the theory of deliberative democracy continues to operate. Examining the source or origin of such thinking may, therefore, be helpful in reorienting our current understanding of the moral life, which will be the purpose of later chapters.

Key to seeing Rousseau as the foundational thinker in the autonomy tradition is appreciating the thread that runs through so much of his philosophy, which is engaged in a refutation of the mechanistic materialism that had gripped eighteenth century intellectual life, along with the determinism and moral relativism that that position entailed. Rousseau's opposition to the most prominent and forceful defenders of materialism, most notably Thomas Hobbes, was based principally on the moral and political implications of this way of thinking, namely, the denial of the freedom of the individual will and the sanction of the political doctrine that might makes right.[2] In response to this materialist outlook, Rousseau drew on a tradition of European Platonism, which, in spite of its less conspicuous reputation at the time, was in fact robust and impressive in its principal exponents.[3] It is in this context—situated within an ongoing debate between a proto-utilitarian materialist philosophy and a substantial body of Neoplatonic idealism—that Rousseau developed and articulated his metaphysical views, which may be seen as providing the foundation for much of his moral and political philosophy.

In response to the challenge posed by materialism, Rousseau drew upon the well-known Platonic doctrine that reality is comprised of material and immaterial substances and that human beings, themselves constituted by both, identify their bodies with the former and their souls with the latter.[4] This "metaphysical dualism," as a number of commentators have referred to it,[5] asserts not only the dignity of human nature, insofar as man alone is able to escape the efficient causality of the natural world by resisting his desires and choosing freely, but also the possibility of all that which lies beyond material existence, for example, God and the immortality of the soul. Against the materialism of those such as Hobbes, Diderot, D'Holbach, Helvetius, Locke, and Condillac, Rousseau's philosophy may therefore be seen—both explicitly in his moral writings and implicitly in his political works—as asserting the possibility of immaterial substance and of all that which was irreducible to the physical universe and the laws of causality.

To those interpreters who see Rousseau as committed to refuting naturalism in this manner, the most explicit expression of this position can be seen in the "Profession of Faith" of the Savoyard Vicar in book 4 of the *Emile*. In this section of the text, the vicar reclaims the foundations of morality from the philosophy of materialism by asserting what he deems to be an undeniable "inner sentiment" as the epistemological basis for human knowledge of "God, free will, the soul, and transcendent ideas."[6] The vicar also establishes three "Articles of Faith" as the foundation of religious instruction in accordance with reason, which may briefly be said to include (1) that all motion must either be produced by other motion or be the result of spontaneous, voluntary acts of will, pointing to a Will that must ultimately give motion to the universe; (2) that the subjugation of motion to regular laws is an indication of an ultimate intelligence behind the movement of the universe; and (3) that, the will being distinguishable from the senses, man too is an active and free being, the source of spontaneous actions animated by immaterial substance.[7] Combined with the "inner sentiment" mentioned above, the first and third of these articles indicate that man's will "is a power in him to consent or resist [his senses], a power that is not obliterated by its own defeat, for it still shows itself in the reproach a person directs at himself for any weakness."[8] To be sure, it is worth noting that not all of Rousseau's interpreters subscribe to the notion that the voice of the vicar represents his own views.[9] However, this is certainly a minority interpretation, and with good reason. For the metaphysical beliefs given voice to are consistently endorsed by Rousseau—with reference to both the ideas themselves and their articulation by the vicar—on numerous occasions.[10] Even more important for our present purposes, the "Profession of Faith" provides a metaphysical grounding for the moral and political positions found in Rousseau's *Discourse on the Origin of Inequality* and *The Social Contract*.[11] Consequently, the vicar's statement can not only be seen as consistent with Rousseau's other major works, but also as elucidating the logic of the idea of autonomy that is operative in those texts, which is seminal to the further development of that concept in Kant and later philosophers.

More must be said, however, about the "inner sentiment" upon which Rousseau relies for this knowledge of immaterial substance, for the materialists of his age would certainly have been inclined to interpret "sentiment" in corporeal terms, that is, as having a foundation that was ultimately "sensual" rather than "spiritual."[12] With this appeal to sentiment, Rousseau mines a conception of nature that is more than the "mere mechanism" or nature-as-system found, for example, in the materialist account of D'Holbach's *Système de la nature*; rather, it is one that refers to the nature-as-emotion that pertains instead to the feelings of which Rousseau believes man is uniquely capable.[13] Against the mere passivity of sense impressions, Rousseau's appeal to sentiment is thus an allusion to the irreducible experience of "conscience," which he sees as an active faculty in human beings, independent of the material world.[14] It is the sense of the indeterminateness of one's actions—not the will itself but the *feeling of* the will to which the word "conscience" refers—whereby Rousseau acknowledges the self as a spirit independent of all matter. In short, Rousseau is affirming the intuition that establishes man as an originator of undetermined action, spontaneous and autonomous in a manner that is similar (though not identical) to God,[15] thus pointing to the inference that is clear in the vicar's movement from the first to the third article of faith above.

Consequently, Rousseau identifies the conscience of man with the soul and even—as Plato had long before asserted—the "eternal verities" (e.g., goodness, truth, beauty) toward which it is drawn and finds happiness, in opposition to the senses or passions associated with the body to which it may, in moments of weakness, succumb and suffer.[16] As "the part of man related to God,"[17] the soul is guided by the conscience in opposition to the pull of instinct, which is the guide of the body. Conscience is thus "the voice of the soul amidst the passions," which are themselves "the voices of the body."[18] It is conscience, the "sacred voice of nature," to which man must look for guidance in fulfilling his duties toward others: "I have only to consult myself as to what I want to do: all that I feel to be good is good, all that I feel to be bad is bad."[19] The vicar's tribute to the moral authority of conscience and its likening man to the divine culminates in his well-known description of its infallibility:

> Conscience! Conscience! Divine instinct, immortal voice from heaven; sure guide for a creature ignorant and finite indeed, yet intelligent and free; infallible judge of good and evil, making man like to God! In thee consists the excellence of man's nature and the morality of his actions; apart from thee, I find nothing in myself to raise me above the beasts—nothing but the sad privilege of wandering from one error to another, by the help of an unbridled understanding and a reason which knows no principle.[20]

Conscience, for Rousseau, is the God-like part of man, both in the sense that it is pure spirit and in that it facilitates man's apprehension of the good, for God himself is conceived as "Perfect Goodness."[21] In *Julie*, Rousseau makes the connection not only between each human soul and God,[22] but between each of these souls and one another, a bond that the destruction of the body upon death does not eliminate.[23] All of these souls are part of nature—once again, understood in Rousseau's sentimentalist sense—and, as such, have nature's universal principles, its eternal laws, written in their hearts.[24]

But how, one might ask, would it be possible to differentiate the "inner voice of God" from all other "voices," especially those of the passions, which lead contrarily toward the pursuit of one's selfish, material interests? The greatest difficulty in making such a distinction, on Rousseau's account, lies not in listening vigilantly for a divine revelation to be spoken from some external, cosmic source, but in eliminating these other "voices" coming from the world of sense experience, which obscure or make inaudible the "sacred voice of nature" that he believes is already within every human being. The great obstacle, in other words, is all those pressures from the experiential realm, which would impose themselves upon the will—determining what is otherwise undetermined—and thus interfering with the will's attunement to conscience. These forms of coercion, Rousseau discovers, are not only to be found in the appetites that stir responses from our bodies, but in all other experience that would determine the will and thus preempt its free choice. In particular, Rousseau is concerned with patterns of lived experience that would predispose us to particular behaviors, that is, rote responses that would ultimately mitigate opportunities for undetermined choice. Indeed, this is not unrelated to his concerns about the appetites, since our submission to the latter can often be attributed to their indulgence becoming a matter of routine or habit. For Rousseau, habits are like instincts that have been acquired through repeated behavior—which become, quite literally, a second nature (in the naturalistic sense)—thus stripping man of his spirituality, sinking him to the level of an animal in the reflexivity of his responses.[25] This shaping of man through concrete experience, which Rousseau refers to as his "perfectibility,"[26] in one sense cuts against the freedom of the will, insofar as it points toward the possibility of shaping or determining the range of individual action. And it is here that one begins to see what is added by Rousseau to the metaphysical dualism of his ancient predecessors, which is his sensitivity to the threat that past experience—at both the individual and collective level—poses to the freedom that Rousseau believes is "the most precious of all [man's] gifts."[27]

The implications of Rousseau's wariness regarding historical experi-ence are profound, particularly for those ancient, church authorities whose interpretations of the divine will in scripture invariably rely on the accounts of others' experiences and are thus twice removed from the inner voice of conscience. Characterizing Rousseau's view of divine revelation promulgated by ecclesiastical authority, Ernst Cassirer explains the radically individualistic consequences for Rousseau's account of religious knowledge: "Religious cer-tainty can never be anything but the certainty arrived at by the individual self. . . . It can never be a certainty acquired through external knowledge and testimony."[28] He continues, "Even if we could convince ourselves of the 'objective' truth of such tradition, the very form of its proof would suffice to rob it of all religious content. The abundance of empirical and historical evidence cannot bring us closer to the real origin of religious certainty but draws us ever farther away from its original source."[29] Again, the "original source" of religious knowledge is the spiritual voice of nature, or conscience, which alone is morally authoritative for Rousseau. Whereas the emphasis had shifted during the Reformation from faith in a tradition of expert interpretation to faith in the unaided individual's understanding of the revealed Word of God, Rousseau thus goes much further, resisting all appeals to scripture, which invariably rely upon others' experiences of the divine.[30] In place of traditional religion, Cassirer says, Rousseau's "religion of freedom" or autonomy, whose apotheosis is the sovereign individual, guided by nothing other than his own inner light, refuses all such dependence on the experience of others.[31] Therefore, the autonomous will, along with a wariness of all experience that could determine that will, defines the metaphysical foundation of Rousseau's philosophy, which manifests itself in his other major works.[32]

Historical Experience and the State of Nature

Rousseau thus bases the logic of individual autonomy on a metaphysical dualism he inherits from the ancient tradition of philosophical rationalism, combined with a new emphasis on the threat that historical experience allegedly poses to the moral freedom of the individual. In the next two sections, it will be argued that this logic of autonomy underpins Rousseau's moral and political thought, which is subsequently built upon by Kant and other thinkers. In the *Discourse on the Origin of Inequality*, Rousseau famously describes the "natural state of man," or man in the state of nature, as a place in which human beings lived prior to the institutions of civil and political society.[33] Most importantly, Rousseau establishes a pointed contrast between the forms of human existence in these two states. Whereas man in society is vicious, dependent, exploitative, and generally miserable among his fellow human beings, man in the state of nature is benevolent, free, robust, and generally blissful in relative isolation from others. The history of Western civilization, for Rousseau, is the development of institutions that are responsible for these differences, enshrining inequalities of power and wealth, along with the oppression by those who possess the latter of those who do not. In short, these institutions corrupt human goodness or virtue and are responsible for the evils that occur when human beings make gains at one another's expense.[34]

But what is the role of Rousseau's account of the state of nature and this contrast that he presents between man in nature and man in civil and political society? At the outset, it is worth noting the organization of the text of the *Second Discourse*, whose division into part 1, on the natural state of man, and part 2, on the historical development of the economic and political institutions in Western society, underscores this contrast. In other words, if the only purpose of the state of nature were to identify the beginning of the long historical process of institutional decline, there would seem to be no need for this division into separate sections. Rousseau's text could, in its entirety, have simply told the story of historical devolution, in which the state of nature was merely the starting point of that lengthy narrative. That is to say, the entire text could, essentially, have resembled part 2 of the work as it was actually written, beginning with the state of nature and ending with Rousseau's depiction of contemporary Western institutions. In this regard, it is interesting that Rousseau does, in fact, begin part 2 of the *Second Discourse* with the state of nature as a point of historical departure from which later developments slowly emerge. In light of these observations, one is left to conclude that part 1, which is devoted to a much lengthier treatment of the state of nature by itself, must serve a purpose other than simply establishing a starting point for the historical narrative that follows.

Furthermore, Rousseau indicates in his preface to the *Second Discourse* that there is a need to distinguish what is "natural" in man from those attributes given to him by the development of our historical institutions.[35] However, what is meant by "natural" here is not merely what was *historically* original in man but that which is in accordance with "nature," understood in the *normative* sense of the term.[36] In other words, it is here that Rousseau first connects his *Second Discourse* to the second part of the question posed by the Academy of Dijon for their essay competition to which his discourse is a response: "What is the origin of inequality among men, and *is it authorized by the natural law?*"[37] Rousseau's answer, in the simplest of terms, is that inequality is not authorized by the natural law because such inequality is ultimately the result of an arbitrary series of historical developments that are in no way dependent on "essential" attributes in man. Part 2 of the *Second Discourse* is thus aimed at showing the contingency of these developments, which sprang from chance happenings, path dependencies, and so on, not anything intrinsic to human flourishing. However, to answer the academy's question more completely, taking into account its normative component, part 1 of the *Second Discourse* must first establish the standard against which these arbitrarily developed institutions have fallen short.[38] It is necessary, in other words, for part 1 of the *Second Discourse* to set up this contrast: before we encounter man as he actually is or has actually developed in society, we must first comprehend man as he ought to be, or "what the human race could have become,"[39] by which Rousseau means the qualities, attributes, or characteristics of man that, ideally speaking, might have been chosen as worthy of cultivation. Without laying out this normative standard in part 1 of the *Second Discourse*, Rousseau would not only have failed to answer the second part of the Academy's essay question but would, for that matter, have undertaken little more than an exercise in early historical anthropology, foregoing all such normative claims.

This reading of the *Second Discourse* finds textual support in the preface, where Rousseau denies any concern with historical accuracy with respect to the state of nature. Rousseau's normative intentions are clear when he writes, "It is no light undertaking to separate what is original from what is artificial in the present nature of man, and to have a proper understanding of a state which no longer exists, which perhaps never existed and which probably never will exist, and yet about which it is necessary to have accurate notions *in order to judge properly our own state*."[40] In establishing the state of nature, in other words, Rousseau is preparing the ground for judging our political institutions as they actually exist. Elsewhere in the preface, he lends further support to the idea that the state of nature acts as such a standard when he states, in reference to the natural law tradition, "It is this ignorance of the nature of man which throws so much uncertainty and obscurity on the *true definition of natural right*."[41] Indeed, one of the central points of Rousseau's preface to which he devotes substantial space is criticizing traditional natural law thinking, since one of the principal concerns of this intellectual patrimony pertains to the discovery of criteria that can serve as the basis for assessing political institutions, which Rousseau believes it has not performed well, since such criteria are ultimately traceable to the institutions that have developed historically.

Rousseau, in an odd way, may actually be seen as part of this natural law tradition, since he likewise reflects on what is essential to human nature, thus giving man his dignity and establishing criteria for judging institutions, while nonetheless rejecting the conclusions of that intellectual tradition regarding the content of these attributes and principles. For Rousseau, two of the most prominent features that define man in the state of nature are the freedom of the will, that is, the power to resist physical impulse, along with the goodness or innocence of the soul.[42] In the first instance, Rousseau is rejecting mechanistic materialism, as well as the dependence on others that defines human life in commercial society. In the second instance, he is rejecting all pessimistic conceptions of human nature, whether of a Christian, utilitarian, or other philosophical variety. In calling attention to these features in the abstract, Rousseau is providing a reference point or standard, informed by the potential in human beings conceived at their very best. Institutions that sustain these ennobling features of man may be considered just, while those that would discourage or inhibit these features may, conversely, be seen as "contrary to natural right."[43] In short, the freedom and goodness of man in Rousseau's state of nature provides regulative, normative criteria by which the institutions of existing society are to be judged.

The antinomy that Rousseau establishes between what is essential and natural, on the one hand, and what is artificial and historical, on the other, is thus central to his contrast between the state of nature and society.[44] For Rousseau, it is precisely because the state of nature does not exist in any particular place, historically speaking, that it can serve as this standard against which any society can be judged. In this regard, one might say that the state of nature as a standard is not, as some have contended, ahistorical, but more accurately should be conceived as *anti-historical*. In other words, it is not that Rousseau is oblivious to, ignores, or neglects our historically derived institutions when he asserts this normative standard in the state of nature. On the contrary, he is acutely aware of the historicity of such institutions, and it is precisely against or in opposition to the latter that his standard is defined—to maintain its purity, natural right must be perfectly abstract, existing in no particular place or time.[45] The state of nature must be, in the most literal sense, a utopia, that is, no place (*ou topos*). Otherwise, Rousseau believes his own civilization and its historical experience, which he sees as thoroughgoingly corrupt, would have contributed, in some way, to the standard against which that very civilization was to be measured.[46] In doing so, one would essentially have replicated the error of all those Rousseau had criticized for attributing to "nature" that which was acquired by man in society. Therefore, in telling his readers that the state of nature is "a state which no longer exists, which perhaps never existed and which probably never will exist," Rousseau must be seen, in the most explicit terms, as placing his standard of right outside of the realm of historical experience.[47] Western history furnishing any part of this standard, on his view, would have corrupted the criterion of assessment itself. Consequently, Rousseau sees the state of nature as establishing a standard that is radically a priori, in no way informed by the actual historical experience of Western civilization. Its severance from the latter is—and indeed must be—complete.[48]

Although the use that Kant makes of Rousseau's thinking and his own contribution to the autonomy tradition will be discussed at greater length in chapter 2, it is worth pausing briefly here to note that Kant's understanding of Rousseau's state of nature echoes that which has been articulated in the foregoing analysis. In Cassirer's words, "[Kant] regarded Rousseau's theory not as a theory of what exists but of what should be, not as an account of what has been but as an expression of what ought to be," and, therefore, he saw in the state of nature "not a constitutive but a regulative principle."[49] Later, he further elaborates this point, explaining that "Kant never takes the idea of the *homme naturel* in a purely scientific or historical sense, but rather ethically and teleologically."[50] The state of nature is thus understood by Kant as establishing man's "primary function,"[51] that is, "primary" in the sense of being preeminent or having fundamental value and dignity, not in any chronological or anthropological sense. Cassirer concludes, "Kant esteems Rousseau for having recognized and honored man's distinctive and unchanging end," a project that Cassirer says Kant aimed to further develop in his own work.[52] It is, therefore, not difficult to see in Rousseau's sharp separation of the state of nature from history the foundation having been laid for Kant's more explicit philosophical separation of the moral realm from that of the experiential, that is, the realm of human autonomy, as distinguished from the realm of man's physically or empirically determined actions. This influence, along with Kant's own modification and development of Rousseau's thinking, will be discussed at greater length in chapter 2.

The General Will and the Problem of Abstraction

The previous section argued that the state of nature in Rousseau's thought functions as a normative standard against which the institutions of society are to be measured for the purpose of making judgments about their justice or injustice, legitimacy or illegitimacy. Prominent among the features exhibited by man in part 1 of the *Second Discourse* are the freedom of the will and the benevolence of the soul, which part 2 of that text aims to show are lacking in Western society as it has historically developed. This negative role of critiquing existing institutions, however, is only one side of the regulative function of Rousseau's state of nature. For it also serves the positive role of informing his ideal or theory of the just regime, that is, the social contract, which in promoting or cultivating these features of human nature conforms to that same standard.[53] While Rousseau acknowledges that there is no possibility of returning to a presocial or precivilizational state of nature[54]—this is already implied by his disclaimer that such a state "probably never existed"—he sets out to cultivate through the political institutions proposed in *The Social Contract* the same ennobling features of human nature that he had envisioned in the thought experiment of the *Second Discourse*.

However, this aspiration leaves Rousseau with an immediate difficulty, which resides at the heart of *The Social Contract* and is explicitly confronted in the famous predicament posed at the beginning of that text: "to find a form of association . . . by means of which each person, joining forces with all, nevertheless obeys only himself and remains as free as before."[55] In this statement, Rousseau forthrightly acknowledges the challenge that arises in asserting as his normative standard the situation of man in the state of nature: he has demanded that political institutions furnish what is seemingly antithetical to their very nature—the radical freedom of individuals who are in no way subject to the coercive authority of society.[56] Rousseau's well-known response to this self-imposed quandary, the general will, entails an exchange of the "natural freedom" in the state of nature for the "moral freedom" of society, whereby its members become united in a single will aimed at their common good.[57] The social contract allegedly solves Rousseau's dilemma, therefore, by arguing that the latter form of freedom is at least the moral equivalent of the former, thus leaving man "as free as before" he entered political society.[58]

Moral freedom, which is the self-legislation or "mak[ing] and follow[ing] one's own rules,"[59] emerges only in society where living among others while mutually attempting to satisfy interests gives rise to conflict, or at least the potential for conflict, and, with it, the moral or immoral treatment of one another. No such situations arise in the state of nature, where humans are blissfully isolated from each other and entirely self-sufficient. However, the interdependence and lack of self-sufficiency in society creates the feeling of vulnerability, in that resources are now more difficult to obtain, and thus more scarce and precious for all. It is here that morally significant choices arise as a result of this scarcity and the ensuing social organization, whose normative ideal is the social contract. Moral freedom, unlike the natural freedom of the state of nature, points toward the self-limitation that is necessary for cooperation. Still, it is important to see the seeds of this moral freedom or autonomy in our natural freedom in the state of nature, even if man did not yet have occasion for the exercise of these moral powers. Man's newly acquired moral freedom should thus be seen as the full development of his natural freedom into autonomy, made possible under circumstances of mutual need, in which the choices of individuals have the potential to become moral and, in the larger sense, their institutions to become just.

How is it, then, that the basis for these institutions, that is, the general will, is to take effect or to be adopted by all so as to bring about Rousseau's just society? Or, what precisely is the principal obstacle to be overcome in order for this moral freedom to become realized in the general will? Similar to what was seen in the discussion of sentiment above, what Rousseau perceives as the main impediment to the realization of the general will is the members of society acting upon any of the experiential bases of human volition, which obscure or silence the voice of conscience. As David Lay Williams succinctly puts it, "the principle of justice is nothing other than 'conscience' for Rousseau, and the principle of conscience is that which speaks to us from the depths of our hearts. It is that which precedes the maxims of culture, convention, opinion, or the passions and eventually serves as the standard by which to judge all norms."[60] In this summary statement, one sees references to that which precludes individuals from identifying their wills with the general will—culture, convention, opinion, or the passions—each of which in its own way is informed not by the "divine voice" or "inner voice" of conscience, but by the concrete, embodied experience of the passions or of other persons, living or deceased. Precisely because of their experiential nature, each of these as the basis of conduct is thought to degrade human beings, depriving them of their dignity that, as Rousseau says in the *Second Discourse* and in *Emile*, is found in the spirituality of the free will. Only the latter achieves the transcendence of the autonomous subject, which is identified with the individual and society who rise above the determination of their wills by material impulse, on the one hand, and the historical inertia of customs, habits, or practices from the past, on the other.

Having ruled out these experiential bases of individual volition, what becomes apparent is that the general will could never be a mere alignment of the empirical wills of all citizens, or what Rousseau calls "the will of all."[61] Furthermore, once one excludes these various "voices" of experience within each person, all that remains is the voice of conscience, that is, the goodness that is within each person and that Rousseau had identified as one of the prominent features of man by nature. As a result, the general will cannot be just any convergence or alignment of wills, but points only toward certain outcomes, which is to say, it points toward the agreement of strictly benevolent wills, or an objective understanding of what is good or just for all in society's political institutions. Consequently, what must be noted here is that there is not only a procedural component to the general will, insofar as individuals become self-legislating or self-determining beings in the exercise of their moral freedom, but also a substantive or constitutive element to it, since individuals who are good or benevolent by nature will only treat one another in certain ways.[62] This is to say that in light of man's benevolence, which is attributable to his empathy or compassion (*pitié*), each individual identifies with the perspective of all other persons, and, in doing so, will see them as equals by virtue of man's capacity to imagine others' suffering as if it were his own.[63]

Although it is obvious how man's natural benevolence would be extinguished by the selfishness or egoism (*amour propre*) that Rousseau attributes to the historical development of Western society, it is perhaps less obvious how he sees such benevolence as not only compatible with but intimately related to the self-love (*amour de soi*) that he likewise observes as fundamental to human nature.[64] In *The Social Contract*, Rousseau actually describes benevolence as an extension of this self-love (*amour de soi*), applying the same regard one has for oneself to all other persons.[65] There is, in other words, "an identification of each citizen with all others" in the social contract, such that the love of self and love of mankind are actually conceived by Rousseau as a species of the same emotion.[66] Rousseau's characterization of the rectitude of the general will underscores this supersession of the love of self (*amour de soi*) by the love of all others: "Why is the general will always in the right, and why do all constantly will the happiness of each person, unless it is because *there is no one who does not apply this word each to himself and who does not think of himself when voting for all?*"[67] In this mutual identification of all citizens, the general will comes to be seen as more than simply an alignment of individual wills in the same direction or upon the same object, even if that were the common good of society. For what is neglected by such a characterization would be the degree to which all must be united in this universalization or extension of the love of self to all others.

Consequently, the general will must be comprehended as each citizen seeing his will and his interests as not merely aligned with, but as *identical to* that of all others—there are not multiple wills that point toward the same conclusions, on Rousseau's account, but a single will that belongs to all. This conception of society's will as one is paramount for Rousseau's theory, as without it the individual citizen may be in agreement with all others on what is the common good, but he does not truly "obey *only* himself and remain as free as before." For each citizen truly to become self-ruled (*auto *nomos*) in Rousseau's sense, it is not enough for one merely to agree or consent to the laws that govern him. Rather, he must *identify with* or see as his own the will that issues such legislation.[68]

What facilitates the unity of these many wills into one is the general will's grounding in the spiritual or the metaphysical, which is to say, only that which truly bridges or overcomes the particularity that separates each individual from all other citizens. Nothing that is experiential, therefore, may be seen as part of the general will. For the latter's basis in concrete experience would obviate both the spontaneous freedom of all who partake in it and their universal empathy (*pitié*) and attendant benevolence vis-à-vis all others. The condition of human beings in Western society contrasts sharply with this utopian ideal—the egoism (*amour propre*) that has been enshrined in man and his institutions represents both the empirical determination of the will and the partiality of human beings toward themselves in the patterns of behavior they have developed. But ours would not be the only society that would fall short in this regard. For only the autonomous self, that is, the self that is a priori and thus divorced from the particularity of experience embodied in any concrete, historical life, can satisfy the demands of Rousseau's social contract, which requires the cultivation of these features of human nature established by the state of nature. This is to say, only the will that is of a purely abstract, spiritual nature can qualify as both free from empirical determination, on the one hand, and empathetic and thus benevolent toward the whole of society, on the other.

Rousseau's anti-historical characterization of the general will must therefore be seen as thoroughgoing, always with this ideal in mind of the freedom of the will and equal treatment of others, which in its purest form is only achievable absent the empirical determination and division of society he attributes to concrete experience. It is for this reason that Rousseau requires that the general will always be expressed as abstract principles, so as to exclude from it all existing cases to which it might be applied, which would entangle citizens in controversies that relate to their particular, historical lives. With regard to the law, Rousseau thus designates its application to the executive power, from which he believes the people's voice must be strictly separated. The corollary to this separation is the assignment of the legislative power to the general will, since Rousseau sees only prospective (thus lacking all history), regulative rules as unencumbered by such particularity and thus the proper expression of the undifferentiated will of the community. With regard to its content, Rousseau further stipulates that a truly general will "must be general in its object as well as in its essence . . . and that it loses its natural rectitude when it tends toward some individual and determinate object."[69] The general will may not even refer to any particular activity or areas of life (thus avoiding historical experience), whose identification in the law would affect some citizens differently than others, thus rendering it partial. Likewise, Rousseau excludes from the general will's content the possibility of referring to particular members of the community (thus avoiding historical persons), since this would overtly treat some citizens differently than others. In sum, Rousseau takes measures necessary to exclude all historical experience and its concrete particularity from the law, or codifications of the general will. With respect to its form, it must refer to its objects prospectively, without regard to historical cases. With regard to its content, it must be restricted to such a degree that neither particular "objects," nor particular persons or groups may be mentioned in its expressions.[70]

Historical Particularity and the Autonomy Tradition

In chapters 4–6 of the present work, it will be argued that this separation or divorce of morality from its historical particularity made possible by the work of Rousseau has become problematic for the way we think about moral and political deliberation. For now, it is merely worth anticipating these later developments from the vantage point of Rousseau's philosophy. Ryn notes well the various problems that arise for practical law making associated with such abstract thinking. To summarize those criticisms: "Rousseau's purpose is to establish the absolute authority of the general will of the people. To accomplish that he feels the need to keep it untainted by all arbitrariness and particularism. . . . In so far as he wants to preserve the generality, and thus the morality, of the general will, he is forced to make of it a meaningless abstraction and in so far as he wants to present it as a real, positive force in politics dealing with concrete matters, it loses its generality."[71] Ryn thus argues that Rousseau's hostility toward historical experience and his separation of the latter from the law renders the general will wholly impractical in addressing concrete political problems. In other words, the law actually *needs* particularity, or reference to particularity, in order to perform its proper function of ordering the lives of the concrete members of an ethical community.

A similar argument will be made in the present work with regard to particularity and moral and political deliberation. Conceiving the general will as divorced from all historical particularity abstracts from what is essential to the expression of true moral imperatives, which is the experience of concrete interlocutors who must inevitably give voice to such moral and political priorities. In connection with this, it will be argued that one of the most acute problems that emerges from Rousseau's philosophy is the utopian belief in limitless deliberation, that is, one that is infinitely inclusive or boundless with regard to its interlocutors and thus possible on the most extensive scales. This is to say that the strict separation of historical particularity from the general will, as inherited by later thinkers, masks a significant limitation with respect to genuine or authentic deliberation, which is the need for the shared experience of the ethical life. Rousseau's problematic conception of moral knowledge viewed standards of judgment in explicitly anti-historical terms, whether in the metaphorical/intuitive terms of the state of nature or the more rationalistic precepts of the general will. In either case, moral judgment must be stripped of all reference to historical experience and its particularity—in the former case, to preserve the purity of the standard and, in the latter case, for its identification as belonging to all and thus fulfilling that standard in society.

However, insofar as language is always embedded in a particular set of historical customs, habits, and practices—indeed, may itself be seen as one such set of practices—it must be recognized that concrete patterns of living both facilitate and delimit the shared meanings that constitute any discourse that has real normative force or resonance, and thus the possibility of persuasion. In other words, similar to the need for particularity Ryn identified in the law, it may be observed that genuine deliberation requires particularity in order to function—as capable of the normative "pull" of any argument with real discursive force and the capacity for meaningful mutual appeal. What is gained with every move in the direction of abstraction for the sake of universal agreement is lost in terms of the referentiality and proximity to concrete experience, whose richness and texture move and compel our minds in specific directions. To be sure, it must be kept in full view that Rousseau is not a deliberative democrat and that such contemporary theories do not, properly speaking, belong to him. Indeed, there is a certain irony in seeing deliberative democracy as the legacy of Rousseau's thinking, since he argues that the proper formation of the general will actually *precludes* deliberation among the members of his social contract.[72] Still, Rousseau's influence within the democratic tradition looms large. And the separation or severance of morality from man's historical life in subsequent generations of thinkers appears inconceivable without his seminal articulation of the general will and the abstraction that defines its universalization.

It was noted at the outset of this chapter that Rousseau did not emerge from nowhere but that he exacerbates existing fault lines between reason and experience, which can be traced back to ancient political philosophy. Having acknowledged this important lineage from which his thinking derived, it is worth looking forward as well, recognizing that just as Rousseau is not without a history that precedes his thinking, neither is he without a legacy that follows him and connects us, his present-day interpreters, with his work. Indeed, we do not receive Rousseau directly or in an unmediated manner from the eighteenth century, but always in the light of those who follow him and were influenced by his work. Most prominent among Rousseau's interpreters, it is Kant who gives a more systematic and rigorous formulation to the prominent features of Rousseau's philosophy highlighted in this chapter, thus furthering the development of the autonomy tradition and giving shape to modern democratic theory. With regard to these essential features of Rousseau's philosophy, Cassirer says, "We hear their echo and reverberations in the most essential and crucial theses of the Kantian ethics."[73]

Most conspicuously in Kant's moral philosophy, Cassirer notes that the first formulation of the categorical imperative, which requires one to act only in accordance with maxims that may be universally adopted, corresponds remarkably closely with Rousseau's general will.[74] He further observes that the second formulation of the categorical imperative, which requires treating others only as ends in themselves and never as a means to an end, further echoes Rousseau's theory of education in *Emile*, which says that every pupil must be educated for his own sake and not for the sake of others.[75] The common thread that unites these moral imperatives is the identification of freedom, understood as autonomy or self-determination, with morality, and the reciprocal view that immorality is the determination of one's actions by empirical forces, or what Kant refers to as heteronomy. In Kant's legal and political theory, Rousseau's general will and its supporting dichotomy between the realm of freedom and morality, on the one hand, and the realm of coercion and historical experience, on the other, are similarly evident. Cassirer thus observes that in his philosophy of law Kant strictly divides questions of legal right, or *quid juris*, from questions of legal fact, or *quid facti*, and, in connection with this distinction, he flatly dismisses the significance (and possibility) of such a thing as the establishment of a social contract through historical experience.[76] The importance of the concept of the social contract, for Kant, is rather the *regulative idea* of a contract from the point of view of determining a political order's legitimacy. He thus sees the notion of the social contract as pointing to the surrender of individual freedom in order to regain it in union with the other members of society as similar to Rousseau's vision of transforming natural freedom into moral freedom.[77] This, Kant insists, is the sole basis for measuring the legitimacy of a political order, its absence implying a form of subjection at the hands of others. The strictness of Kant's conclusion with respect to what constitutes political legitimacy thus appears similar to the Manichean division between the realms of morality and history in Rousseau's philosophy, which says that historical experience must be eliminated from the choices of the will in order for individuals to be truly free and moral. It is this intellectual influence, along with its further development along distinctively Kantian lines, that will be the subject of the following chapter.

Notes

1. In calling attention to these central characteristics or features of the autonomy tradition, the focus will be to a large extent (though not exclusively) on prominent secondary literature—both in this chapter and in the following chapter—which has itself informed and helped constitute the lens through which Rousseau's and later Kant's thinking have been understood within contemporary democratic theory. It is important to recognize that the autonomy tradition has not been received by deliberative democrats over the last several decades in a direct or unmediated fashion from Rousseau (or Kant) but represents an understanding of his and subsequent writers' ideas that has developed over time, facilitated by intervening generations of interpreters (e.g., Ernst Cassirer, Charles Hendel) who emphasized particular aspects of his philosophy. Subsequent authors are always part of the ongoing conversation and it is impossible to hear these original voices without also hearing the echoes of these other interpreters.

2. David Lay Williams, *Rousseau's Platonic Enlightenment* (University Park: Pennsylvania State University Press, 2007), xviii, 3.

3. Ibid., 28. Williams argues that Europe was not only sympathetic to idealism at the time but that Platonism was "a widespread mode of thinking in modern Europe" and the fact that Rousseau was influenced by this Platonism "should not be surprising in this context." In his section "Rousseau's Familiarity with the Modern Platonists," he identifies those in this tradition who likely influenced Rousseau's thinking the most: Descartes, Leibniz, Malebranche, Lamy, and Fenelon. Ibid., 50. Other works that emphasize the importance of Platonic philosophy for the development of Rousseau's thinking include Ernst Cassirer, *Rousseau, Kant, Goethe: Two Essays*, trans. James Gutmann, Paul Oskar Kristeller, and John Herman Randall, Jr. (Princeton, NJ: Princeton University Press, 1947), and Charles Hendel, *Jean-Jacques Rousseau: Moralist* (New York: Bobbs-Merrill, 1962).

4. Williams, *Rousseau's Platonic Enlightenment*, xix.

5. See, for example, ibid., xvx, 30, 31; Lee MacLean, *The Free Animal: Rousseau on Free Will and Human Nature* (Toronto: University of Toronto Press, 2013), 98; Robin Douglass, *Rousseau and Hobbes: Nature, Free Will, and the Passions* (Oxford: University of Oxford Press, 2015), 11; Timothy O'Hagan, "Taking Rousseau Seriously," *History of Political Thought* 25, no. 1 (2004), 83.

6. Williams, *Rousseau's Platonic Enlightenment*, 61–62, 93.

7. Jean-Jacques Rousseau, *Emile, or On Education*, trans. Barbara Foxley (Waiheke Island, NZ: Floating Press, 2009), 522, 525–26, 538.

8. Hendel, *Jean-Jacques Rousseau*, 147.

9. See, for example, Roger Masters's interpretation of the "Profession of Faith," which follows Leo Strauss's skepticism regarding Rousseau's belief in natural right. According to Masters, the dualistic metaphysics expressed by the vicar may be seen as "detachable" from the rest of Rousseau's moral and political philosophy. Both thinkers ultimately interpret Rousseau as a positivist based on their interpretation of the general will as not having any objective basis, but as fundamentally grounded in nothing more than an alignment of wills or human convention. See Roger Masters, *The Political Philosophy of Rousseau* (1968; Princeton, NJ: Princeton University Press, 2016), 72. See also Arthur Melzer, *The Natural Goodness of Man: On the System of Rousseau's Thought* (1978; Chicago: University of Chicago Press, 2016), 30; Victor Gourevitch, "Recent Work on Rousseau," *Political Theory* 26, no. 4 (1998), 554.

10. The arguments of the vicar thus appear in Rousseau's own voice in his personal correspondence, as well as in his *Reveries of the Solitary Walker*. Williams, *Rousseau's Platonic Enlightenment*, 63. Lee MacLean examines the content of this correspondence in considerable detail and determines that "the preponderance of evidence indicates, we surmise, that the *Profession of Faith* really does contain much of Rousseau's own position about metaphysics and religion." MacLean, *The Free Animal*, 122–23. See also the similar conclusions reached in the respective interpretations of Douglass, *Rousseau and Hobbes*, 11, and O'Hagan, "Taking Rousseau Seriously," 82–83.

11. As Williams succinctly asserts: "Morality grounded in free will seems to be at the very core of not only his metaphysical speculations but also his politics." Williams, *Rousseau's Platonic Enlightenment*, 70.

12. Ernst Cassirer, *The Question of Jean-Jacques Rousseau* (New York: Columbia University Press, 1954), 90–91.

13. Ibid., 106–7.

14. Ibid., 108–9.

15. See MacLean, *The Free Animal*, 110–12, for a discussion of the theological implications of Rousseau's conception of God as an active spirit vis-à-vis passive matter, which MacLean believes to be Manicheism.

16. Hendel, *Jean-Jacques Rousseau*, 146–47.

17. Ibid., 146.

18. Ibid., 152.

19. Ibid., 152 and 154, quoting Rousseau.

20. Rousseau, *Emile*, 560.

21. Hendel, *Jean-Jacques Rousseau*, 146. That Rousseau's idea of moral conscience ultimately points to "an analogous religious sentiment, a feeling of the reality of perfection and love of the Good or God," according to Hendel, ultimately echoes the idea of divine grace found in the Platonic and Augustinian thinking of Malebranche (see 131).

22. Cassirer describes Rousseau's view of God in Kantian terms as "sovereign in the realm of ends," a spirit with authority over all such spirits, as it were. Cassirer, *Rousseau, Kant, Goethe*, 54.

23. Hendel, *Jean-Jacques Rousseau*, 134. This idea that the immaterial soul survives the death of the material body has obvious echoes of the argument for the immortality of the soul in Plato's *Phaedo*.

24. See the numerous occasions on which Rousseau invokes the idea of God's laws written in the heart of man detailed in Williams, *Rousseau's Platonic Enlightenment*, 73–76. Rousseau employs this or similar language, for example, "engraved indelibly on the human heart," throughout his work. The phrase originates in Romans 2:14–15, though it is often associated with St. Augustine, who repeats the words of Paul in various contexts. St. Augustine uses the terms eternal law, law of nature, and law of conscience interchangeably and, therefore, Rousseau's use of "conscience" in the manner described above would appear to place him within this Platonic-Augustinian natural law framework, albeit in a highly modified way. More will be said on the relationship to this tradition of thought later in this chapter.

25. See Jean-Jacques Rousseau, *Discourse on the Origin of Inequality*, trans. Donald A. Cress, introduced by James Miller (Indianapolis: Hackett, 1992), 25–26.

26. See ibid. James Miller says it is "with a certain deliberate irony" that Rousseau gives this term, "perfectibility," to man's ability to be shaped in this manner, since it implies not one particular model of perfection but that "the possibilities for being human are both multiple and, literally, endless." Miller, introduction in ibid., xiv–xv. Consequently, Miller argues, perfectibility is for Rousseau the "corollary" of freedom, since the habits that man acquires from such shaping differ from natural instincts, in that they are "plastic" and capable of great variation rather than being "fixed" (xiv). It is important to note, however, that to see perfectibility as implying freedom in this way depends, crucially, on the individual being the autonomous chooser of whatever new habits he acquires. Hence the remark above that this shaping or molding of man in Rousseau's concept of "perfectibility" must certainly be recognized for its coerciveness.

27. Ibid., 61.

28. Cassirer, *The Question of Jean-Jacques Rousseau*, 116.

29. Ibid., 117.

30. Ibid., 118.

31. Cassirer, *Rousseau, Kant, Goethe*, 45–46.

32. Rousseau is explicit on numerous occasions that religion and faith are foundational for morality and highly important for politics. See Heinrich Meier, *On the Happiness of the Philosophic Life: Reflections on Rousseau's Reveries in Two Books* (Chicago: University of Chicago Press, 2017), 223.

33. Rousseau, *Discourse on the Origin of Inequality*, 18–44. The focus in the present analysis is on the *Second Discourse* because the emphasis here is on Rousseau's legacy, and this is the most widely read of his works that contrast man in nature with man in society and highlight the historical developments that contribute to this division. The *Discourse on the Arts and Sciences*, or *First Discourse*, shares this framework but has been far less influential. Rousseau's *Discourse on Political Economy*, or *Third Discourse*, is unlike the first two, insofar as it is more constructive, anticipating his thinking about the general will in *The Social Contract*, and it is for this reason that he no longer makes use of the antithesis between nature and history in that text. Rousseau's emphasis in the *Third Discourse* and *The Social Contract*, one might say, is on the theoretical conformity of ideal political institutions to the standard of right, as opposed to the disjuncture between that normative standard and the actual development of historical institutions in Western society described in the first two discourses.

34. Rousseau's account of the state of nature effectively reverses much of traditional Christian thinking about human nature, which had attributed social ills to the innate sinfulness of man inherited from the Fall. As a number of commentators have noted, Rousseau's declinist narrative of Western history essentially modifies the story of Genesis, and, in doing so, transfers the problem of evil from man to society. This transference of the responsibility for evil from individual to society is well documented by Irving Babbitt. See his account in *Democracy and Leadership* (1924; Indianapolis: Liberty Fund, 1979), 99. Contrary to Williams' interpretation of Babbitt, the latter's critique of Rousseau is thus aimed not at demonstrating Rousseau's denial of free will tout court but with his modification of moral responsibility by identifying it with collective as opposed to individual choice and action. Consequently, when Babbitt says that Rousseau denies "a struggle between good and evil *in the breast of the individual*," it is the latter phrase, that is, the locus of this struggle, that needs to be emphasized, not the former taken by itself. Williams quoting Babbitt in *Rousseau's Platonic Enlightenment*, 99. Emphasis added. For Williams's critique of Babbitt, see 99–101.

35. Notwithstanding his prominent inversion of the doctrine of original sin (see note 34 above), Rousseau's most explicit engagement on the subject of human nature in this text is not with Christian thinking but with that of Thomas Hobbes, a fellow social contract theorist, who had described the state of nature as egoistic, competitive, and distrustful on purely materialist grounds. Hobbes claimed that these antisocial instincts were observable in society, though sufficiently mitigated by the sovereign's threat of physical punishment to allow for peaceful cooperation. Rousseau refers explicitly to Hobbes when he rejects the method of

attributing to "nature" instincts that, far from being innate, were in fact acquired over time in society. See Rousseau, *Discourse on the Origin of Inequality*, 35. The problem with Hobbes's account, for Rousseau, is similar to that which he has with Christianity—each assumes that man could never be other than he is because each operates with a fixed, pessimistic conception of human nature. There is, as a result, a bias toward the status quo of political affairs built into these accounts of human nature, based on an unwillingness to question the assumption that man is at his core egoistic, as one observes in Western society as it actually or currently exists. One's justifications for the institutions of society, Rousseau believes, are thus based on a false set of assumptions regarding what is "natural," which merely reflects what has in fact developed, historically. For Rousseau, such justifications of political institutions based on the inevitability of what is already in existence in society are ultimately tautological.

36. For an account of the numerous conceptual uses of the term "nature" in Rousseau, see Ludwig Siep, "Rousseau's Normative Idea of Nature," *Redescriptions: Political Thought, Conceptual History and Feminist Theory* 4, no. 1 (2000): 53–72, http://doi.org/10.7227/R.4.1.5.

37. Ibid., 16. Emphasis added.

38. Claes G. Ryn writes, "Whatever else it is, [Rousseau's] state of nature is a normative and analytic concept." Claes G. Ryn, *Democracy and the Ethical Life: A Philosophy of Politics and Community*, 2nd ed. (1990; Baton Rouge: Louisiana State University Press, 2001), 104. Robin Douglass similarly remarks that for Rousseau, "nature" represents "a regulative normative standard," against which political institutions are to be judged. Douglass, *Rousseau and Hobbes*, introduction, 8–13. It is for this reason that at the start of his discussion of the state of nature, Rousseau proposes examining man from his "metaphysical and moral side," and he uses this as a lead-in to his discussion of the free will, one of man's defining attributes in the state of nature, which Rousseau says exhibits the spirituality of the soul. Douglass, *Rousseau and Hobbes*, 76–78. Also emphasizing the normative character of the state of nature, Cassirer says that the question the latter attempts to answer, "What is man?" cannot be settled through "ethnography or ethnology," but is in reality the question of "What ought [man] to be?" Rousseau's inquiry into the nature of man, Cassirer argues, seeks to uncover his authentic or true self, an archetype carried within every human being. Cassirer, *The Question of Jean-Jacques Rousseau*, 50–51, 65.

39. Rousseau, *Discourse on the Origin of Inequality*, 17.

40. Ibid., 12. Emphasis added.

41. Ibid. Emphasis added.

42. These are obviously not the only features of man in Rousseau's state of nature. Other such characteristics may be said to include his ignorance of morality, his robust constitution, his general happiness, and so on. These are all sufficiently important to Rousseau to warrant their inclusion in his account. However, the features identified above have been singled out with an eye to the development of

the autonomy tradition and their subsequent importance as values within contemporary democratic theory.

43. Rousseau, *Discourse on the Origin of Inequality*, 71. This phrase is taken from the concluding sentence of the *Second Discourse*, in which Rousseau provides his ultimate assessment of the institutions in Western society. Self-preservation (*amour de soi*) has been transformed into selfishness or egoism (*amour propre*), while more or less subduing entirely our natural empathy (*pitié*), with the aid of a reason that rationalizes serving only one's self-interest. Rousseau paints a picture of complete mutual dependence, which denies autonomy not merely to some but to all (even the wealthy and powerful) members of society, effectively transforming human nature.

44. This sharp contrast between nature and history is expressed most vividly in the "Preface" of the *Second Discourse* in Rousseau's metaphor likening man in nature to Plato's "statue of Glaucus," which prior to having been disfigured by the elements had looked more like "a god." Ibid., 11. Rousseau's depiction of man prior to the advent of social institutions is conveyed in highly metaphysical terms. Immediately following this metaphor, he describes man in the state of nature as "being active always by certain and invariable principles," and with a "heavenly and majestic simplicity whose mark its author had left on it."

45. Deliberate abstraction from our historically received institutions is what Rousseau believes the great philosophers who preceded him failed to undertake in their own reflections on natural right. It is with this aspiration to greater abstraction in mind that he suggests what will be needed is "even more philosophy than is generally supposed" and shortly thereafter when he poses the rhetorical question, "What experiments would be necessary to achieve knowledge of natural man?" Ibid., 12. Emphasis in the original. The answer implied is precisely the anti-historical thought experiment that is the state of nature.

46. The aim of avoiding historical experience informing his standard of right is so complete or thoroughgoing, it defines even Rousseau's well known method of writing, as he seeks to escape the influence of Western society on his thinking by fleeing to the bucolic environs of Saint-Germain, where he takes long strolls in the woods to reflect on man's true nature. See James Miller, introduction in ibid., viii.

47. It is in this same spirit that Rousseau famously says, "Let us therefore begin by putting aside all the facts, for they have no bearing on the question." Ibid., 17. Facts have no bearing on the question of what is right by nature; Rousseau is in a more radical way than ever before "putting aside" the question of what is for the question of what ought to be.

48. Cassirer says that Rousseau "denied all appeals to the experience of centuries. The verdict of the past had no validity for him." Cassirer, *The Question of Jean-Jacques Rousseau*, 71.

49. Cassirer, *Rousseau, Kant, Goethe*, 10.

50. Ibid., 20.

51. Ibid., 26.

52. Ibid.

53. In this regard, Rousseau is following the ancients, for whom questions of justice are not limited to institutions conceived separately from the individuals therein, as one finds in liberal political thought among those such as John Locke. Rather, the fundamental question of justice is about how regimes contribute to the good or virtuous character of their citizens, which Rousseau addresses both in his critique of Western society in the *Second Discourse* and in his proposed ideal society in *The Social Contract*. Both of these major works emphasize the type of person or citizen formed within their respective societies, which Rousseau sees as decisive for the justice or injustice of the regime. However, as will be seen below, Rousseau's anti-historical standard is ultimately at odds with the concrete texture or particularity of moral and political life, which even ancient rationalists such as Plato recognized as unavoidable for the formation of character and as contributing to different treatment of the various types of citizens under the law.

54. Rousseau is explicit on this point: "But human nature does not turn back. Once man has left it, he can never return to the time of innocence and equality." Rousseau, *Rousseau juge de Jean-Jacques*, third dialogue, quoted in Cassirer, *The Question of Jean-Jacques Rousseau*, 54.

55. Jean-Jacques Rousseau, *Rousseau's Political Writings*, trans. Julia Conaway Bondanella, ed. Alan Ritter (New York: Norton, 1988), 92.

56. It is in this problematic established at the beginning of *The Social Contract* that Rousseau exhibits what Robert Spaemann calls "the utopian goal of the abolition of authority." Spaemann, quoted in Stephen K. White, "Reason and Authority in Habermas: a Critique of the Critics," *The American Political Science Review* 74, no. 4 (1980), 1010. In short, Rousseau envisions a political order in which the coerciveness of institutions has essentially been rendered nonexistent by virtue of every member of society joining together to become the author of every law.

57. Rousseau, *Rousseau's Political Writings*, 95–96.

58. Cassirer argues that, for Rousseau, the exchange of natural for moral freedom results in a vastly superior situation for man, an understandable conclusion in light of some of Rousseau's remarks regarding this transformation. However, Cassirer presses the point to an extreme, such that his account of what is gained by entering political society all but eviscerates the value of the state of nature in Rousseau's work. See Cassirer, *The Question of Jean-Jacques Rousseau*, 56. Cassirer's efforts to show Rousseau's anticipations of Kant's conception of autonomy and the priority of the latter for Rousseau at times seem heavy-handed. See the similar assessment in Peter Gay's introduction to Cassirer's book (24). Still, Cassirer's influential and perspicacious account of the conceptual connections between these two thinkers makes him a valuable interpreter for understanding the logic of autonomy and the intellectual development of the autonomy tradition.

59. Ibid., 96n1.

60. Williams, *Rousseau's Platonic Enlightenment*, 93. When Williams says that "the principle of conscience" is "the standard" that precedes these various forms of experience, I take his interpretation of Rousseau to be consistent with my own. I have likewise argued that conscience or sentiment is, for Rousseau, the faculty for apprehending what is right by nature. The state of nature, then, is an expression of that standard through an extended metaphor, whereas a "principle" is a more rationalistic articulation of what is right by nature. Though his nomenclature differs slightly, I take the spirit of what Williams is arguing in his interpretation of Rousseau to be largely consistent with what I have argued. Similar to Cassirer, Williams later relates Rousseau's general will to Kant's moral philosophy, and it may be in anticipation of that analysis that he uses the more rationalistic, Kantian language. See Williams, *Rousseau's Platonic Enlightenment*, ch. 7, "Kant's Conception of the General Will: The Formalist Interpretation," 207–35.

61. Rousseau, *Rousseau's Political Writings*, 100.

62. More will be said about this in chapter 3, where it will become apparent that the legacy of these two sides of the general will in Rousseau's thinking is a split or dichotomy in contemporary theories of deliberative democracy, which have come to emphasize either procedures or outcomes in their normative conceptions of deliberation.

63. See Rousseau, *Discourse on the Origin of Inequality*, 14, 36–38. Once again looking ahead to chapter 3, more rationalistic concepts such as Habermas's universalization principle (U), which entails what he calls "ideal role taking" or the "universal exchange of roles," would appear inconceivable absent the centrality to human nature that Rousseau ascribes to *pitié*.

64. The two principles prior to reason, which Rousseau says are fundamental operations of man in the state of nature, are self-love (*amour de soi*) and empathy (*pitié*), and it is the latter that inspires benevolence. Ibid., 14, 38.

65. Ryn, *Democracy and the Ethical Life*, 114.

66. Ibid.

67. Rousseau, *Rousseau's Political Writings*, 102. Emphasis added. See also Ryn, *Democracy and the Ethical Life*, 114–15.

68. See Ryn, *Democracy and the Ethical Life*, 111–12.

69. Rousseau, *Rousseau's Political Writings*, 102.

70. See the excellent discussion in Ryn, *Democracy and the Ethical Life*, 120–27, upon which the foregoing paragraph has drawn.

71. Ibid., 125–26.

72. Rousseau, *Rousseau's Political Writings*, 101.

73. Cassirer, *Rousseau, Kant, Goethe*, 32.

74. Ibid.

75. Ibid., 32–33.

76. Ibid., 34–35.

77. Ibid., 35.

Chapter 2

Kant Formalizes the Divorce

The Newton of the Moral World

It is well known that the thinking of Rousseau exercised a powerful influence on Kant. Not only did Kant have a portrait of Rousseau that hung on the wall of his spartanly decorated home in Konigsberg, but—in what is probably the most famous story of their relationship—Kant's regimented walking routine, by which his fellow citizens were said to be able to set their watches, was interrupted just once, as a result of his having been engrossed in Rousseau's *Emile*.[1] Perhaps the second most famous testimony of the profound effect that Rousseau had on Kant's thinking comes from Kant himself, in a series of remarks accompanying his *Observations on the Feeling of the Beautiful and the Sublime*, written in approximately 1765, just two years after this initial encounter with the *Emile*.[2] Frequently said to mark a turning point in Kant's thinking, he confesses in these marginal notes that while his earlier intellectual pursuits had strictly aimed at improvement in human knowledge, Rousseau alerted him to the hidden meaning and import of the moral universe. Likening Rousseau to a "Newton" in the discovery of this invisible order, Kant says: "Rousseau straightened me out . . . I learned to honour mankind."[3] After this encounter, science and the attainment of knowledge was, for Kant, no longer valuable for its own sake. He believed its worth only to be found in the service and advancement of the rights of man.[4]

Looking beyond these biographical accounts to the substance of Kant's philosophy, the present chapter aims to further illuminate the intellectual roots of the autonomy tradition by examining important features of Kant's thinking that were inherited from Rousseau. In what follows, it will be argued that Kant ultimately proceduralizes the aforementioned dualism transmitted to him by Rousseau, along with the latter's anti-historical conception of right, which had a detrimental influence on subsequent generations of democratic theory. For, in Kant's more systematic philosophical approach, there lies a further entrenchment of the cleavage that Rousseau had explicitly established between historical experience and morality. The intellectual inheritance of the autonomy tradition, it will be argued, consequently promotes an illusory view of the moral life, which comprehends moral principles in formalistic terms, conceptualizing the latter as abstract entities that are separate or distinct from the concrete ethical life from which they ultimately derive.[5] The consequence for contemporary democratic theory and for political philosophy more broadly has been a failure to comprehend the essential role of historical experience for the shared meanings and values presupposed by any genuine deliberation.

Freedom and Universalization

Kant's most prominent intellectual debt to Rousseau is his conceptualization of freedom, understood as the individual exercising his capacity to choose absent determination of the will by forces internal or external. In this way, freedom is defined by the independence that Rousseau had identified with the autonomous will in both *Emile* and the *Second Discourse* and, ultimately, the moral freedom associated with the general will in *The Social Contract*. This idea of freedom as autonomy is articulated by Rousseau in these works in a somewhat inchoate manner but transformed by Kant into a procedure of the rational intellect,[6] most prominently in his moral philosophy.[7] Both of these thinkers agree, as well, that if the ideal of freedom is conceived in terms of this autonomous activity of the will, and if violation of the will's sovereignty or authority over one's actions is considered an affront to our fundamental human dignity, then the legitimate terms of political association require everyone willing the public acts that would coerce society's members. In short, just laws are those that all members of society can will, since only the latter are capable of preserving their freedom. For both thinkers, it is in this manner that the autonomy of each subject can be upheld.

This respect for individual autonomy, ensured through institutions that require and themselves instantiate the universal will of society, Cassirer argues, is the legacy of Rousseau's emphasis on law or the form of law, which appears to shape both Kant's moral and his political thought.[8] Cassirer thus devotes particular attention to Rousseau's *Discourse on Political Economy*, where he indicates how it is that law, more than any other instrument or human convention, contributes to the fulfillment or realization of this higher form of freedom.[9] For here we see that it is Rousseau's idea of law as a "universal voice"[10] that resolves his fundamental paradox of authority transformed into freedom, insofar as law's generality has the capacity to eliminate what is otherwise alien and coercive to the individual will. Rousseau elaborates: "These wonders are the work of Law. It is to Law alone that men owe justice and liberty; it is this salutary organ of the will of all that makes obligatory the natural equality between men; it is this heavenly voice that dictates to each citizen the precepts of public reason, and teaches him to act in accordance with the maxims of his own judgment, and not to be in contradiction to himself."[11] It is the interchangeability of perspectives, Cassirer shows, that gives law its impartiality and, ultimately, the equality with which it treats citizens. Of course, not all law fulfills this function for Rousseau, but only that which unifies the wills of society in such a manner as to represent their shared interests. In other words, in addition to the form of the will's expression being that of law, which makes it general, the substance or content of what is willed must be general as well. Still, there is here in the *Third Discourse* an early glimpse of Rousseau's sense that there is a quality in law as such that contributes to the liberation of political subjects, in that it treats them impartially or equally. That quality is law's capacity for generality or abstraction from particular persons and circumstances, which is later featured in *The Social Contract*. By consistently refusing to subject others to conditions from which an individual would be exempt, law precludes one from being "in contradiction" with oneself, an insight that anticipates law's potential to structure or proceduralize the duty that Kant identifies vis-à-vis others' free wills.

For Cassirer, it is this uniformity of treatment and the interchangeability of subjects in law that so clearly resembles and anticipates Kant's understanding of moral conduct as the coherent or noncontradictory universalization of that which one wills. In the categorical imperative, therefore, we see the demand of removing references to oneself and the requirement of treating others in a manner identical to ourselves with respect to the maxims of our actions. We see this affinity with the general will most clearly in the first formulation of the categorical imperative, described by Kant as the principle of universal "legislation" for this resemblance to the consistency and impartiality of law.[12] Though consonant with the other formulations of the categorical imperative, Kant's emphasis here is on the avoidance of self-contradiction, which echoes Rousseau's reference to law's avoidance of "contradiction" for its citizens in the *Third Discourse*, as well as the impartiality in the treatment of subjects in *The Social Contract*.[13]

Kant's appropriation of the general will is not limited to his moral philosophy. In Kant's philosophy of law, Cassirer notes, this same idea finds its most explicitly political expression, as Kant sees the universal will of the people as the identical basis for the legitimate exercise of political authority: "It obligates every lawgiver to promulgate his laws in such a way that they could have arisen from the united will of an entire people, and to regard every subject, in so far as he desires to be a citizen, as though he had joined in assenting to such a will. For that is the touchstone of the legitimacy of every public enactment."[14] Other commentators have echoed these observations pertaining to the nature of this influence of Rousseau's general will on both Kant's moral and political thought. George Armstrong Kelly likewise calls attention to the ideal of autonomy when he refers to Rousseau's "liberty which is self-enacted law" and its fundamental importance for Kant's opposition to both Scholastic theology and the hedonistic school of empiricism.[15] Shortly thereafter, Kelly points to the corresponding institutional expression of this ideal when he says, "It is also possible to detect fundamental connections between Rousseau's ideal model of political legitimacy and the *societas sociorum* of Kant in which individual wills would be made reciprocally co-restrictive by the 'laws of freedom' of a juridical commonwealth or republic."[16]

More recently, Williams has similarly identified the origin of Kant's ideal of autonomy in the thinking of Rousseau, noting in general that "Rousseau was frequently given to insisting on the autonomy of our acts in order to regard them as moral."[17] And later, in greater detail, he shows how the guarantee of this freedom, which was the achievement of Rousseau's general will and social contract, shapes Kant's understanding of both the "original contract" of society as well as all legitimate legislation.[18] Finally, Richard Velkley, whose most penetrating study of the intellectual relationship between these thinkers will be taken up later in this chapter, succinctly summarizes the influence as follows: "Rousseau's place in the Kantian endeavor is normally conceived in terms of the contribution of Rousseauian formulations about self-legislative freedom, in the *Social Contract*, to the related Kantian formulation about the supreme moral law, the categorical imperative."[19] Rousseau's idea of the general will, which aims to preserve the independence of the free will under the circumstances of social life, is thus well recognized as having been appropriated within Kant's moral and political thought. What remains to be established, however, is whether Kant's doing so reflects assumptions similar to Rousseau's regarding the relationship between morality and historical experience. For this is the feature of the autonomy tradition that will be the focus in the discussion of contemporary political thought in the next chapter.

Kant's Dualism and the Problem of Historical Experience

In his study on the thinking of Rousseau, David Lay Williams begins his final chapter, which is dedicated to Rousseau's influence on Kant, with the observation that "Jean-Jacques Rousseau has never been known as an especially abstract philosopher."[20] With this remark, Williams aims to convey Rousseau's antipathetic attitude toward the metaphysical tradition, along with the romantic strain running through works, such as the *First* and *Second Discourse*, that demonstrate an aversion toward intellectualism with regard to the study of human affairs. Williams substantiates his claim by noting several of Rousseau's disparaging comments with respect to the "jargon" and "absurdities" of classical metaphysics, and he makes the additional observation that Rousseau's writings rarely engage in epistemological and metaphysical arguments, as was the case with many of his contemporaries.[21] It was Kant, Williams contends, the more systematic and rigorous of the two philosophers, who was left the task of rationally conceptualizing the insights of Rousseau regarding freedom and morality that had inspired him. Consequently, Williams concludes that Kant's role in this intellectual relationship was to render in more abstract and explicit philosophical terms the latent metaphysical underpinnings of Rousseau's thinking, which had been incompletely theorized throughout his various works.

However, Williams's interpretation, correct though it may be about Kant's more systematic method of inquiry, fails to capture the abstract nature of Rousseau's reflections on moral and political life, which ultimately became his legacy—together with Kant—through the writings of thinkers who followed them in the tradition of democratic theory. For, with this focus on the thinkers' different modes of thinking and writing, Williams fails to appreciate that there is in Rousseau's philosophy an abstraction that transcends his more romantic articulation of the ideal of autonomy. Notwithstanding Rousseau's tendency to express himself in a more intuitive or imaginative form than Kant, his thinking established an outlook vis-à-vis historical experience that contributed significantly to the development of a more abstract understanding of morality, of which Kant was the inheritor. Thus, one cannot simply conclude that, because Kant was articulating his thinking about morality in the language of philosophical reason or through the use of concepts of the intellect, the latter were necessarily more abstract than the thinking of Rousseau.[22] For imagination as well as reason is capable of abstraction, as one sees, most prominently, in the case of Rousseau's romantic imagination, which contains explicit, self-conscious departures from the "facts" of human experience.[23] The question of whether a thinker is culpable of the charge of abstraction thus depends not on the use of reason or imagination per se, but upon the latter's fidelity (or lack thereof) to historical reality. Consequently, it may be said that what is definitive with regard to the quality of abstraction is the fundamental separation or severance of the ultimate moral standard from the realm of concrete, historical life. The most prominent illustration of this departure from or explicit rejection of historical reality is Rousseau's state of nature, which renders the autonomy tradition complicit in this tendency from the very beginning. It is thus the aversion to historical experience as contributing to moral standards that, properly speaking, defines the abstract or formalistic quality of the thinking of both Rousseau and Kant, along with that of subsequent writers in the tradition of democratic theory.[24]

In his study of Kant's philosophy, Richard Velkley lays out the crucial, formative period during which Kant came under the influence of Rousseau, which he identifies as 1764–65, when Kant composed his *Remarks* on the *Emile*.[25] During this decisive period of Kant's intellectual development, Velkley explains, he came under Rousseau's belief that there are no determinate purposes in nature, as previous philosophers had assumed, but that "culture indefinitely transforms nature rather than perfecting determinate potentials within it."[26] Kant's position, nevertheless, like Rousseau's, is far from relativistic, as Kant's statement cited above regarding man's dignity and his rights clearly indicates. Instead, Kant recognizes a source of moral worth in man that is tied to his ability *not* to have his historical life—which is seen, similar to Rousseau, as something "artificial"[27]—determine his purposes for him.

Consequently, the fundamental law that this "Newton" of the moral world discovers, for Kant, is that man's distinctive moral worth resides not in an essential nature, understood in terms of a *telos* or some predetermined purpose, but in his ability to resist the impulsion of historical experience and to become a self-determining agent. With Rousseau, Kant thus discovers the invisible order of the individual as an end, who may freely will or determine his own destiny, rather than having it determined for him by nature from without. As such, human dignity is located in this resistance to or escape from the allegedly dehumanizing force of historical experience, which is seen as diminishing our ennobling faculty, that is, the free will that allows one to be an autonomous agent. This is Kant's development of the logic of Rousseau's dualistic metaphysics, given voice to by the Savoyard Vicar in *Emile*, along with the will that escapes the coerciveness of concrete experience in that text and the *Second Discourse*. History, which Rousseau believes is "accidental and arbitrary," because otherwise unchosen, becomes for Kant as well a force that opposes the freedom of the will, whose diminishment is always seen as a moral loss.[28]

By contrast, exercising one's agency as a moral end entails becoming a cause independent of a chain of empirical causes and, therefore, becoming the initiator of one's own chain of causality, in a manner similar to the Creator. In doing so, one has the potential to initiate or direct the environment that shapes what one is to become, opening the door to our self-creation or "perfectibility."[29] Characterizing Rousseau's view, James Miller explains that our very capacity to be molded or shaped by our circumstances creates opportunities, paradoxically, for the self-direction of the subject: "because we are free, we may always change our minds, change our habits, and change our social institutions. We can, in principle, start over again."[30] As a result, one is not free from history per se, in the sense that one is always impervious to or unaffected by the latter's causality, so much as one may be formed by a history that one's free will had a role in choosing or directing. Man stands not beyond history, but is capable of resisting complete determination by it, which allows him to choose the circumstances that shape the person one ultimately becomes or, collectively speaking, to participate in the choice of the people one is to become. History still shapes us, on Rousseau's account, but it also has the potential—always and without limits defined by nature—to be shaped by us.

Of course, the implication of such thinking about history—that one can choose the circumstances by which one is shaped or formed—is to elevate the importance, or raise the stakes, of the moment of free choice or willful assertion vis-à-vis one's historical circumstances. The moment that "perfectibility" is seen as more than the admission, with the ancients, of the inevitable molding of an individual's character by one's community, but as the radical freedom of self-creation without limits defined by nature, one elevates the importance of this choice. It is critical, therefore, to understand the nature of this willful assertion that Kant, following Rousseau, believes man is capable of undertaking, amid or within the flux of historical experience. There is an ambiguity in Kant's concept of the will that, Lewis White Beck explains, Kant aims to clarify by introducing the fundamental distinction between *Willkür* and *Wille*.[31] While the former indicates "the spontaneous initiation of a causal series as emerging in an act of will," the latter refers to "the source of the law to which this spontaneity is subject as also a will."[32] This can be expressed by the analogy that the will has both an "executive" and a "legislative" function, which is to say, an ability to initiate undetermined action (*Willkür*), as well as issue its own commands to itself (*Wille*). The former, on Beck's account, can thus be seen as the independence of the arbitrary will that escapes determination by the natural world, while the latter is the choice of principles or maxims legislated to that will, which must likewise be completely undetermined or free, lest there be determinate purposes in nature.

While the morality of our actions requires both of these aspects of the free or autonomous will, for Kant, it is the spontaneity in *Willkür* that is attributable to the same effort in Rousseau to account for the will's escape from the determination of our actions by concrete experience. Clearly, this represents Kant's initial indebtedness to Rousseau's metaphysical dualism, in that there is a need for strict separation or escape of the agent from the empirical or historical world, which is seen as threatening the individual's freedom and dignity. However, Kant applies the logic behind this separation to *both* aspects of the will that he identifies—the individual as an agent lacking a *telos* must be the source of spontaneous endeavor (*Willkür*) *and* the free choice (*Wille*) that gives direction to those actions, if they are not to be seen as determined by heteronomous inclinations or the decisions of previously existing persons. Influenced as well by Rousseau's insight into the "legislative" aspect of freedom mentioned in the previous chapter, Kant thus identifies and distinguishes *Wille* as a separate dimension of autonomy— one must not only exercise causal agency but self-legislate the principles or purposes toward which one acts. To be free, one must be the undetermined agent behind both the decision (*Willkür*) to act and the basis (*Wille*) for one's actions. Heteronomy is seen to threaten freedom as an impetus of action as well as a ground of choice, both of which strive to maintain the purity of the free will against the incursions of the empirical realm. In this way, one sees in Kant's ethics a self-conscious articulation and further development of the cleavage between the realm of morality and the realm of experience. Dividing the will into two parts, Kant thus extends the requirement of independence from the world of concrete experience to both elements in order for the individual to achieve true autonomy.

According to Velkley, Kant's concern for the freedom and morality of the will, which he acquired while reading Rousseau in the 1760s, also became the driving force behind Kant's later "critical" writings and, indeed, his entire philosophical system. He thus notes that this early period, during which Kant is composing his *Dreams of a Spirit-Seer Explained by the Dreams of Metaphysics*, is when the distinction between the noumenal and phenomenal—the freedom of the spirit and the coerciveness of experience—first makes its appearance in Kant's writings. For Kant, Velkley says, "morality opens up the possibility of a metaphysics of a new sort, concerned with objects produced by or implied by the activity of a free will ('noumenal' objects) and transcending the whole realm of sense ('phenomena') to which theoretical science is limited."[33] As a result, the framework of the noumenal-phenomenal division in Kant's metaphysics can, to a significant degree, be traced to this priority regarding the freedom of the will and the escape from empirical determination inherited in his practical philosophy from the thinking of Rousseau, which later informs his epistemological concerns.[34]

In his *Grounding for the Metaphysics of Morals*, Kant thus demonstrates the connection between the important idea of the autonomy of the will and his separation of the noumenal and phenomenal realms. Simultaneously appropriating while also modifying the idea of "spontaneity" transmitted via Rousseau's concept of man's perfectibility, Kant here connects the latter with the faculty of reason, which he actually describes as "pure spontaneity" to emphasize its independence from all empirical determination.[35] Representing the purity of the noumenal realm, reason demonstrates the ability to avoid the heteronomy of the will, that is, the latter's dependence on contingency and external determination. It is reason, therefore, that Kant identifies as that part of the self that is not just capable of *acting* (*Willkür*) outside the realm of concrete experience, but also *choosing* (*Wille*) purposes that are similarly autonomous or independent of empirical phenomena. In this way, one's transcendent or rational self is conceived in purely nonempirical terms:

> Therefore a rational being must regard himself qua intelligence (and hence not from the side of his lower powers) as belonging not to the world of sense but to the world of understanding. Therefore he has two standpoints from which he can regard himself and know laws of the use of his powers and hence of all his

actions: first, insofar as he belongs to the world of sense subject
to laws of nature (heteronomy); secondly, insofar as he belongs
to the intelligible world subject to laws which, independent of
nature, are not empirical but are founded only on reason.[36]

We live in two worlds, as it were, and Kant maintains that our actions only
become moral insofar as they are ordered by the agent who both resists
determination of his actions, in the first place, and chooses or legislates
purposes for himself, in the second place, both of which are conditions that
must be obtained beyond the realm of concrete experience.

Michael Sandel, whose seminal critique of John Rawls's political philosophy similarly connects the ideal of autonomy in contemporary political
thought to the noumenal-phenomenal division inherited from Kant's moral
philosophy, succinctly explains this indebtedness in terms of a "transcendental
self": "*Qua* object of experience, I belong to the sensible world; my actions
are determined, as the movements of all other objects are determined, by
the laws of nature and the regularities of cause and effect. *Qua* subject of
experience, by contrast, I inhabit an intelligible or super-sensible world;
here, being independent of the laws of nature, I am capable of autonomy,
capable of acting according to a law I give myself."[37] In other words, we are
our moral and autonomous selves, undetermined by empirical forces only
when we operate in the noumenal realm, which is to say, in the realm of
actions and choices that are free or independent of coercive, heteronomous
experience. Conversely, we diminish our highest faculty, our capacity for
self-determination or freedom conceived as autonomy, insofar as our actions
and choices reflect the influence of such experience. It is the reason or
intellect, for Kant, which now represents the spontaneous agent or moral
end, that stands apart from the flux of history and empirical determination
in all respects.[38]

Though he similarly emphasizes the role of Rousseau's concept of perfectibility in Kant's ideal of autonomy, William Galston does not see in this
a reason for Kant to have been wary of historical experience as a threat to
man's freedom. Rather, Galston focuses more narrowly on Kant's disavowal
of appetite and the threat that the latter poses to freedom and morality.
In other words, Galston affirms the argument here that Kant inherits from
Rousseau a traditional metaphysical dualism, according to which the will
as a self-creating force must overcome the imposition of experience. However, for Galston, there is no extension of the latter beyond the hedonistic
tradition's understanding of experience as corporeal desire. Consequently,

far from inheriting Rousseau's anti-historical sensibility, Galston reads Kant as a proto-historicist, whose understanding of our social and institutional development accounts for the emergence of the faculty of the rational intellect, which allows man to progress from his instinctual, physical origins to the eventual achievement of republican freedom and peaceful cooperation within and among societies.[39] As a result, Galston is critical of Kant for his failure to explain the metaphysical nature of reason, insofar as he sees the emergence of reason from our experiential selves as contradictory, posing irresolvable paradoxes for Kant. For the purposes of the present project, the question that must be confronted is whether Kant, as Galston contends, may not have had the negative view of historical experience that has been attributed to him here as an inheritance from Rousseau.

Although there is much common ground between Galston's argument and the present study regarding the metaphysical dualism shared by Rousseau and Kant, his analysis unjustifiably narrows the idea of "experience" in Kant and, as a result, overlooks the anti-historical character of his thinking inherited from Rousseau. For, although Galston is correct in observing Kant's attack on the "eudaimonistic tradition,"[40] which is manifest in Kant's admonishments of happiness as a motivation to the performance of duty, his relegation of experience to the problem of appetite fails to recognize the breadth of the difficulty that Kant sees all phenomena presenting for the heteronomy of the will and the morality of one's choices. The problem of experience as a source of duty, for Kant, is linked principally to the latter's contingency or variability, a difficulty that is raised as much by the particularity of the historical life as it is by the fleeting and individualistic nature of desire. Our rational, transcendent selves, according to Kant, cannot be seen as subject to the vicissitudes of the phenomenal realm if they are to remain free or autonomous.

Williams, who contends that Rousseau transmitted a Platonic metaphysics to Kant, instead rightly highlights Kant's broader aversion to the particularity of experience as such. In his appropriation of Rousseau's general will, Williams argues, Kant is thus articulating a Platonic ideal of justice from which all particularity has been expunged.[41] And in the *Critique of Pure Reason*, he further asserts, Kant argues for Plato's radically transcendent ontology in virtually all respects: "[Kant] says that Plato properly abstracts from all experience, without which virtue would be 'something that changes according to time and circumstance, an ambiguous monstrosity not admitting of the formation of any rule.'"[42] Consequently, it is the contingent and variable nature of experience that is the cause of Kant's aversion, which implies a broader problem than an attempt to preserve freedom and morality from the assaults of the eudaimonistic tradition, even if, as Galston contends, the latter is conceived more broadly so as to include Aristotelianism. As Williams explains, "The only stable, transcendent, and true foundations of normative thought [for Kant] lie abstracted from *all* experience."[43] In short, such variation or contingency would, for Kant, imply the dependence of the will and its choices on the fleeting times and places of historical life, and this would threaten man's freedom, as much as when it is rooted in the impulse of desire.

The additional evidence supporting the idea that Kant was the inheritor of Rousseau's anti-historical, metaphysical dualism is Kant's statements indicating his support for the emancipatory project of the Enlightenment. Viewed in the context of Kant's remarks about the Enlightenment as an approach to human affairs that would liberate mankind from the dogmas of tradition, particularly that of religious authority, the opposition between the free moral will and historical experience that has been claimed for Kant appears substantiated and unsurprising. According to Velkley, the practical goal of "emancipating man from human nature," as nature was conceived by utilitarian naturalists such as Hobbes, or within the teleological systems of theologians, was central to Kant's aspiration of establishing a position of neutrality toward all human ends or purposes.[44] In other words, the knowledge that nature does not settle the question of man's purposes but leaves the latter to each rational being to determine individually would be a liberating or emancipating force for human agency. By contrast, naturalism and theological orthodoxy were each seen by Kant as denying reason its proper role in the determination of human ends, thus depriving individuals of their inherent freedom and dignity.

It is in the spirit of emancipating humanity from traditional dogma, which had affirmed such purposes, that Kant articulates his famous critique in "What Is Enlightenment?" Here, he admonishes those who would rely on the "tutelage" of such scientific and religious authorities, that is, traditional social institutions from which human beings were said to be emerging.[45] Kant's remarks in this essay regarding the illegitimacy of religious doctrines and legal agreements that extend over time, which he describes as "a crime against human nature," similarly points to the threat of historically received institutions to the natural freedom and dignity of man.[46] The emancipatory goals of the Enlightenment project are thus consonant with an anti-historical view of freedom conceived as autonomy, which was central to Kant's philosophical purposes after his initial encounter with Rousseau. In the context of Kant's explicit call for emancipation from traditional authority, the tension between the undetermined will and historical experience in Kant's metaphysical dualism thus appears further corroborated.

Scientific Morality

Notwithstanding the rejection of Williams's suggestion that Kant rendered Rousseau's ideas more abstract by articulating them in a more philosophical manner, there is a sense in which Kant does contribute to an accentuation of the division between morality and historical experience. In addition to his denial of any purposes in nature and his explicit critique of social authority, what further contributes to the anti-historical understanding of morality in Kant's writing is his aspiration to make the articulation of the supreme moral principle serve the progress or improvement of human affairs, an aim that connects his moral philosophy to the scientific aspirations of the Enlightenment project.[47] As an avowed disciple of Rousseau, this should be seen as rather ironic, when viewed in the light of Rousseau's animadversions against the narrative of Enlightenment progress, particularly in the *First* and *Second Discourse*.[48] However, Kant is undeniably more optimistic than Rousseau regarding the possibility of social progress resulting from theoretical reflection and learning and, more specifically, a more scientific account of moral truth, which he believed Rousseau's thinking had (however ironically) facilitated.[49]

Kant's modification of Rousseau through his emphasis on reason, as opposed to sentiment, as the faculty that achieves the freedom and morality of the will, must be seen in precisely this light. For, as Williams notes, Kant sees reason as a more reliable basis on which to rest man's duty, for which he was seeking a lawlike certainty or regularity that resembled scientific, even mathematical, forms of knowledge.[50] In other words, much as Kant agreed with Rousseau on the benevolent potential of the feeling of empathy, he believed that any such emotion would be "weak and always blind,"[51] incapable of motivating consistent behavior, which he associated with the patterns in the universe observed in the natural sciences. The importance of reason, for Kant, was that it could establish laws that rigorously enforced the benevolent impulse of man that Rousseau had identified as the first principle or foundation for morality. Self-legislated by the noumenal will, such laws were not seen as predetermined purposes in nature but grounded in human freedom itself.

In his *Beautiful and Sublime*, just as Kant was coming under Rousseau's influence, he expresses this notion of universalizing affection toward others, which was to be established as an invariable principle or rule of conduct:

> When universal affection toward the human species has become a principle within you to which you always subordinate your actions, then love toward the needy one still remains, but now, from a higher standpoint, it has been placed in its true relation to your total duty. Universal affection is a ground of your interest in his plight, but also of the justice by whose rule you must now forbear this action. Now as soon as this feeling has arisen to its proper universality, it has become sublime.[52]

For Kant, universal affection is, as Rousseau had asserted, the ground of justice, but as emotion, Kant believes it lacks the reliability of a rule to which one must consistently subordinate one's actions. Rousseau, it will be recalled, identified universal affection or empathy (*pitié*) with the extension to all of the self-love (*amour de soi*) that man is said to possess in the state of nature. However, from Kant's perspective, this extension or universalization can only be realized through the use of the rational intellect, which all human beings are known to possess. For this fundamental dignity of human choice, or man as an end, is perceived by the individual both in himself and others. Consequently, each being recognized as possessing an independent will (in the sense of both *Willkür* and *Wille*) and maintaining sovereignty over his actions, any permanent arrangement of moral conduct would entail the noncontingent systematization of such recognition.

It is here that Kant's understanding of our duty toward others can be seen in the light of his intellectual relationship to Rousseau. Viewed from this perspective, it is the transformation of Rousseau's idea of universal affection into a consistent, lawlike principle, apprehended not through the emotions, which Kant saw as unreliable, but the more rigorous and methodical operation of practical reason. For reason, which is the intellection of the noumenal self, seen as severed from all temporality, is alone believed capable of withstanding the vicissitudes of concrete experience. While Kant sees Rousseau as correct and profound in identifying human freedom as the end that any system of morality must serve, he is interpreted by Kant as failing to see sentiment as residing within empirical nature—understood, that is, as part of our sense experience—and thus vulnerable to the contingency of the phenomenal realm.

By contrast, reason was thought to be capable of achieving the precision of mathematics, geometry, or formal logic, and thus would not be susceptible to such uncertainty. The lynchpin of this system of thought, therefore, is the possession of pure practical reason by every individual, since that would allow for assumptions about the interchangeability of perspectives and the correctness of judgments regarding "universalizability." It is chiefly this condition—the epistemological extirpation of the particularity of all subjects—that points to the possibility of formulating moral rules or codes of conduct, which would be acceptable to all: "Everything in nature works according to laws. Only a rational being has the power to act according to his conception of laws, i.e. according to principles, and thereby has he a will."[53] Therefore, rules or principles are essentially employed by Kant to achieve what Rousseau had once identified as the great achievement or "wonder" of law—their ability to abstract from the particularity or individuality of persons and circumstances, refusing to differentiate among the subject or objects of any proposed action, such that one's role could always be reversed with another while arriving at identical conclusions regarding an action's propriety.

Consequently, where the ancients had once seen the law's formalism as simultaneously an advantage and a disadvantage in the resolution of moral and political questions,[54] Kant saw only the former and believed the reversibility of perspectives that the form of law achieved to be the sine qua non of moral and political decision-making. In the next chapter, it will be seen that contemporary thinkers who take their bearings from the autonomy tradition come down on different sides of the question of whether legitimate laws or policies are those that appeal to all in terms of their form or substance. In other words, though these thinkers all prioritize the generality or impartiality that Rousseau and Kant believed to characterize moral conduct and just politics, they place their emphasis variously on procedures, outcomes, or some combination thereof. What is important, for present purposes, is their inheritance from Rousseau and Kant of this division between morality and historical experience. For it inaugurates an understanding of morality as divorced from the historical life, which is to say, severed from the particular contexts in which moral imperatives emerge and have their meaning. As will be seen, the reification or hypostatization of abstract moral principles has consequences for our thinking about moral and political discourse. For it encourages an understanding of deliberation that is limitless with regard to the inclusion of interlocutors, insofar as they are no longer understood as tied to particular, historically rooted ways of living.

Notes

1. Ernst Cassirer, *Rousseau, Kant, Goethe: Two Essays*, trans. James Gutmann, Paul Oskar Kristeller, and John Herman Randall, Jr. (Princeton, NJ: Princeton University Press, 1947), 1.

2. Susan Shell, *The Embodiment of Reason: Kant on Spirit, Generation, and Community* (Chicago: University of Chicago Press, 1996), 81.

3. Kant, cited in George Armstrong Kelly, *Idealism, Politics, and History: Sources of Hegelian Thought* (New York: Cambridge University Press, 1969), 92.

4. Susan Shell, *The Rights of Reason: A Study of Kant's Philosophy and Politics* (Buffalo: University of Toronto Press, 1980), 22.

5. The charge of "formalism" is one of several traditionally leveled at Kantian ethics. See Onora O'Neill, "Kantian Ethics," in *A Companion to Ethics*, ed. Peter Singer (Oxford: Blackwell, 2003). There are a number of different problems critics have raised in association with this term. While some have alleged that formal rules are too indeterminate to be useful in guiding ethical conduct, others have, conversely, seen such rules as overly rigid and insensitive to the needs of particular circumstances. Still others have argued that action-guiding ethical rules by themselves are inadequate to motivate ethical behavior. The problem to be addressed in the present study, which is ultimately concerned with the autonomy tradition's legacy in contemporary political thought, is the conceptualization of moral principles as reified entities, seen as separate from the interlocutors who draw on them.

6. It must be acknowledged that although Kant's philosophy is justly described as more "rationalist" than that of Rousseau, the general will, as G. D. H. Cole observes, is certainly a "rational" will in the Kantian sense. Admittedly, Kant's universalizing procedure, performed by the operation of practical reason, is what grounds the categorical imperative, whereas Rousseau's general will is an expression of the feeling or sentiment that is said to be written on the heart of man. However, the benevolence of man's natural sentiment points toward the wish for equality manifested in the general will. Thus, as Cole succinctly states, "The 'rational' precepts of the General Will . . . find an echo in the heart of [Rousseau's] 'natural' man." G. D. H. Cole, introduction to *The Social Contract and Discourses by Jean-Jacques Rousseau*, trans. G. D. H. Cole (Toronto: Dent, 1923). Consequently, though Rousseau's theory is grounded in emotion and Kant's in reason, it is this universalization of the will that represents the true "rationality" or consistent application to all subjects that is the moral core of both philosophies.

7. Although Kant's political and legal thought will also be discussed, the principal focus in this chapter will be his moral philosophy, since it has been the most influential for the development of the autonomy tradition. The primary source will thus be his *Grounding for the Metaphysics of Morals*, though other works will be referenced as well. See Immanuel Kant, *Grounding for the Metaphysics of Morals*,

3rd ed., trans. James W. Ellington (1785; Indianapolis, IN: Hackett, 1993). Also important for Kant's ethical theory is his *Critique of Practical Reason* and, to a lesser extent, his *Metaphysics of Morals*, both of which are similarly concerned with the question of duty and the establishment of the supreme principle of morality. See Immanuel Kant, *Critique of Practical Reason*, trans. Werner S. Pluhar (1788; Indianapolis: Hackett, 2002); *Metaphysics of Morals*, trans. James W. Ellington (1797; Indianapolis: Hackett, 1983).

    8. See Cassirer, *Rousseau, Kant, Goethe*, esp. 25–35.

    9. Ibid., 30–31; Jean-Jacques Rousseau, *Rousseau's Political Writings*, trans. Julia Conaway Bondanella, ed. Alan Ritter (New York: Norton, 1988), 92.

    10. Cassirer, *Rousseau, Kant, Goethe*, 30.

    11. Cassirer quoting Rousseau in ibid., 31.

    12. Immanuel Kant, *Grounding for the Metaphysics of Morals*, 15.

    13. Cassirer, *Rousseau, Kant, Goethe*, 31–32.

    14. Ibid., 35.

    15. George Armstrong Kelly, "Rousseau, Kant, and History," *Journal of the History of Ideas* 29, no. 3 (1968): 347.

    16. Ibid., 348.

    17. David Lay Williams, *Rousseau's Platonic Enlightenment* (University Park: Pennsylvania State University Press, 2007), 220.

    18. Ibid., 224–26.

    19. Richard Velkley, *Freedom and the End of Reason: On the Moral Foundation of Kant's Critical Philosophy* (Chicago: University of Chicago Press, 1989), 7.

    20. Williams, *Rousseau's Platonic Enlightenment*, 207.

    21. Ibid.

    22. Engaging in philosophical reasoning does not per se diminish the concreteness of one's thinking. For it is possible to conceive of philosophy in ways that are more or less abstract, due to the degree of correspondence that the latter has to historical reality. Philosophy can thus be seen as departing more or less radically from the concrete material of human history while becoming no more "philosophical" for its radicality. The quality of abstraction is, therefore, not a characteristic of philosophy as such, but indicates a lack of adherence or faithfulness to the truth of historical experience. For Claes Ryn, a prominent critic of Rousseau and the abstract character of his thinking, such fidelity to historical reality is implied by the term "philosophical reason," properly understood. He explains, "Philosophical reason is . . . historical, not in the empirical-positivistic sense, but in the sense that it is closely attentive to the experiential facts of the enduring but evolving human consciousness. If philosophical reason has some understanding about the goal of human existence, it is not because it enjoys privileged access to 'ideal' truth or norms of perfection, but because it has knowledge about the permanent *categorial structure* of human life, of the formal conditions of goodness, truth and beauty

as historically manifested in practical action, art and thinking." Claes G. Ryn, "Philosophical Reason: Historical, Systematic, and Humble," in *Humanitas* 6, no. 2 (1993): 85–86. Emphasis in the original.

23. Once again, see Rousseau's most explicit and deliberate aim to depart from such "facts" in *Discourse on the Origin of Inequality*, trans. Donald A. Cress, introduced by James Miller (Indianapolis: Hackett, 1992), 17.

24. Although O'Neill explicitly connects "formalism" and "abstraction," she nonetheless divides these into separate categories of criticism, arguing that while the charge of "formalism" alleges that the categorical imperative is an empty doctrine, that of "abstraction" concedes that the latter contains some principles, but maintains that these are too vague or indeterminate to guide one's choices. O'Neill, "Kantian Ethics," 181–82. This distinction, which is relevant for the study of Kantian ethics, has no bearing on the present study, which is less concerned with the "action guiding" nature of moral principles than with the shared meaning (or lack thereof) when they are used in the justification of political positions. For the purposes of my analysis, I thus use the terms "formalistic" and "abstract" interchangeably.

25. Velkley, *Freedom and the End of Reason*, esp. ch. 3.

26. Ibid., 62. In this observation, Velkley thus echoes James Miller's remark about the irony with which Rousseau uses the term "perfectibility" in his description of man in the state of nature. See chapter 1 of the present work.

27. Ibid.

28. Ibid., 64.

29. Ibid., 26. William Galston is among the most thorough in his discussion of Rousseau's idea of man's "perfectibility" and its connection to the ideal of autonomy. Galston uses "spontaneity" to characterize this Rousseauistic expression of freedom, and he clearly sees it as anticipating Kant's concept of autonomy but, curiously, does not explicitly connect this to Kant's discussion of spontaneity as a constituent part of the freedom of the will (*Willkür*) to be discussed below. See Galston, *Kant and the Problem of History* (Chicago: University of Chicago Press, 1975), 116–23.

30. James Miller, introduction to Rousseau, *Discourse on the Origin of Inequality*, xvii.

31. Lewis White Beck, "Kant's Two Conceptions of the Will in Their Political Context," in *Kant and Political Philosophy*, ed. Ronald Beiner and William James Booth (New Haven, CT: Yale University Press, 1993), 39.

32. Ibid.

33. Velkley, *Freedom and the End of Reason*, 108, 200.

34. The influences on Kant's thinking that reflect this metaphysical dualism throughout his life's work are, to be sure, numerous and complex and cannot exclusively be attributed to Rousseau. Furthermore, this is obviously a dualism that, in the larger sense, pervades the philosophical climate of the seventeenth and eighteenth centuries. It is therefore important to note that Rousseau's transmission to Kant of an anti-historical, metaphysical dualism is not intended to rule out the influence

of others on Kant's thinking, such as Leibniz and Berkeley vis-à-vis his idealism. See Kant, *The Critique of Pure Reason*, trans. Werner S. Pluhar (1781; Indianapolis: Hackett, 1996). Nevertheless, with respect to Kant's moral and political philosophy, the stamp of Rousseau's conception of freedom as autonomy, which is defined in opposition to concrete experience as a normative basis for the exercise of a moral will, is unmistakable.

35. Kant, *Grounding for the Metaphysics of Morals*, 53.

36. Ibid.

37. Michael Sandel, *Liberalism and the Limits of Justice*, 2nd ed. (Cambridge: Cambridge University Press, 1998), 9.

38. Notwithstanding his indebtedness to Rousseau discussed above, it is worth noting Kant's modification of the general will here. For Rousseau had seen reason as a faculty emerging from history and the development, in particular, of language, in part 2 of the *Second Discourse*. Kant, by contrast, more closely tracks the mind-body dualism of Descartes with regard to the operation of reason or the intellect. The immaterial realm or realm of the spirit in Rousseau's dichotomy is instead occupied by the "heart," "feeling," "instinct," "inner voice," or "conscience" of natural man, which he describes as directly inspired by the divinity, as discussed in the previous chapter. See also note 6 above. More will be said on the relationship between reason and emotion in Rousseau in the final chapter.

39. See Immanuel Kant, "To Perpetual Peace: A Philosophical Sketch" (1795), in *Perpetual Peace and Other Essays* (Indianapolis: Hackett, 1982).

40. Ibid., 133.

41. Williams, *Rousseau's Platonic Enlightenment*, 216. The point can obviously be pressed too far, and Williams comes close to doing so. It is anachronistic, for example, to read into Plato an aversion to historical particularity stemming from a concern with the problem of historicism, since historical consciousness only emerged in Western philosophy in the late eighteenth and early nineteenth centuries and thus would have been inaccessible to him. Still, Williams's interpretation of Kant as echoing Plato's aversion to particularity supports the present argument. Where I part company with Williams is my argument that Kant and Rousseau went further than Plato in their establishment of an anti-historical conception of right and critique of tradition.

42. Ibid., 216–17.

43. Ibid., 217. Emphasis added.

44. Velkley, *Freedom and the End of Reason*, 18.

45. Kant, "What Is Enlightenment?," in *Perpetual Peace and Other Essays*, 41.

46. Ibid., 44.

47. See, in particular, Kelly, *Idealism, Politics, and History*, 89–104.

48. Ibid., 94.

49. Kelly, although admiring of Cassirer's analysis of the relationship between Rousseau and Kant, raises criticisms that point to Cassirer's failure to appreciate

Kant's significantly more optimistic attitude toward the future and the possibility of human progress. See Kelly, "Rousseau, Kant, and History," 348.

50. Williams, *Rousseau's Platonic Enlightenment*, 218, 233.

51. Kant, cited in ibid., 213.

52. Kant, cited in ibid., 213.

53. Kant, *Grounding for the Metaphysics of Morals*, 23.

54. Thus, for Aristotle, law's general or abstract character, while allowing it to encompass a broad range of activity, also precludes it from anticipating the contingent nature of particular cases, which gives rise to the need for judges and decisions of equity. See Aristotle, *Nicomachean Ethics*, trans. W. D. Ross (New York: Oxford University Press, 2009), 98–99 (1137b–1138a).

Chapter 3

Democracy's Deliberation

Over the course of the last several decades, the autonomy tradition of Rousseau and Kant has enjoyed somewhat of a renaissance in contemporary democratic theory. Frustrated by extant theories of democracy that understood political legitimacy in terms of majoritarian voting and the aggregation of individual preferences, scholars began to scrutinize this standard as inadequately capturing the ideal of collective self-determination that is conceived as central to the idea of democracy. The problem with the "aggregative" model, it was argued, was that it reduced democratic governance to a procedure for determining winners and losers in the large-scale promotion of individual preferences.[1] While this might be seen as fair for its equal treatment of those preferences, it was argued, in no meaningful sense could those who were on the losing end of such a process be seen as authors of the policies to which they were bound, or self-determining agents. As a result, a number of scholars began to articulate the theory known as "deliberative democracy,"[2] which required citizens' participation in discussions over the policies by which they were to be governed, so that through a process of mutual justification and persuasion, policy decisions might come to be seen as belonging to the people as a whole, rather than simply a majority.[3] Even if citizens were not ultimately convinced or brought into agreement with one another's views, the process of giving reasons for one's position was seen as treating others as equal participants in and coauthors of political outcomes. Such decisions, even where deep cleavages remain, can be seen as collectively fashioned, in contrast to a process that merely counts up interests, "while keeping our fingers crossed that [others'] are outweighed."[4]

The central concern of the deliberative turn in contemporary democratic theory is therefore with the authenticity of democracy, that is, its fidelity to the ideal of collective self-determination, which is seen as requiring a deep commitment to public communication in the pursuit of others' agreement or consent to the policies that govern them.[5] As noted in chapter 1, it is somewhat ironic for Rousseau to be identified as the intellectual forebear to the theory of deliberative democracy. For he was explicit that the citizens in his social contract should be *prohibited* from conversing with one another and potentially interfering with the formation of an authentic general will.[6] However, despite this disagreement with respect to means, the end sought by Rousseau and his intellectual progeny was ultimately the same—the fundamental concern with autonomy that is at the heart of this political project. Contemporary deliberative democrats thus share with the autonomy tradition the goal of reconciling freedom and authority, or, more precisely, showing political authority to be compatible with the priority of respecting individual freedom.[7] Only, instead of prohibiting discussion in order to promote the general will, deliberative democrats actually insist upon reason-giving or justification for policies. By requiring that policies be justified to all other members of society, or with reference to "reasons that all can accept,"[8] deliberative democrats are similarly motivated by the aspiration to universal endorsement or sanction of the coercive authority to which citizens are bound. For this is thought to establish—even if in a weaker sense than Rousseau or Kant may have wished—the authorship of all citizens of the laws by which they are governed.

But how, it might be asked, could one expect reasons that are universally acceptable to exist in modern democratic societies, which are typically characterized by an enormous diversity of outlooks with respect to ultimate values, or the ends of human life? Deliberative democrats provide different answers to this difficult question, but it is their common grounding in Kant's conception of universal reason that principally supports this contention. In this chapter, these foundations of the deliberative turn in contemporary democratic theory will be examined in order to identify key assumptions that have informed its development. At the trunk of this intellectual family tree or genealogy, one encounters Jürgen Habermas and John Rawls, two of the most prominent political theorists of the late twentieth century, coming from the Continental and Anglo-American philosophical traditions, respectively, who explicitly endorse and elaborate the theory of deliberative democracy.[9] Key pieces of their writing will be examined, as well as that of others, such as Amy Gutmann and Dennis Thompson, along with Joshua

Cohen, whom they influenced and who were themselves influential. After identifying the conceptual framework within which this conversation has taken place, the chapter will proceed to argue two main points. First, it will further support the contention, which was briefly asserted at the end of the previous chapter, that the intellectual roots of deliberative democracy are discoverable in the autonomy tradition inherited from Rousseau and Kant. Second, it will show that as a result of this lineage, deliberative democracy contains the metaphysical dualism that has already been associated with this tradition, which results in a utopian conception of a limitless body or group of interlocutors. It will then be the task of subsequent chapters to reconceptualize the relationship between deliberation and tradition, the precondition of *genuine* deliberation, which will require collapsing this metaphysical dualism inherited by contemporary democratic theory.

The Uses of Public Reason

The perspective from which it is necessary to view this convergence in the thinking of Habermas and Rawls is their common background in Kant's practical philosophy and the attempt to identify the proper procedure for resolving questions of justice.[10] Both of these thinkers follow Kant in seeing such questions as matters of fairness or impartiality between conflicting interests, which are resolvable at a general, abstract level, in contrast to narrower questions of ethics.[11] While particular traditions contain distinct conceptions of happiness and virtue, the "moral point of view" instead points toward universal moral imperatives that, in Habermas's terms, transcend the particularity of the lifeworld.[12] Both thinkers, therefore, ascribe to reason a role that is deemed suitable for the circumstances of the modern, pluralistic society, insofar as the intellect's capacity for distantiation from traditional ways of life allows for the possibility of adjudicating, impartially, between a variety of such narrower perspectives. Kant's various formulations of the categorical imperative were intended to capture the rational acceptability of the maxims or principles supporting one's actions, which is central to the moral point of view. And, despite their modifications, it is this same idea of free subjects treating one another reciprocally as equals that inspires the procedural frameworks of both Habermas and Rawls. "In the Kantian tradition, respect for the individual is tied to the freedom of each to act on norms she can herself accept as right and concern for the general interest to the impartiality of laws that all can agree to on that basis."[13] Where differences between these thinkers arise is with respect to our knowing what is acceptable, or the appropriate method for testing the validity of such norms.

Habermas develops his revision of Kantian ethics over the course of several years, but its most systematic exposition is found in his "discourse ethics,"[14] where he "reconstructs" the validity test of the categorical imperative to establish its basis in intersubjective communication, rather than individual consciousness. Drawing on work in the pragmatics of language by Karl-Otto Apel, Habermas shows that, in every speech act made by a competent speaker, certain unavoidable presuppositions are subscribed to, which he terms the "transcendental-pragmatic presuppositions of argumentation."[15] Principal among these presuppositions is the implicit desire for rationally motivated agreement, indicating that the logical structure of argument itself may be said to rule out "all external or internal coercion other than the force of the better argument."[16] Building further upon this insight, Habermas deduces a number of "symmetry rules" that he believes any speech act must adhere to in order to avoid a performative contradiction: that each subject is allowed to participate in discourse, that each is allowed to question any assertion, introduce any assertion, or express himself in any way, and that none of these rights may be abridged by coercion.[17] In short, whenever we seek to persuade or gain the assent of another competent speaker, offering them the opportunity to accept or reject the validity of a given assertion, our speech implicitly points to the ideal of coercion-free discourse, or what Habermas famously refers to as the "ideal speech situation."[18]

Habermas's reliance on language theory has important implications for his revision of Kantian ethics and what he believes is required to test the validity of norms. For it is conformity to the symmetry rules outlined above that warrants discourse's assessment of a truly free consensus among subjects. And it is discourse, therefore, that becomes the appropriate mechanism for testing the rational acceptability or justice of any norm.[19] As a result, Habermas shows that the impartiality entailed in the moral point of view is no longer capable of being discerned, as Kant once believed, through theoretical reflection on a norm's universalizability, but instead must be discovered in communicative action among subjects themselves, the outcome of which the philosopher has no privileged knowledge.[20] The universalization of norms, to be sure, still has a role in this procedure, as participants in such a discourse may not merely be strategic, but must adopt the perspectives or vantage points of all others, an attitude that Habermas refers to as "ideal role taking" or the "universal exchange of roles."[21] Still, this attitude is to be adopted not by the lone theorist who tests norms for logical inconsistency or self-contradiction, but by participants in actual discourses, who engage in discursive testing in order to determine mutual acceptability, that is, the terms of cooperation to which all can agree.[22]

In light of this insistence on practical discourses to determine the validity of norms, Habermas's reconstruction of the moral point of view is said to distinguish itself from that of others, such as Kant and Rawls, who treat monologically problems of justice that demand dialogical resolution.[23] In other words, it emphasizes that the rational acceptability of norms finds its ultimate expression in a consensus among competent speakers or a "common will," rather than speculation by those who may be insensitive to the particular perspectives of those affected by its adoption.[24] The conception of public reason in the discourse ethics is, therefore, defined procedurally, which is to say, only in terms of requiring the universalization of perspectives and discursive testing among those affected, not in terms of specific principles determined through theoretical or a priori reflection. Indeed, Habermas is insistent, particularly in his dialogue with Rawls, that all questions of public deliberation must remain entirely open and undetermined in advance of such discourses.[25] And it is for this reason that Habermas is often contrasted with Rawls as having a more authentically "republican," orientation toward the public use of reason.

Furthermore, it is not only the substance of public reason that is unrestricted for Habermas, but also the participants who are to constitute this "public" that deliberates. Defining its contours broadly, Habermas understands the latter to encompass not only public officials, such as legislators, judges, and bureaucrats, but also "unofficial networks of private people communicating about public matters," whom he sees as constituting the very "nervous system of the public sphere."[26] As a result of this extension, it becomes difficult to distinguish the public from the private sphere on Habermas's account, whose conception of "public" and "public reason" encompasses not only all competent speakers but all competent speech at every level of society, including that of the lifeworld.[27] Habermas's republican proceduralism, and the indeterminacy that it entails, is so thoroughgoing that it is brought to bear even on the outcomes of public deliberation themselves. For such resolutions, according to Habermas, must never be conceived as settled or fixed but remain forever susceptible to further discussion and modification.[28] Even the constitution, whose very purpose is, at least in part, to fix procedures for collective regulation of the public sphere, should be viewed as continually under revision, a project that is never complete but requires constant revisiting in light of changes in circumstances and in the people themselves.[29]

However, just as Habermas's proceduralism levels charges at those, such as Rawls, who would preempt the resolution of substantive questions properly left to public deliberation, so has he incurred criticism from these very scholars in relation to his own account of public reason. These scholars claim, in the first place, that the problem with Habermas's proceduralist account is that it fails to take seriously the problem of value pluralism, which threatens convergence on universally acceptable justifications, particularly with its unrestricted conception of public reason. And, in the second place, there are a number of scholars who fear that even if a consensus were to emerge, Habermas has provided insufficient protection for core liberal values, such as fundamental rights and liberties, which are especially vulnerable to the vicissitudes of broad public participation in political discussions. In short, those such as Rawls perceive a utopianism in Habermas, who is said to place too much faith in republican procedures to ensure that a consensus among deliberators would either be likely or just.

Having been accused of utopianism in connection with his own seminal work, *A Theory of Justice*, Rawls becomes concerned with constructing a more realistic theory of liberalism, which provides a practical basis for the ideal of "justice as fairness," than he had previously articulated.[30] In *Political Liberalism*, Rawls thus addresses this concern by developing the idea of an "overlapping consensus" of "reasonable comprehensive doctrines," which helps him to build both stability and fundamental liberal principles into his theory from the outset.[31] According to Rawls, the focal point of such a consensus is a "political conception of justice," by which he means a set of shared convictions in the public political culture that is "freestanding"; that is, it is independent from and does not presuppose any comprehensive religious, philosophical, or moral doctrine.[32] To be sure, Rawls is clear that the political conception of justice is not merely a modus vivendi, allowing for peaceful coexistence amid the fact of pluralism. Although based on a consensus that is indeed oriented toward mutual accommodation, Rawls's theory of political liberalism is more than just a pragmatic political arrangement. In a well-ordered democratic society, Rawls explains, the overlapping consensus contains the moral principles that all citizens are free and equal and that the society should be a fair system of cooperation.[33] Moreover, he fully acknowledges that citizens will embrace the political conception of justice because of its connection to each individual's comprehensive moral outlook. It is this connection, in fact, that motivates each to refrain from imposing their comprehensive doctrines upon others, a commitment to toleration that Rawls identifies with a society of "reasonable pluralism."[34] Still, in spite of this moral grounding, the idea of a *political* conception of justice indicates that whenever such values are invoked in arguments regarding our political, social, or economic institutions, they are "presented without saying, or knowing, or hazarding a conjecture about" the particular comprehensive doctrine that supports them.[35] Their use in public justification, in other words, must be strictly "political, not metaphysical."[36]

For Rawls, the existence of reasonable pluralism in a democratic society is what facilitates this highly circumscribed form of justification. For the orientation toward tolerance in the public political culture of a democracy informs a unique relationship among citizens. Rawls distinguishes this from the (previously mentioned) aggregative model of democracy, in which citizens express only interests and preferences, as well as the more dogmatic conception where the whole truth of comprehensive moral doctrines is asserted by their adherents.[37] In contrast to both of these, Rawls says that democracy entails a "duty of civility," which requires that when we appeal to one another with moral reasons, we do so without reference to the deeper religious, philosophical, or moral foundations of our positions. Consequently, his theory of political liberalism requires an appeal to the truth that is limited by what "each could reasonably expect that others might endorse as consistent with their freedom and equality."[38] Rawls thus identifies the public use of reason with this duty of civility that requires citizens to justify their positions in terms that are strictly inclusive: "The point of the ideal of public reason is that citizens are to conduct their fundamental discussions within the framework of what each regards as a political conception of justice based on values that the others can reasonably be expected to endorse and each is, in good faith, prepared to defend that conception so understood."[39] Because all individuals in a society of reasonable pluralism recognize the illegitimacy of using state power to impose their comprehensive moral doctrines on others, each citizen is expected to censor their own appeal to the latter when they enter the public arena.[40]

The ideal of democratic citizenship that Rawls puts forth thus conceives of public reason in terms of the identification and exclusive use of "political values."[41] In this way, the public sphere is a "special domain" where the political conception of justice alone sanctions the use of state coercion.[42] A strict division between public and private therefore distinguishes Rawls's thinking from that of Habermas, particularly its removal of the most controversial and divisive issues from public deliberation. For Rawls, public reason is seen as facilitating the coexistence of diverse comprehensive doctrines, while recognizing that their most fundamental disagreements are irreconcilable, often involving incommensurable values. Reasonable moral agreement, which is grounded in mutual respect for others' status as equal citizens, becomes the basis for the conduct of democratic politics. Rawls further indicates that the content of public reason, which forms in the public political culture of such societies, is "broadly liberal in character."[43] This means that although there are a variety of "liberalisms" that may emerge from public deliberation—justice as fairness being just one of them—each ensures the priority of basic rights, liberties, and opportunities.[44] This is not to say that there is no room for dissent in the public sphere. Rather, Rawls believes that with these priorities pertaining to the basic structure of society, disagreement can take place within safe boundaries, as it were, knowing that outcomes of deliberation are precluded from violating fundamental liberal values.[45] These substantive commitments vis-à-vis all citizens, together with the procedure of universal justification, Rawls sees as facilitating a form of disagreement that does not threaten or undermine political legitimacy: "We should sincerely think that our view . . . is based on political values everyone can reasonably be expected to endorse. For an electorate thus to conduct itself is a high ideal the following of which realizes fundamental democratic values not to be abandoned simply because full agreement does not obtain."[46] Public reason, on Rawls's account, provides a basis for tolerable diversity of belief, identifying strict boundaries, both substantive and procedural, which allow citizens to agree to the terms of their disagreement.

This framing of the issues surrounding public reason in terms of procedure and substance has shaped much of the literature concerning deliberative democracy.[47] Gutmann and Thompson, whose work has also been influential, define their deliberative ideal as an attempt to overcome the "deadlock" between "procedural democrats" and "constitutional democrats," represented by Habermas and Rawls, respectively.[48] While they distance themselves from the pure proceduralism of Habermas's discourse ethics, their attempt to reconcile the competing "republican" and "liberal" priorities nonetheless places them closer to Habermas than to Rawls. In the first place, Gutmann and Thompson are clearly averse to what they see as the speculative attempt to identify substantive principles prior to actual deliberation by the members of a society.[49] And, for similar reasons, they explicitly reject the proposal of Rawls to bracket or set aside disagreements of a metaphysical nature.[50] To be sure, the position of Gutmann and Thompson is not that there should be no "principles of preclusion," that is, principles that restrict certain types of appeals and even particular issues from the public forum. However, they echo Habermas in their argument that the range of permissible discourse should be substantially wider than most constitutional democrats allow.[51]

In the second place, Gutmann and Thompson also rely on "principles of accommodation," which qualify not the content of public reason but its practice by requiring "mutual respect," which is said to surpass or transcend the liberal concept of tolerance. In other words, these principles point beyond regulating the content of deliberation, instead promoting standards for the manner in which positions are publicly held. Gutmann and Thompson see mutual respect as embodied in a certain "deliberative . . . character," which exhibits a "family of dispositions," such as open-mindedness, sincerity, consistency, flexibility, and magnanimity.[52] Because both procedure and substance are informed by the reciprocity at the heart of the moral point of view, Gutmann and Thompson conclude that it is impossible to give ultimate priority to either one of these two principles over the other, and that it is better to see them as justly limiting each other whenever the need arises in the service of that end.

Similarly attempting to overcome the impasse between procedural and constitutional democrats, Joshua Cohen reconciles the value of fundamental liberties and self-government in a manner that ultimately places him closer to Rawls. According to Cohen, the familiar tension between the liberties of the ancients and those of the moderns has created somewhat of a false dilemma within democratic theory. Or, at least, it is a dilemma that fails to appreciate the demands of democratic governance according to the deliberative conception. For democratic decisions to be authorized by the citizens as a body, collectively, Cohen contends that all must be treated as free and equal—*free* from the coercive imposition of others' fundamental values and *equal* participants in discussions that shape public decisions. This, he explains, is the basis for the requirement that arguments must be made with reasons that all can accept, since this establishes equality for citizens in their contributions to policy formation while maintaining their freedom in qualifying how they are to be ruled by others. Cohen then explains that it is through this very procedure of universal justification that certain substantive outcomes may be ruled out. In requiring justification in terms that all can accept, in other words, we are guaranteed certain limits or restrictions with respect to what it is possible to justify to one's fellow citizens.

What Cohen calls the "principle of deliberative inclusion"—justification using reasons that are acceptable to all others—thus has a way of guaranteeing negative liberty without adverting to a priori principles.[53] He illustrates this with the case of religious liberty. Policies that are to coerce religious believers in a manner that forces them to do what is against their faith, or refrain from doing what their faith requires, must be justified to them in terms that would need to override their most fundamental convictions.[54] Such beliefs must be seen by others neither as preferences capable of being bargained away nor simply moral positions one might be persuaded to revise. Rather, they are seen as imposed from without and, as such, create fundamental obligations for the faithful. Complying with the principle of deliberative inclusion demands justification with reasons capable of superseding or outweighing such sacred duties.[55] However, Cohen argues, the recognition by others that such justifications are unavailable requires them to respect the right of adherents *never* to be coerced in this manner. As a result, the principle of deliberative inclusion is said to guarantee the liberty of conscience and worship, or "free exercise" of religion.[56] Cohen's attempt to overcome the division between procedural and constitutional democrats ultimately places him closer to Rawls than to Habermas. For it takes as given and as part of the reality of living within the fact of pluralism, the irreconcilable nature of deep metaphysical disagreements and, as a result, declares such matters to be external to public reason. While Cohen shares with Gutmann and Thompson the desire to overcome the divide between procedure and substance, this consequence of the principle of deliberative inclusion echoes Rawls in its reliance on the removal of such matters from discussion.

Deliberation and the Autonomy Tradition

While the idea of public reason aimed at the universal justification of political positions first emerged in these early discussions regarding deliberative democracy, the concept has its roots in the autonomy tradition that can be traced back to Kant and Rousseau.[57] For it was the idea of the general will, first articulated in Rousseau's *Social Contract*, that was responsible for the notion that democratic legitimacy requires citizens to become the authors of the laws by which they are to be governed. This idea has inspired not only those who draw directly on the political philosophy of Rousseau but also those who follow in the footsteps of Kant's moral philosophy and its central concept of the categorical imperative. Looking back to Rousseau's early articulation of the ideal of autonomy, one sees an anticipation of the public reason debate regarding procedure and substance, insofar as Rousseau concerns himself with both the process of citizens' participation in politics and the justice of outcomes for those who live under the law. In short, the general will is concerned with the status of each citizen as both ruler and ruled. It will be argued here that the republican and liberal values that are at stake in these contemporary discussions arose out of an ambivalence in Rousseau's thinking about autonomy.[58] For he leaves unresolved within the idea of the general will a latent tension between these competing concerns, which becomes more pronounced as democratic theorists have employed the contemporary analogue of "public reason," in order to confront the challenge that pluralism poses for the political legitimacy of democratic societies.

Christopher Bertram has remarked that Rousseau not only anticipates recent discussions regarding the role of public reason in establishing political legitimacy,[59] but that his social contract can actually be understood as codifying public reason into law.[60] Bertram argues that advocates of public reason, insofar as they are divided between procedural and constitutional democrats,[61] are echoing an equivocation in Rousseau's writings about the general will.[62] Therefore, he shows how Rousseau vacillates and actually tries to "blur" the distinction between a "transcendent" or objective conception of the common will of citizens and a "democratic" or procedural conception that identifies the common will strictly with their agreement, whatever that may be.[63] Noting this ambiguity in Rousseau's thinking, Bertram speculates on how these priorities might be reconciled, arguing that it is possible to read Rousseau as "committed to [both] a hypothetical and a procedural view, such that the general will would indeed emerge from the collective decision-making of citizens, just in case the right conditions for its emergence were actually in place."[64] In other words, just procedures create the conditions under which objectively just outcomes may be expected to emerge from citizens' collective decision-making. Habermas and others have attempted, in similar fashion, to ensure liberal political outcomes through the stipulation of ideal deliberative procedures, often claiming that an illiberal consensus is an indication of distorted or coerced forms of communication. The important point here is not whether this attempt at reconciling liberal and republican values has been successful, but that one notes the same tension or dynamic at work in Rousseau's general will that one later sees in one of the foremost exponents of public reason.

The autonomy that is achieved in the general will is a conception of freedom in which individuals must be treated as moral ends, insofar as they are directed only by their own will. When all subjects will the common or general will, as opposed to their private interests or inclinations, each is united in a will that belongs to other citizens, yet is adopted as one's own will. In order to align the numerous individual wills of society in this way, citizens must will only what is in the public interest, or the common good. As a result of universalizing their wills in this manner, each may be said to acquire a new type of freedom, Rousseau's "moral freedom," and escape the coercion of others. In doing so, one is rendered free in two senses—in one's capacity as both ruler and ruled. As the author of the will that rules over oneself, each may be said to determine his own destiny, and as one whose will remains uncoerced by others, there is no external imposition of another's will.[65] The former entails participation in the process of creating legislation, while the latter is concerned with one's treatment under the law and the substantive limits to legislation needed to preclude coercion. For Rousseau, both of these priorities may be seen as satisfied in the general will because both types of coercion may be obviated when all converge on the common good. However, such an alignment of wills is only possible when, as discussed previously, the self that is conceived purely in noumenal terms is separated from, or independent of, the experiential or phenomenal self that is specific to one individual. Otherwise, desires and interests make an individual will narrow and particular and threaten the unity that guarantees each will's escape from empirical determination.

Kant is seemingly motivated by both of these concerns as well in his development of the categorical imperative. However, his understanding of the nature of practical reason renders his test of the morality of any action an operation of the solitary intellect. This has the effect of establishing hypothetical limits on conduct based on reason's ability to identify actions that are irreconcilable with the reciprocal actions of others, or those that fail the test of universalization. Kant's pure practical reason, in other words, while not generating its own maxims, could deduce negative prohibitions on the acceptability of hypothetical actions. As previously discussed, Habermas sees the theoretical or monological nature of any such test by itself as problematic from the point of view of post-conventional society where the diversity of perspectives within the whole are based not only on the individual's interests, but also the morally pluralistic nature of modern life. His supplementation of the universalization principle (U) in his own thinking with the discourse principle (D) is designed to overcome this difficulty of Kantian ethics. Put in the terms of the present discussion, Habermas's critique of Kant can be seen as recognizing the one-sidedness that Kant represents in the autonomy tradition, which favored substantive limitations on the treatment of subjects over the procedural requirement of participation in public decisions. Others who follow Kant are similarly concerned with the justice of outcomes and derive constitutionalist conclusions from tests that resemble or further elaborate the categorical imperative. While Kant himself derived few conclusions with regard to the substance of such agreements—often resulting in the charge that the categorical imperative represented an "empty formalism"—the fuller development of this reflective method in mechanisms such as Rawls's veil of ignorance deduced specific, absolute limits with regard to what freedom requires.

Having inherited this tradition from Rousseau and Kant, Habermas and Rawls can each be seen as principally concerned with one of these particular dimensions of autonomy and as giving that priority or precedence over the other, as if they were rendering more consistent or systematic one of the central moral impulses in Rousseau's *Social Contract*. Habermas's view of public reason as unrestricted deliberation aimed at a universal agreement thus emphasizes the republican principle of self-determination and is a revision of the perceived overemphasis in Kant's categorical imperative on objectivity, while Rawls's political constructivism is more concerned with the justice of outcomes and may be seen as a political application and further development of Kant's moral philosophy.[66] While there are differences between their respective positions, as discussed earlier in this chapter, they are joined in the belief that the aim of uniting one's will with that of all others is the surest way to promote freedom as autonomy. The proximity or convergence in their thinking can therefore be explained by the fact that public reason seeks to satisfy the concerns about autonomy of each for their respective reasons. For Habermas, public reason aims at a consensus over norms that are universally acceptable (U), confirmed through a testing process that involves broad participation in practical discourses (D). For Rawls, public reason entails the limitation of claims to justice that are strictly political (not metaphysical), so that all citizens are left uncoerced by legislation that reflects no particular set of metaphysical commitments. Gutmann and Thompson and Cohen have, each in their own way, tried to reconcile these competing concerns with procedure and substance, though each ultimately emphasizes one or the other of these two priorities relating to autonomy.

What is key and unavoidable for each of these thinkers, regardless of the priority of deliberative procedures or the substantive outcomes of deliberation, is the possibility of reasons or justifications endorsed by "all." The ideal of autonomy, in other words, is only conceivable when the universalization of wills is conceivable, based on its uniting or converging with the wills of all other participants in discourse. But this ultimately implies that at the center of the idea of public reason resides a metaphysical dualism that is similar to that which was observed in Rousseau's general will—a unity of all wills that depends on their identity, or possibility of convergence, beyond the limitations of the phenomenal or historical realm.[67] For what is common or shared in justifications to all, like the general will, cannot be particular if one is to avoid the coerciveness that is implied by less than universal endorsement. Such justifications are ultimately conceived as lacking historical particularity and the narrowness of perspective that the latter entails, and they are shared by an implied community of reasoners that, for this same reason, must not be susceptible to temporal restrictions.[68] The persons with whom one unites one's will, therefore, having been stripped of their historical character or particularity, can be seen as akin to noumenal selves, lacking the distinctiveness that would interfere with the universalization of wills and threaten the freedom of citizens, whether in their capacity as rulers or ruled.[69]

Constitutionalists and proceduralists alike share in this assumption insofar as they retain what Habermas calls the "moral point of view," which was originally conceptualized in Rousseau's general will and then more fully elaborated by Kant's categorical imperative and the use of pure practical reason. The implication of bringing this dualism into political deliberation and justification is that in order for the ideal of autonomy to be conceivable, the impediments to one's discursive appeals that are historically particular and exclusive must be seen as both illegitimate and theoretically capable of being transcended, that is, they are excluded from the consensus of which only the noumenal will or self is a part. The "all" assumed in each characterization of what establishes political legitimacy—for example, justification to all others or using specifically "reasons that all can accept"—can therefore be seen as implying an agreement among deliberators that is radically non-exclusive with regard to perspectives, since limitation is synonymous with the particularity that, ipso facto, renders autonomy problematic. However, if this is the necessary implication of the Rousseauian-Kantian inheritance of "the moral point of view," public reason must ultimately assume not only the existence of such universal reasons, but universal reasoners who would be capable of their apprehension and employment in discourse. Such individuals are implicitly seen as joining together with others in what is essentially a noetic realm of public principles or reasons that, in order for all to remain free, must never be limited by the parochial nature of their historical backgrounds. In the following section, the criticism will thus be raised that deliberative democracy has, in this way, tacitly posited or relied upon the notion of a limitless community of interlocutors and, for its refusal to allow such exclusion from its consensus, has essentially done away with any meaningful conception of community.

The Community without Limits

The idea of using public reason to achieve a universal justification of political positions relies upon the key premise that universally acceptable reasons both exist and are recognizable to all citizens in contemporary democratic societies. Deliberative democracy, insofar as it is influenced by the autonomy tradition, affirms this by asserting that just norms are grounded not in any particular worldview, but in a form of universal rationality that can become distantiated and thus abstracted from the particularity that constitutes the ethical life, or what Hegel refers to as *Sittlichkeit*.[70] The recognition of this potential for universal justification, according to Habermas and Rawls, has become increasingly accessible to individuals of various cultural and ethical backgrounds in modern, pluralistic societies, since the bonds of custom and tradition have come under increasing strain and opened the door for a conception of justice that is rationally accessible to all. Consequently, paired with the idea of a limitless or potentially universal speech community is the employment of a historical narrative that declares our awareness or recognition of these conditions to be a uniquely modern phenomenon. This historical narrative belonging to the theory of deliberative democracy will be examined in more detail in a later chapter.[71] For now, the question of what is assumed with regard to the existence of such justifications or reasons must be further examined, in order to establish the fundamentally utopian nature of such thinking about democratic societies and the fact of political pluralism.

In light of what has been said, it comes as no surprise that those who contemplate the possibility of universal authorization of the law see the mere majoritarianism of the aggregative model of democracy as problematic. For this fractures the citizenry and their disparate wills, sanctioning the rule of private interests that belong only to some, while denying the loss of freedom among those who are in no way authors of the law and are ruled according to others. The narrowness of perspective adopted by citizens within the aggregative model is principally attributable to its grounding in the satisfaction of individual desires or preferences. However, for the autonomy tradition, more than hedonistic interests are seen to be a threat or impediment to the universalization of wills needed for the realization of freedom. It is also the particularity of the ethical life, or historical patterns of living, that jeopardize the consensus upon which autonomy depends. For, in either case, what narrowly belongs to one individual or group of individuals, by virtue of their concrete experience or phenomenality, is permitted to direct the lives of others such that freedom is compromised. The reconciliation of freedom and authority, consequently, is seen by deliberative democrats as similarly jeopardized by the conditions of moral pluralism as much as it is by interest assertion and aggregation in the public sphere, due to the threat that this poses to the universality requirement in the ideal of autonomy.

As a result, the imperative of merely deliberating, unqualified by the adoption of "the moral point of view," is insufficient to address the problem that pluralism poses for political legitimacy, according to deliberative democrats. For even the most genuine or earnest appeals from one's narrow ethical perspective may fall on deaf ears, given the deep metaphysical commitments upon which political disagreements are based within contemporary democratic society. How, then, is it possible to contend with the threat that pluralism poses to autonomy, since some citizens will invariably find themselves in the minority on particular political issues? The aspiration of many deliberative democrats is achieving political legitimacy through universal justification so that even when there is failure to reach specific policy agreements, political disagreement is underpinned by an alleged or implied unity among interlocutors, which is to say these theorists posit a unity of moral wills resembling the general will that allows for alleged authorship even of policies with which one disagrees. Though admitting that perfect agreement on matters of law and policy is not possible, the prospect of identifying exclusively with one's "universal" self in public matters raises the hope of containing such divisions within this broader normative consensus. We can, it is believed, agree to the terms of our disagreement or "agree to disagree," thus reconciling freedom and authority in a new way under the conditions of pluralism. Autonomy can be preserved for all, it is believed, if each agrees to abide by the requirement of treating others as ends, insofar as we seek to justify ourselves with reasons that are acceptable to everyone. In doing so, we allow for mutual authorship of the law, in that each individual denies his or her narrow, historical form of life the right to rule over others.

In his critique of Habermas, Robert Spaemann characterizes this aspiration to universal agreement for the sake of preserving autonomy in political society as the "utopian goal of the abolition of authority," and he similarly relates Habermas's idea of universal rationality to Rousseau's general will.[72] In doing so, Spaemann identifies a danger in Habermas's thinking, long associated with the general will, which is the potential it affords for suppressing dissent while claiming to speak on behalf of "the true will of the people." This is the well-known temptation of the democratic strain of thinking within the tradition of positive liberty. While Spaemann is correct in identifying this as a real danger of such theories, it ought to be acknowledged that there is, additionally, a less conspicuous though likewise detrimental problem associated with this form of democratic utopianism. The issue is that such imagined agreement can obscure the true, concrete source of all genuine deliberation—the historical patterns of living constitutive of real community, in which shared experiences provide the true ground of mutual appeal and justification. While denying that traditional ways of life may serve as a proper source of legitimacy, due to their ethically particular and thus narrow perspectives, deliberative democrats in the autonomy tradition operate as if all speakers within large, pluralistic democracies can be treated as members of a single group of interlocutors, or "community," whose shared rationality could allow for universal justification. Only now, "community" is tacitly understood as an association of reasoners whose communication is abstracted from and thus untinged by the experiences of any particular ethical tradition. In order to assert this possibility, Habermas and others must neglect, if not entirely redefine, what it means to have a "community" of speakers, while implicitly and sometimes even explicitly positing the existence of new forms of communication that have superseded those of traditional, shared patterns of living.

To be sure, Habermas forthrightly admits that the knowledge that is gained through the use of practical reason is acquired and developed in the lifeworld and, for that reason, he believes his discourse ethics cannot be accused of taking for granted this generative context of communication, as various "neo-Aristotelian" scholars have alleged.[73] However, in order for practical reason to preserve "intact its universalistic core" and remain faithful to the Kantian idea of the moral point of view, Habermas also maintains that such knowledge must not merely grow or develop as one is socialized *into* the lifeworld but must actually point *beyond* it: "Practical knowledge can all the more readily claim to be knowledge the more radically we open ourselves to others and expand our local knowledge and ethnocentric outlook—indeed, extend our community in a virtual manner such that our discourse ultimately includes *all subjects capable of speech and action*."[74] The lifeworld, it may be said, has instrumental value with regard to intersubjective communication, and beyond that, Habermas believes, reason must transcend the authority of traditional norms. As with Rousseau's anti-historical metaphysical dualism, the normative status of practical reason is conceived in Habermas's account in terms that are either universal and moral or particular and immoral. And, as with Rousseau's general will, "the moral point of view" remains elusive even when the good that is common to a particular subgroup with a shared historical life is contemplated.[75] Moral knowledge, on Habermas's understanding, is identified with a collective, developmental maturity, insofar as citizens have transcended the narrow and parochial view of the traditional ethical life into which they were originally socialized.[76]

If the binding power of traditional forms of life has been attenuated, what is left that generates the authority necessary to ground any moral obligations? For Habermas, modernity does not leave us adrift in a skeptical or relativistic posture vis-à-vis social interaction resulting from this attenuation of *Sittlichkeit*. Rather, he sees hope or promise in the very rationality that was responsible for the weakening of traditional forms of life. Regardless of one's ethical tradition, Habermas believes, what always remains in communicative action are the presuppositions of argumentation—the normative implications of the reciprocity implied within any discourse from which Habermas derives his principle of universalization (U), which is at the heart of validity conferring discourses (D). However, this derivation—from a speech act undertaken within a particular linguistic framework to a universal moral principle—trades on an ambiguity. The alleged "universality" from which the principle (U) is derived is discerned from a perspective thought to transcend all particular forms of life, which claims to observe a normative attribute that is universally present in discourse as such: the implicit offer to reject, accept, or respond in any way to the assertion contained in any speech act. Yet this "universality," even if it were a quality or characteristic *of all* communication, certainly ought not to be mistaken for an offer that is made *to all* speakers. That is to say, such utterances are not invitations implicitly extended to all persons, across all traditions and cultures, which ultimately may be said to encompass all competent speakers, or the whole of humanity. To be clear, this is certainly not to say that communication is impossible across such traditions and cultures. Rather, it is to acknowledge that although every tradition may, implicitly make such offers within its speech acts, these communicative appeals presuppose more than just the formal conditions of reciprocity.[77]

To locate this linguistic offer or invitation to respond as the "normative core" of deliberation, in other words, is to abstract away from the *content* of such utterances, focusing exclusively on their *form*. Yet content is what furnishes the concrete texture, richness, and genuine meaning to any form of communication. And it is for this reason that such offers are made, typically and most effectively, to limited, particular groups of interlocutors, who draw on specific, shared experiences, to which such utterances are intimately related. Consequently, if one signals a certain normative import or recognition of the other speaker as the latent presupposition of one's speech, as Habermas is wont to declare, it is not all competent speakers everywhere to whom such recognition is implicitly accorded, but the competent speakers of a circumscribed speech community, whose linguistic competence, crucially anticipated by a given speaker, is grounded in historically preexisting patterns of meaning.

However, the consequence of operating within Habermas's dualistic framework, in which cognitive rationality is thought to be universal and post-metaphysical, and ethical substance is particular and metaphysical, comes with a price. For his insistence on the "universality" of his transcendental-pragmatics—one that transcends the particularity of all forms of life—results in the inability to recognize even the most basic limits to practical reason. The acknowledgment that the latter is informed by the lived experience of a temporally bounded people would, under the conditions of modernity and pluralism, render its judgments parochial, for Habermas, and thus representative of only a narrow perspective. Reason, when viewed in this way, must be capable of apprehension by all who have been emancipated from such shared, historical experiences, along with the boundaries that would exclude those on the outside—pluralism, in other words, must be recognized precisely because such ethical traditions have been weakened. As a result, historical particularity and the standards it engenders becomes, by definition, limited and ethnocentric. However, since the moral point of view is defined in opposition to all that is experiential and particular, it is unclear, for Habermas, how there could *ever* be legitimate boundaries or contours that define such a group or community of competent speakers. Indeed, Habermas appears to believe practical reason is essentially incapable of any such limitation: "If each individual community can achieve 'knowledge' (in not just a metaphorical sense) concerning what is good for it, it is far from obvious why this practical knowledge should not be extended in an intercultural direction and become so thoroughly emancipated from provincial limitations that it orients itself to what is *equally good for all*."[78]

Defending his theory against neo-Aristotelian charges of abstraction, Habermas does not shrink from the theoretically infinite extension of interlocutors in the moral point of view, the outer limits of which are defined only by speaking competence *as such*. Doubling down on this extension, Habermas affirms the ideal of an "unlimited communication community and a universal discourse," which "preserves the characteristics of a transcendental socialization and invokes the social bond that unites humanity as a whole."[79] Notwithstanding his emphasis on actual discourses in the (D) principle, this illimitability of normative criteria—in short, this utopianism—must be seen as stemming from his identification of practical reason with "the moral point of view." For what is tested of norms, "practical" though such discourses may seem, is precisely their conformity with the latter's *universalization principle* (U), that is, the *complete* or total reversibility of all perspectives by individuals who are capable of "distanc[ing] themselves temporarily from the normative spectrum of all existing life."[80] Having divorced themselves from their acculturated, historical experiences and norms of the lifeworld, the perspectives of these selves must therefore "become *completely reversible* in all relevant respects,"[81] a view that is incompatible with the particularity of a historical form of life.

When practical reason aspires to such abstraction, there simply can be no justifiable basis for exclusion from a "community" of reasoners. However, this formulation results in the effective elimination of any genuine deliberation and meaningful concept of a speech community, since reason's endless extension results in a correspondingly endless expansion of interlocutors, or at least, all human beings who are capable of communicative action per se, while neglecting the concrete linguistic practices that furnish their meaning. The idea of community, on Habermas's account, thus no longer represents a unique form of human relationship—one that has developed by living together over time and sharing iterative (though never identical) experiences among particular persons—but merely describes a *similarity* that exists among all human beings insofar as they have some capacity for rational communication. To infer from this the fundamental condition of political justification, what must be denied is the contribution made to meaningful discourse by the historicity of experience.

As mentioned earlier in this chapter, Rawls's thinking appears to undergo a change between the publication of *A Theory of Justice* and *Political Liberalism*, in which he abandons the idea that the members of a well-ordered society might converge on the principles of justice as fairness, in favor of the idea that the latter represents merely one comprehensive doctrine that affirms a political conception of justice, which is the focal point of an overlapping consensus. Yet the idea of what Habermas calls the moral point of view, inherited from the Rousseauian-Kantian autonomy tradition, under-pins Rawls's thinking throughout this evolution, with the result that both works may be seen as characterized by the utopian aspiration to universal agreement, notwithstanding Rawls's efforts to ground a more "realistic" con-sensus in *Political Liberalism*. With regard to his earlier work, Patrick Neal has observed that in *A Theory of Justice*, it is Kant's ideal of autonomy that informs Rawls's concept of the original position, whose aim is to further elaborate Kant's ethics in a political direction.[82] Rawls is therefore explicit that "the original position interprets the point of view of noumenal selves,"[83] which, in excluding the narrow interests of phenomenal beings, points to the alleged universal acceptability of the choices that are made behind the veil of ignorance.[84] Without this assumption, the deduction of principles of justice from his thought experiment would not be warranted: "The person's choice as a noumenal self I have assumed to be a collective one. The force of the self's being equal is that the principles chosen must be acceptable to other selves. . . . This means that as noumenal selves, everyone is to consent to these principles."[85] Rawls, it may be observed, relies here on a similar reversibility of perspective among subjects associated with Habermas and the universalization principle (U).

In *Political Liberalism*, the idea of "everyone" or "all" is admittedly transformed by Rawls out of a concern for the realism of his theory. How-ever, Rawls's idea of a political conception of justice nonetheless remains driven by the aim of universal acceptability and individual autonomy. In other words, the strategy for achieving consensus differs from that of *A The-ory of Justice* in that it is based on an overlap between existing "reasonable comprehensive doctrines."[86] But the goal of universal authorship of law and policy remains the ultimate end of Rawls's theory. Consequently, the political conception of justice that Rawls articulates is, notwithstanding its allegedly historical grounding, still abstract in *Political Liberalism*, so as to ensure the ostensible universality of the consensus among comprehensive religious, philosophical, and moral doctrines. Such convergence on the "principles" of political liberalism, divorced as they are from the concrete practices of the ethical life is thus ultimately illusory. Rather than advocating deliberative appeals based in concrete patterns of living among particular groups, which would necessarily be limited in scale and thus exclusive vis-à-vis the whole of society, Rawls's identification of the contents of his overlapping consensus takes the form of "principles" and "doctrines"—in reality, conceptual reifi-cations or hypostatizations of once historically lived experiences—which are rendered sufficiently abstract so as to make them appear noncontroversial or capable of universal adoption. As a result, Rawls's alleged consensus in *Political Liberalism* trades on the superficial existence of such "reasons that all can accept" by virtue of an abstraction in each instance from experiential particulars. In fact, the reality regarding Rawls's consensus is substantial differences in the potential meaning of such conceptualizations, which reveals itself upon their interpretation by ethically diverse interlocutors at the level of practice and the various circumstances in which such principles inevitably need to be applied.[87]

Severed from their historical contexts, Rawls's universal principles or reasons to which public appeals must be made—such as the provision of "basic liberties," "equality of opportunity," or a "fair system of cooperation"—are capable of acquiring a multitude of diverse meanings, at times even pointing in the direction of rival or opposite political conclusions. These differences of interpretation emerge once abstract principles are translated into the experiential orientations of the concrete persons who must apply them. However, such indeterminate principles are hardly a workable basis for Rawls's idea of public reason, since those meanings vary dramatically depending on the concrete interpreter, and thus are unconvincing or uncompelling to persons of diverse ethical orientations. Consequently, Rawls's overlapping consensus, which serves as the underlying agreement for his principles of public reason, may be seen to rest on a tenuous foundation, the universality of its principles' appeal being conceivable only if the historicity or phenomenality of deliberators is abstracted from, such that their understanding of these principles can be asserted as theoretically reversible and thus capable of persuasion.

The idea of a moral consensus that underpins political disagreement and facilitates large-scale justification is also connected to a novel and indeed questionable conception of community—often implicit, though occasionally explicit—in the Rawlsian conception of deliberative democracy. If the aggregative model of democracy fractures and particularizes the members of society, the deliberative model, by contrast, can be seen as bringing citizens together in recognition of one another's equal membership in the political order. This alone is believed to establish legitimate political association in the age of pluralism, since the latter's grounding in the ethical life and traditional community is conceived by some deliberative democrats as no longer plausible. Thus, Cohen boldly claims, "if political community depends on sharing a comprehensive moral or religious view, or a substantive national identity defined in terms of such a view, then reasonable pluralism *ruins* the possibility of political community."[88] Furthermore, and perhaps more controversially, deliberative democrats such as Cohen who stipulate Rawlsian restrictions on justification claim that their model of public reason actually forges its own bonds of solidarity, furnishing a novel, modern, and inclusive sense of community among interlocutors. In seeking the consent of others to policies that would govern them on their own terms, citizens are thus thought to develop new egalitarian bonds with all other citizens, though with none in particular: "In this assurance of political autonomy, deliberative democracy achieves one important element of the ideal of community. This is so . . . because the requirement of providing acceptable reasons for the exercise of political power to those who are governed by it . . . expresses equal membership of all in the sovereign body responsible for authorizing the exercise of that power."[89] It is in this mutual recognition as equal members of the body politic itself that the value of community is now alleged to be exclusively supported, having replaced the shared practices of historically rooted patterns of living. By seeking others' consent to "binding collective choice" and promoting their autonomy, citizens are said to treat one another as equals, a process that is claimed to form new "solidarities" among them.[90]

However, this novel or uniquely modern account of what generates the bonds of community would appear to place the cart before the horse. For, it claims that mutual justification is capable of contributing to or promoting the value of community, when in fact it is a concrete community and its attendant linguistic and cultural practices that must, in the first place, furnish shared meaning and the values behind the resonance of appeals, in order for any such justification to take place. To posit justification without historical community, in other words, is to see the ethical life (*Sittlichkeit*) and its particularity as not only unnecessary but problematic for communication, at least within the political order of large-scale, pluralistic democracies. In the following chapters, it will be argued that the prejudices that are given to us by these concrete, historical communities are not in fact problematic but are actually *indispensable* to moral and political justification, and, therefore, they can be neglected only at the expense of meaningful deliberation itself.

Additionally, what must be considered in connection with the preceding claim is the familiar challenge just mentioned, which says that "reasonable pluralism ruins the possibility of political community," since it is, in the first place, this avowed feature of modern life that motivates the search for such "solidarities." Both of these concerns are to be addressed in the chapters that follow, in which the case is made for nourishing and sustaining these limited and traditional—though indeed vital—sources of community and ethical orientation. Such experience must ultimately stand in the background of any deliberative engagement, whose justifications have deep meaning and resonance. However much we may desire and seek legitimacy among all-inclusive, pluralistic populations, we may simply have to settle for more realistic—which is to say circumscribed—forms of deliberation, whose experiential and historical nature necessitates their emergence and practice on a more limited scale. For, to deny this challenge and to ignore the degree to which diverse experiences contribute to diverse understandings may, in the long run, undermine more authentic forms of justification and the reasoning that characterizes genuine deliberation.

Notes

1. For the aggregative model, see Kenneth Arrow, *Social Choice and Individual Values*, 2nd ed. (New York: Wiley, 1963); William Riker, *Liberalism against Populism: A Confrontation between the Theory of Democracy and the Theory of Social Choice* (San Francisco: Freeman, 1982); Robert Dahl, *Democracy and Its Critics* (New Haven, CT: Yale University Press, 1989).

2. Some of the earliest references to the term "deliberative democracy" include Joseph M. Bessette, "Deliberative Democracy: The Majority Principle in Republican Government," in *How Democratic Is the Constitution?*, ed. Robert A. Goldwin and William A. Schambra (Washington, DC: American Enterprise Institute, 1980), 102–16, and Cass Sunstein, "Free Speech Now," *University of Chicago Law Review* 59, no. 1 (1992): 255–316. Both of these were later developed into fuller treatments of the idea. See Joseph M. Bessette, *The Mild Voice of Reason: Deliberative Democracy and American National Government* (Chicago: University of Chicago Press, 1994); Cass Sunstein, *The Partial Constitution* (Cambridge, MA: Harvard University Press, 1993).

3. The very success of the theory of deliberative democracy prohibits a comprehensive account of the literature. However, some of the foundational statements related to the idea may be said to include the following: Jürgen Habermas, "Discourse Ethics," in *Moral Consciousness and Communicative Action*, trans. Christian Lenhardt and Shierry Weber Nicholsen (1983; Cambridge, MA: MIT Press, 1990), 43–115; *Between Facts and Norms: Contributions to a Discourse Theory of Law and Democracy*, trans. William Rehg (Cambridge, MA: MIT Press, 1996); John Rawls, *Political Liberalism* (New York: Columbia University Press, 1993); Amy Gutmann and Dennis Thompson, *Democracy and Disagreement* (Cambridge, MA: Harvard University Press, 1996); *Why Deliberative Democracy?* (Princeton, NJ: Princeton University Press, 2004); Joshua Cohen, "Deliberation and Democratic Legitimacy," in *The Good Polity: Normative Analysis of the State*, ed. Alan Hamlin and Philip

Pettit (Oxford: Blackwell, 1989), 17–34; John Dryzek, *Discursive Democracy: Politics, Policy, and Political Science* (New York: Cambridge University Press, 1990); Seyla Benhabib, "In the Shadow of Aristotle and Hegel: Communicative Ethics and Current Controversies in Practical Philosophy," *Philosophical Forum* 21, no. 1 (1989): 1–31; Charles Larmore, *Patterns of Moral Complexity* (Cambridge: Cambridge University Press, 1987); David M. Estlund, "Who's Afraid of Deliberative Democracy? On the Strategic/Deliberative Dichotomy in Recent Constitutional Jurisprudence," *Texas Law Review* 71 (June 1993): 1437–77.

4. "Reflections on Deliberative Democracy," in Joshua Cohen, *Philosophy, Politics, Democracy* (Cambridge, MA: Harvard University Press, 2009), 335.

5. Since these seminal statements of the theory cited in note 3 above, the scholarship on deliberative democracy, both normative and empirical, has continued to grow. For an account of the development of and relationship between the normative and empirical strains of research, see Dennis Thompson, "Deliberative Democratic Theory and Empirical Political Science," *Annual Review of Political Science* 11 (2008): 497–520. For a recent symposium on the normative theory of deliberative democracy, see James M. Fishkin and Jane Mansbridge, eds., "The Prospects and Limits of Deliberative Democracy," special issue, *Daedalus* 146, no. 3 (2017).

6. See Jean-Jacques Rousseau, *Rousseau's Political Writings*, ed. Alan Ritter, ed. and trans. Julia Conaway Bondanella (New York: Norton, 1988), 101. To be sure, the "communication" referred to in this context by Rousseau is that which occurs outside the general assembly (101n1).

7. Rousseau famously describes the fundamental problem that he aims to address in *The Social Contract* as how the individual "while uniting himself with all, may still obey himself alone, and remain as free as before." Ibid., 92.

8. See James Bohman and Henry S. Richardson, "Liberalism, Deliberative Democracy, and 'Reasons That All Can Accept,'" *Journal of Political Philosophy* 17, no. 3 (2009): 253–74.

9. John Dryzek, *Deliberative Democracy and Beyond: Liberals, Critics, and Contestations* (New York: Oxford University Press, 2009), 2. Dryzek cites the major works *Between Facts and Norms* and *Political Liberalism*, respectively, in which Habermas and Rawls self-identify as deliberative democrats. However, as will be seen, these positions emerge from earlier works that did not always adopt this label but nonetheless inform the theoretical positions that later developed.

10. Thomas McCarthy, "Kantian Constructivism and Reconstructivism: Rawls and Habermas in Dialogue," *Ethics* 105, no. 1 (1994), 44.

11. Ibid., 46.

12. Ibid.

13. Ibid., 47.

14. See Habermas, "Discourse Ethics." But see also the earlier development of his position in Jürgen Habermas, "Toward a Theory of Communicative Competence," *Inquiry* 13, nos. 1–4 (1970): 360–75; *Communication and the Evolution of*

Society, trans. Thomas McCarthy (Boston: Beacon, 1979); *Theory of Communicative Action*, 2 vols. (1981; Boston: Beacon, 1984, 1987).

15. Habermas, "Discourse Ethics," 81–82.

16. Ibid., 88–89.

17. Ibid., 89.

18. Ibid., 88. On the ideal speech situation, see "Reflections on the Linguistic Foundation of Sociology: The Christian Gauss Lecture (Princeton University, February—March, 1971)," in Jürgen Habermas, *On the Pragmatics of Social Interaction*, trans. Barbara Fultner (Cambridge, MA: MIT Press, 2001), 85–103.

19. Habermas's reconstruction of the moral point of view should clearly be seen as a procedural theory of democratic legitimacy, whereas he sees justice itself as the *outcome* of discursive testing that is coercion-free, which is to say, discourse that is congruent with the symmetry rules of the ideal speech situation. When only the force of the better argument is operative, the consensus that emerges indicates the rational validity or justice of norms proposed for regulating collective behavior. As will be seen later in this chapter, Habermas's theory aims to be strictly formal or procedural and thus silent on substantive questions of justice.

20. Thomas McCarthy succinctly describes Habermas's revision of Kant as the following: "Rather than ascribing to others as valid those maxims I can will to be universal laws, I must submit them to others for purposes of discursively testing their claim to universal validity. The emphasis shifts from what *each* can will without contradiction to what *all* can agree to in rational discourse." McCarthy, "Kantian Constructivism and Reconstructivism," 45. Emphasis in the original.

21. Ibid., 65. The former phrase Habermas borrows from G. H. Mead. See also "Lawrence Kohlberg and Neo-Aristotelianism," in Jürgen Habermas, *Justification and Application: Remarks on Discourse Ethics*, trans. Ciaran Cronin (Cambridge, MA: MIT Press, 1993), 129. Habermas's principle of universalization says, "(U) All affected can accept the consequences and the side effects its *general* observance can be anticipated to have for the satisfaction of *everyone's* interests (and these consequences are preferred to those of known alternative possibilities for regulation)." Habermas, "Discourse Ethics," 65. Emphasis in the original.

22. Habermas, "Discourse Ethics," 66. The stipulation that the validity of norms must be determined in actual discourses is found in this additional principle: "(D) Only those norms can claim to be valid that meet (or could meet) with the approval of all affected in their capacity *as participants in a practical discourse*" (66). Emphasis in the original.

23. Ibid., 67. Habermas refers, specifically, to Rawls's "original position" in *A Theory of Justice* as an attempt to reason out the substantive, universal principles of justice—the basic liberties and the difference principle—that Habermas believes are more appropriately left to discursive testing (66).

24. Ibid., 67–68.

25. See Habermas, "Reconciliation through the Public Use of Reason: Remarks on John Rawls's Political Liberalism," *Journal of Philosophy* 92, no. 3 (1995): 109–31.

26. McCarthy, "Kantian Constructivism and Reconstructivism," 50.

27. See, for example, Habermas, "Lawrence Kohlberg and Neo-Aristotelianism," 124.

28. Patchen Markel takes this argument further and claims that a vigorous public sphere, on Habermas's account, is highly contentious and therefore constantly challenging old settlements. On his reading, the aspiration to consensus is merely part of Habermas's phenomenological account of the structure of language, not a normative ordering principle for the public sphere. As a result, he believes Habermas's thinking to be compatible with theories of agonistic pluralism. See Patchen Markel, "Contesting Consensus: Rereading Habermas on the Public Sphere," *Constellations* 3, no. 3 (1997): 377–400.

29. McCarthy, "Kantian Constructivism and Reconstructivism," 49.

30. See John Rawls, *A Theory of Justice* (1971; Cambridge, MA: Harvard University Press, 2009). Rawls discusses these concerns about the unrealistic expectations of *A Theory of Justice* in *Political Liberalism*, xix.

31. See Rawls, *Political Liberalism*, 58–66, 144–50. Much controversy has surrounded this attempt. Many see Rawls as having essentially abandoned the critical edge (particularly the egalitarianism) of his earlier work, insofar as he makes justice as fairness one among many possible outcomes of the thought experiment in the original position. The charge is that Rawls's concern with stability in *Political Liberalism* results in an unfortunate conservative turn in his thinking. Joshua Cohen defends Rawls against these charges in "Moral Pluralism and Political Consensus," in Cohen, *Philosophy, Politics, Democracy*, 38–60.

32. Rawls, *Political Liberalism*, 10–11, 25.

33. Ibid., 18–19.

34. Ibid., 58–66.

35. Ibid., 12–13.

36. Ibid., 10, 97. This phrase was made famous by the seminal article in which Rawls (arguably) appears to have abandoned the interpretation of justice as fairness as a privileged conception found in *A Theory of Justice* in favor of the idea found in *Political Liberalism* that justice as fairness is merely one possible candidate for a political conception of justice in a well-ordered, democratic society. See John Rawls, "Justice as Fairness: Political Not Metaphysical," *Philosophy and Public Affairs* 14, no. 3 (1985): 223–51.

37. Rawls, *Political Liberalism*, 219.

38. Ibid., 218.

39. Ibid., 226.

40. Ibid.

41. Ibid., 214.

42. Ibid., 140.

43. Ibid., 223.

44. Ibid.

45. Rawls initially appears to indicate that his conception of public reason and the restrictions on justification that it entails pertain only to "constitutional essentials" and "questions of basic justice." However, he says shortly thereafter that this limitation is only because the latter is, essentially, his test case for the public use of reason, not because he sees it as necessarily limited to the basic structure of society. Rawls says that if its appropriateness can be established for this area of political life, its use in other cases can then be further examined. But even without having undertaken such further inquiry, he points beyond the basic structure when he asserts that "it is usually highly desirable to settle political questions by invoking the values of public reason." Ibid., 214–15.

46. Ibid., 241.

47. Although the emphasis here is on the influence that Habermas and Rawls have exercised on other deliberative democrats discussed in this section, it should not be overlooked that the relationship has sometimes been the reverse. See, for example, *Political Liberalism*, 217n4, 422n68.

48. Gutmann and Thompson, *Democracy and Disagreement*, 26–39, 368–71.

49. Ibid., 16, 37, 55–56.

50. See Gutmann and Thompson, "Moral Conflict and Political Consensus," *Ethics* 101, no. 1 (1990): 64–88.

51. Although Gutmann and Thompson distance themselves from pure proceduralism, even their reliance on principles of preclusion has Habermasian overtones. Consider two of their requirements to determine whether a position is to be precluded from public discourse. One stipulates that arguments must be in conformity with the "moral point of view," which means that one "must presuppose a disinterested perspective that could be adopted by any member of a society whatever his or her circumstances (such as class, race, or sex)." Here, there are obvious echoes of Habermas's universalization principle (U) that he believes must characterize actual deliberation. Another is the requirement that premises to arguments, "should be in principle open to challenge by generally accepted methods of inquiry," which resembles aspects of Habermas's ideal speech situation. Gutmann and Thompson, "Moral Conflict and Political Consensus," 71. Although these may indeed preclude certain substantive positions from the outset, as Gutmann and Thompson clearly demonstrate, it is easy to see how they might just as easily be characterized as procedural requirements. Indeed, Gutmann and Thompson elsewhere acknowledge that procedure and substance at times can easily be mistaken for one another. Gutmann and Thompson, *Democracy and Disagreement*, 49–50. But it is for this reason that the distinction they draw between their position and that of pure proceduralists such as Habermas at times seems rather thin.

52. See Gutmann and Thompson, *Democracy and Disagreement*, 79–85. Thomas McCarthy has noted affinities with Habermas in Gutmann and Thompson's reliance on principles of accommodation, whose strategy for consensus is to keep (civil) conversation going, in contrast to principles of preclusion, which aim to prohibit the most controversial types of discussion. See McCarthy, "Kantian Constructivism and Reconstructivism," 62n31. Gutmann and Thompson compare their position to Locke's theory of religious toleration, which is grounded in the conviction that belief must ultimately be rationally assented to if it is to be genuine. For Gutmann and Thompson, "The secular analogue . . . holds that democratically formed, collective moral judgments by society must be a matter of deliberation: citizens should choose, deliberately, the principles of public morality." Gutmann and Thompson, "Moral Conflict and Political Consensus," 68. Consequently, instead of removing controversial moral questions from the public forum, as Rawls does, they actually allow for public deliberation over the most fundamental, comprehensive moral principles in order to encourage "moral learning" and the possibility of rational persuasion on the substance of public morality and the common good (86–87).

53. Joshua Cohen, "Procedure and Substance in Deliberative Democracy," in *Deliberative Democracy*, ed. James Bohman and William Rehg (Cambridge, MA: MIT Press, 1997), 417.

54. Ibid.

55. Ibid. 417–18.

56. Ibid., 418.

57. Rawls indicates that he borrows the term "public reason" from Kant, who distinguishes public from private reason in his essay "What Is Enlightenment?," while noting that Kant's meaning in this context is different from his own. Rawls, *Political Liberalism*, 213n2. Elsewhere, Rawls attributes the substantive concept of public reason to Rousseau when he asserts, "It is clear . . . that Rousseau's view contains an idea of what I have called public reason. So far as I know, the idea originates with him." John M. Warner and James R. Zink, "Therapeutic Politics: Rawls' Respect for Rousseau," *Review of Politics* 78, no. 1 (2016): 128; quoting John Rawls, *Lectures on the History of Political Philosophy*, ed. Samuel Freeman (Cambridge, MA: Harvard University Press, 2007), xvii. Although Rawls emphasizes the substantive idea's origination in Rousseau's thinking here, both Rousseau and Kant ultimately shape his view. For Rawls's understanding of Rousseau was itself informed by Kant (and the Kantian philosopher, Ernst Cassirer), such that Rawls refers to Kant as Rousseau's "best interpreter." Warner and Zink, "Therapeutic Politics," 129, quoting Rawls, *Lectures*, 200. Habermas, for his part, frames his entire discourse ethics in terms of the autonomy tradition and the idea of the general will. See "Remarks on Discourse Ethics," in Habermas, *Justification and Application*, 51. Stephen White discusses the influence of "the Rousseau-Kant tradition of positive freedom" on Habermas's thinking. He notes Habermas's explicit acknowledgment of "Rousseau's

importance as a forefather of the discursive principle of legitimacy; he [Rousseau] was the first political philosopher to develop clearly a procedural conception of democratic legitimacy, to argue that the basic principle is not derived from nature or God, but purely from the idea of a voluntary agreement among equals." See Stephen K. White, "Reason and Authority in Habermas: A Critique of the Critics," *American Political Science Review* 74, no. 4 (1980): 1013.

58. I have borrowed this insight from Christopher Bertram. See Christopher Bertram, "Rousseau on Public Reason," in *Public Reason in Political Philosophy: Classical Sources and Contemporary Commentaries*, ed. Piers Norris Turner and Gerald Glaus (New York: Routledge, 2017), 248–63; "Rousseau's Legacy in Two Conceptions of the General Will: Democratic and Transcendent," *Review of Politics* 74, no. 3 (2012): 403–19.

59. Bertram, "Rousseau on Public Reason," 248, 253, 262. Bertram mentions Rawls and the idea of the overlapping consensus at various points in this essay, along with the theory of deliberative democracy, as his principal illustration of the contemporary thinking Rousseau anticipates. See also Bertram, "Rousseau's Legacy in Two Conceptions of the General Will," 418–19, where he mentions both Rawls and Habermas as continuing a line of thinking traceable to Rousseau.

60. Bertram, "Rousseau on Public Reason," 248. Bertram speaks somewhat anachronistically about the role of "public reason" in Rousseau's thinking, a term that Rousseau does not generally use and that certainly had not acquired its contemporary meaning. There are two instances in which Rousseau uses "raison publique" in the *Third Discourse*, but nowhere does the phrase appear in his discussions of the general will in the *Social Contract*. Still, Bertram's attribution of the idea to Rousseau may nevertheless be seen as a testament to Rousseau's "contribution to our thinking about public reason" and his "inspiration to advocates of various forms of direct, participatory or deliberative democracy" (259, 262).

61. Bertram uses other language to describe this division, but he has the same dichotomy in mind. He refers to "a view of public reason as involving the actual collective argument, deliberation and decision of the citizenry on the one hand, and a more objective understanding that stresses the reasons that apply to people, independently of whether those people actually acknowledge the reasons." Ibid., 251.

62. Bertram alludes here to just two of the most conspicuous examples of this equivocation. See Rousseau, *The Social Contract*, book 4, chapter 1, where he speaks of the general will as "constant, incorruptible, and pure," in contrast to book 2, chapter 3, where he discusses, "whether the general will can err." Rousseau, quoted in Bertram, "Rousseau on Public Reason," 252. Bertram's fuller exegesis can be found in "Rousseau's Legacy in Two Conceptions of the General Will," esp. 404–7.

63. Bertram, "Rousseau on Public Reason," 251–52.

64. Ibid.

65. In Rousseau's moral freedom, one hears obvious echoes of both the "positive" and "negative" liberty famously identified by Isaiah Berlin. See "Two Concepts

of Liberty," in Isaiah Berlin, *Four Essays on Liberty* (Oxford: Oxford University Press, 1969). However, there is an important distinction between the negative liberty that Berlin identifies and that which is found in the Rousseauian-Kantian tradition. For the ideal of autonomy, objective limits to rule are based on a consensus, perceived or actual, that is, what would be acceptable to, or is accepted among, all citizens, a foundation that introduces an element of contingency into such negative liberties. Berlin was certainly aware of the contingent and thus precarious nature of this ostensible "negative liberty" in the autonomy tradition.

66. It is important to note here that while Rawls (and Cohen) are part of this constitutionalist tradition that is seen as positing "objective" limits to rule, Rawls's political constructivism introduces the contingency mentioned in note 65 into its conclusions, due to its dependence on the acceptability of such limits to all citizens. For, the rights and liberties that Rawls identifies with political liberalism depend (at least in his later work) upon the existence of an overlapping consensus of reasonable comprehensive doctrines, which is claimed to be present only in a particular democratic society or societies.

67. There are obvious objections to this claim from both thinkers to be addressed in the following section. For Habermas, the introduction of (D) was designed precisely to obviate the monological character of discourse and, along with it, thinking about justice that was a priori in a manner similar to Kant. For Rawls, the overlapping consensus of reasonable comprehensive doctrines was to be found in an existing, public political culture that was part of a process of long historical development in Western society. However, I do not find either of these arguments convincing—the persistence of what Habermas calls "the moral point of view" in both thinkers, I will argue, is the vestige of the Rousseauian-Kantian noumenal realm that is necessary for belief in the ideal of autonomy, which represents their shared normative impulse.

68. It may be more accurate to say that there are no limits to the group of interlocutors or "community" of justification other than the exclusion of those who would not universalize their appeals in this way, that is, the intolerant or those who Rawls would say have comprehensive doctrines that are not "reasonable," since this would undermine the formation of collective agreement, or the aspiration to inclusiveness that comes to define both theories of public reason. Obviously, there is always the possibility that some may not be willing to bring their wills into alignment with others. However, the point of contention here is that where such willingness is present, the unity of wills and the boundaries that define the speech community are seemingly limitless.

69. The charge that the legacy of Kant's transcendental self remains within the thinking of these ostensibly "post-metaphysical" thinkers is not new. Such criticisms lie at the heart of what Habermas calls "neo-Aristotelian" or what others have termed "communitarian" critiques, inaugurated by those such as Alasdair MacIntyre, Charles Taylor, and Bernard Williams. See note 73 below.

70. James Gordon Finlayson, though articulating a neo-Hegelian critique of Habermas, concedes too much here, arguing that Habermas's transcendental pragmatics empiricizes the derivation of (D) and even (U) and thus rejects Kant's "two-world thesis." However, Finlayson's critique of Habermas's overly sharp division between ethical and moral norms later implicitly attenuates or at least qualifies this claim. See James Gordon Finlayson, "Habermas' Discourse Ethics and Hegel's Critique of Kant's Moral Theory," in *Habermas: A Critical Reader*, ed. Peter Dews (Oxford: Blackwell, 1999), 29–52.

71. See chapter 6, in which I examine the understanding of "modernity" respectively for both Habermas and Rawls and the role this plays in their arguments. I view this as a complimentary but distinct element of their theories related to questions regarding historical particularity, and thus worthy of its own treatment.

72. Robert Spaemann, "Die Utopie der Herrschaftsfreiheit," *Zur Kritik der politischen Utopie* (Stuttgart: Ernst Klett), 124, quoted in White, "Reason and Authority in Habermas," 1010.

73. Habermas, "Lawrence Kohlberg and Neo-Aristotelianism," 124. For this critique regarding "abstraction from concrete ethical life," see Alasdair MacIntyre, *After Virtue* (Notre Dame, IN: University of Notre Dame Press, 1981); "Does Applied Ethics Rest on a Mistake?," *Monist* 67, no. 4 (1984): 498–513; Charles Taylor, *Sources of the Self: The Making of the Modern Identity* (Cambridge, MA: Harvard University Press, 1989); "The Motivation behind a Procedural Ethics," in *Kant and Political Philosophy*, ed. Ronald Beiner and William James Booth (New Haven, CT: Yale University Press, 1993), 337–59; Bernard Williams, *Ethics and the Limits of Philosophy* (Cambridge, MA: Harvard University Press, 1985); David Wiggins, *Needs, Values, Truth* (Oxford: Oxford University Press, 1987); M. Passerin d'Entreves, "Aristotle or Burke? Some Comments on H. Schnaedelbach's 'What Is Neo-Aristotelianism?,'" *Praxis International* 7, nos. 3–4 (1987): 238–45. I have assessed these critiques from a sympathetic but critical perspective in Ryan Holston, "Deliberation in Context: Reexamining the Confrontation between the Discourse Ethics and Neo-Aristotelianism," *Telos* 181 (2017): 151–75. The upshot of this assessment is that these critiques, while correct in identifying the abstract nature of "procedural ethics," were themselves insufficiently attentive to the historical nature of reason and deliberation. Thus, even MacIntyre, who is often associated with a more historically informed account of reason, frequently succumbs to the premises of modern rationalism. It is for this reason that I have drawn on Gadamer's thinking in the following chapters as an alternative for conceptualizing moral and political deliberation.

74. See Habermas, "Lawrence Kohlberg and Neo-Aristotelianism," 124. Emphasis added.

75. Bertram thus describes Rousseau's view as the "nesting of different levels of individual and collective interests" in which the morality of reasons is relative to the level of generality: "The more general and abstract the identity, Rousseau thinks, the more closely the related reasons approach what morality requires. The more particular and individual the identity, at least as a generalization, the more

disruptive the corresponding volitions are for the peaceful coexistence of people together within society." Bertram, "Rousseau on Public Reason," 250. Although Rousseau appears to embrace the idea in his earlier work of a kind of "cosmopolitan public reason," Bertram argues that he came to endorse a less extreme view in the *Social Contract* that the state (as opposed to all of mankind) represents the level at which individuals might be motivated to bring their reasoning in line with the general will (see 249–51).

76. See his reliance on the developmental psychology of Lawrence Kohlberg in "Moral Consciousness and Communicative Action," in Habermas, *Moral Consciousness and Communicative Action*, 119–33.

77. Incidentally, it would appear that even the formal condition of reciprocity is not implied in all speech acts for the very reason that speakers are not always implicitly equal, even in attempts to reason with one another. For example, parents who engage in speech acts with children often employ reason in order to teach or persuade, but this may not be an open invitation for children to respond in the ways that Habermas suggests. Similarly, employers or supervisors will engage in reasoned assertions with employees that are aimed at informing or instructing and are often not intended as occasions for disputation. Likewise, priests or ministers who give sermons may engage their parishioners in the use of reason, but the relationship and the occasion of their deliverance are clearly not intended as opportunities for rebuttal. Teachers, although sometimes engaging in collaborative inquiry, as the case of the Socratic dialectic, which allows for objections to be made, do not always do so, but will sometimes lecture or instruct in a manner that makes use of reason but is not characterized by a relationship of equality.

78. Habermas, "Lawrence Kohlberg and Neo-Aristotelianism," 124–25. Emphasis in the original.

79. Ibid.,130.

80. Ibid., 131.

81. Ibid. Emphasis in the original.

82. Patrick Neal, "In the Shadow of the General Will: Rawls, Kant and Rousseau on the Problem of Political Right," *Review of Politics* 49, no. 3 (1987): 392. Emphasis in the original.

83. Ibid., 392. Neal quoting Rawls.

84. Ibid., 393.

85. Ibid. Neal quoting Rawls.

86. Rawls identifies the historical source of his political conception of justice as European culture following the Wars of Religion. However, in his hands, the abstractions of social contract theory are further severed from this historically specific way of life and transformed into principles that are conceived as having universal appeal in pluralistic nation-states constituted by hundreds of millions of interlocutors.

87. More will obviously be said about interpretation and the application of norms in the subsequent chapters on Gadamer's thinking. For now, it is worth noting that Habermas has similarly struggled to come to terms with the problem

of application with regard to moral norms that after having emerged from the lifeworld and withstood discursive testing must be reapplied in the context of practical action. See "Remarks on Discourse Ethics," in Habermas, *Justification and Application*, 36–38. For the argument to which he frequently adverts regarding the supplementation of "application discourses," see Klaus Günther, *The Sense of Appropriateness: Application Discourses in Morality and Law*, trans. John Farrell (Albany: State University of New York Press, 1993).

88. Cohen, "Procedure and Substance in Deliberative Democracy," 416. Emphasis added.

89. Ibid.

90. Ibid., 430–31.

Chapter 4

The Rehabilitation of Prejudice

Thus far, it has been argued that genuine or authentic forms of moral and political deliberation have become inconceivable for the intellectual progeny of the autonomy tradition because of its understanding of the relationship between morality and history. That is to say, the normative impulse that the autonomy tradition has imparted to one of the most prominent strains of contemporary democratic theory, the theory of deliberative democracy, views the ethical life (*Sittlichkeit*) or historically rooted community as problematic and incompatible with "the moral point of view," which is believed to be the sole basis for the justification and hence the legitimation of modern political order. However, this disparagement of the ethical life and its neglect as part of political deliberation has fostered a credulity with regard to the possibilities of mutual justification in contemporary democratic societies. For it is believed that large-scale populations—those in the hundreds of millions of persons—might appeal to principles or reasons that can be accepted by all citizens. The cost of this political idealism or utopianism with respect to the source of mutual justification, therefore, is a failure to recognize and support the true, essential foundation of all meaningful deliberation, that is, concrete communities that exist over time.

If the divorce of morality from historical experience was responsible for this misconception of deliberation by contemporary deliberative democrats, it follows that addressing this error will require a collapse of this problematic division, in order to arrive at a sounder understanding of deliberation. The purpose of the present chapter is to begin to reconceptualize the relationship between morality and history and, in particular, the manner in which the ethical life (*Sittlichkeit*), which is not a set of formal principles that can be rationally articulated but part of who we are in our concrete being, is always with us in the moment of deliberation and choice. Consequently, it will be argued, temporal constraints must be taken into account when we conceptualize persons in their capacity as moral and political deliberators. Having established this more embodied, historical understanding of the "principles" that make up who we are as interlocutors, the chapter that immediately follows will be in a position to propose an alternative conception of moral and political deliberation.

The present chapter thus turns to Gadamer's practical philosophy for this reconceptualization of the relationship between morality and history. While much better known for his theory of interpretation, or philosophical hermeneutics, the work of Gadamer in the decades following the publication of *Truth and Method* on a broad range of topics (e.g., ethics, politics, religion) articulated philosophical insights into the nature of human choice (*prohairesis*) in the concrete or practical situation.[1] As will be seen, these views are not easily separated from but are properly understood as intertwined with his philosophical hermeneutics. For, according to Gadamer, interpretation or understanding is the ontologically universal condition of human being in the world,[2] and therefore its appearance in the context of other forms of human *praxis* is merely indicative of our effective-historical consciousness (*wirkungsgeschichtliches Bewusstsein*), the way in which all human understanding involves the mediation of old and new experience and, as such, must be conceived as always already under way. Yet, each horizon of understanding, far from being a discrete perspective unto itself, contributes to a continually developing whole or synthetic comprehension of the world in which we live. In this way, Gadamer's practical philosophy is not a separate area of subsequent intellectual interest in his life's work, but an extension of philosophical hermeneutics to the moment of human choice and action and the unceasing development of human consciousness.

The Historicity of Truth

In part 1 of *Truth and Method*, Gadamer traces the epistemology of the modern human sciences, which culminates in the hermeneutical "method" of Wilhelm Dilthey, back to its origins in Kantian and post-Kantian Romantic aesthetics.[3] For it was under Dilthey, Gadamer argues, that elements in the Romantic theory of knowledge had inadvertently and ironically played a role in bolstering the "scientific" credentials of modern social science. By furthering Romanticism's continual tendency to truncate its understanding of human experience, Dilthey was successful in providing the human sciences with a new basis for objectifying and studying historical phenomena.[4] As Schleiermacher's biographer, Gadamer argues, Dilthey seized on the latter's atomized and radically subjective concept of experience (*Erlebnis*) for the purpose of establishing discrete units of historical life that, if retrievable, would allegedly provide the historian with a fundamental datum or fact that lay beneath each piece of historical writing. With Schleiermacher, Dilthey thought that the uniqueness of each experience expressed in a historical text could be overcome and comprehended through a process of "divination" on the part of the interpreter.[5] Thus, by assuming, again with Schleiermacher, a "preexisting bond" between all historical forms of life, Dilthey was able to see each piece of historical writing as at once evidence of a radically unique human experience and open to discernment by the modern investigator.[6] Such investigation, or interpretation, would thus take the form of reconstructing the psychological state of the author and the experience manifested in the written expression.[7]

The problem Gadamer has with Dilthey's influence on the development of the human, particularly the historical, sciences is that this ideal of investigation "obliges one to sever one's bond with life, to attain distance from one's own history, which alone makes it possible for that history to become an object."[8] In other words, standing over a piece of historical writing as an object of investigation, treating it as code for the datum of experience whose precise exposition is necessary for accurate understanding, loses sight of the possibility of there actually being something "true" in the content of what is said.[9] What Gadamer terms "historical consciousness" represents this objectification of historical phenomena. It implies treating such phenomena as mere expressions of historical life, whose precise meaning appears discernible only through the tacit assumptions of pantheistic metaphysics and a corresponding false sense of simultaneity among interpreter and object of inquiry.[10] In this way, the particularity of both is not so much overcome but neglected or forgotten, so that the social scientist examining historical phenomena may be thought of as external to the world of his object of study, thus ostensibly resembling the natural scientist. For Gadamer, this understanding that emerges in the interpreter represents a distorted relationship with the past, in which historical phenomena no longer speak to us and our lives but are merely "there" to be observed, like artifacts in a museum.[11] Recovering the possibility of truth or knowledge of reality, as opposed to mere "facts," is thus central to Gadamer's genealogy of the human sciences. In order to achieve this recovery, Gadamer sees it as necessary to turn away from the truncated, subjective conception of experience that the human sciences have inherited from Kant and Romanticism and to return us to the more historically informed and embedded conception of experience (*Erfahrung*) that one finds in the thinking of Hegel. The latter is thus intended to overcome historical consciousness and make us, through the very acknowledgment and engagement of our historical particularity, receptive to the truth that lies within the past by way of a genuine, that is, nondistorted, encounter with it.

Once Gadamer's critique of the modern human sciences is placed in this context, his fundamental concern with our relationship to the past begins to emerge. For Gadamer, we have come to see ourselves standing at a distance before our historical world, an epistemic pathology that is traceable to the demotion of our particularity by Kantian and post-Kantian aesthetics. As a result, we relativize and neglect the past's truth claims. Gadamer thus laments the fact that Schleiermacher's aim to reconstruct the psychological state of the historical author requires that the investigator examine his texts "independently of their claim to truth" such that he "disregards [their] content as knowledge," and this represents the central problem Gadamer identifies in parts 1 and 2 of *Truth and Method*.[12] In the last section of part 1, which is entitled "Reconstruction and Integration as Hermeneutic Tasks," Gadamer highlights the centrality of confronting this issue. Here he establishes an opposition between Schleiermacher's lifeless "reconstruction" of authorial experience and Hegel's important aim of integrating the past into the life of the present. Gadamer suggests the primacy of this integration for his philosophical hermeneutics in order to overcome the distorted relationship between past and present brought about by historical consciousness: "It is not only the written tradition that is estranged and in need of new and more vital assimilation; everything that is no longer immediately situated in a world—that is, all *tradition*, whether art or the other spiritual creations of the past: law, religion, philosophy, and so forth—is estranged from its original meaning and depends on the unlocking and mediating spirit that we, like the Greeks, name after Hermes: the messenger of the gods."[13]

The proper role of hermeneutical understanding, for Gadamer, must now be seen as an integration, assimilation, or mediation of past with present, so that this estrangement of the past may be overcome. Gadamer's critique of historical consciousness can thus be seen as centrally focused on the nature of this "estrangement" of the past, which he sees as a severing or atomizing of time that puts the truth content or knowledge contained within history in jeopardy for the present. Indeed, Gadamer's philosophical hermeneutics becomes truly compelling only when the truth or knowledge contained within the past is seen as being *at stake*.[14] Consequently, the epistemological purpose of *Truth and Method* is to recover the possibility of truth in interpretation and understanding by promoting a true integration of the past with the present, a decidedly normative purpose that defines Gadamer's magnum opus.[15] In contrast to Schleiermacher's objective of reconstructing the past, which effectively tears both phenomenon and interpreter from their historical worlds, Gadamer follows Hegel's aim of engaging in "thoughtful mediation [of the past] with contemporary life."[16] It is only through such mediation and engagement with the past, that is, treating the past as speaking to the life of the present, that the possibility of its having real truth content could be restored. Gadamer believes, above all, that properly mediated or nondistorted interpretation of the past will always entail the latter's "application" to the life of the present. Doing away with the distorted subject-object relation inherited from nineteenth century hermeneutics will thus involve restoring the art of applying texts to the present situation of the interpreter. To do so, Gadamer uses theology and law as models of interpretive practice for his hermeneutics. Proper understanding and engagement of the past will thus mirror the way that interpretation in these fields always has an eye to the meaning—as in the case of interpreting scripture or statute—of a text specifically for present circumstances. Appropriating the application entailed in both of these models of interpretation, Gadamer aims to recover our ability to "respond to what [a text] has to tell us."[17]

This restorative project regarding our engagement with the past relies on the recognition that our historically particular perspectives, that is, our prejudices (*Vorurteile*), actually facilitate rather than simply occlude, human knowledge. Appropriating Heidegger's original insight that all being (*Dasein*) is historically conditioned, Gadamer observes that our prejudices not only are unable to be removed from understanding, but that such prejudices are in fact the essential precondition for our understanding anything. For Gadamer (and Heidegger), there is always a "fore-conception" or "fore-projection" of historically conditioned presuppositions that facilitate understanding, insofar as they allow us to anticipate and revise expectations of meaning, thus contextualizing in prior experience that which we seek to understand.[18] For Gadamer, this hermeneutical process of projection, revision, and re-projection of fore-meaning more truly characterizes how understanding operates than the view of modern social science, which aims at the removal of all prejudice (*Vorurteil*) from interpretation. Strains of Enlightenment thinking that seek to rationally examine all of our prejudices are thus called into question by this notion that no thought, even that which performs such examination, is unsupported by prejudice. To be sure, Gadamer does believe that our knowledge is made partial, and at times is even impaired, by the particularity of our situatedness. However, this recognition is understood by Gadamer as compatible with the idea that knowledge is also made possible or facilitated by our having a historically particular vantage point on what is "said." In this way, Gadamer views our historical embeddedness as the helpful lens through which we come to know reality but that always approaches that reality from a particular, and thus limited, perspective.

In light of the structure of hermeneutical understanding that Gadamer appropriates from Heidegger, it is thus not only a delusion to think that we can remove all of our prejudices from our understanding, but the attempt to do so may have detrimental consequences.[19] For, the systematic attempt to view the past scientifically or in a distantiated manner may cause us to turn a deaf ear to the past's truth claims and its insights into the nature of reality. According to Brice Wachterhauser, it is Gadamer's indebtedness to Hegel that helps him to overcome this error, collapsing Kant's division between reality-in-itself and reality-for-us, by demonstrating that reality is actually given to us through our historically and linguistically conditioned representations.[20] This is not to say that the reality we become aware of is ultimately "constructed," in a pragmatic sense, such that we are merely given "a world" of meaning in some arbitrary or relative fashion. Rather, what is given to us is a particular vantage point from which *reality-in-itself* can be perceived. What Wachterhauser describes as Gadamer's "perspectival realism" thus implies that "human knowing always depends on language and history, on a context of commitments and practices to show the thing itself in a certain way."[21] This means that we never have complete access to truth, but that we do gain the kind of insight into the nature of reality that comes with perspective or situatedness. Wachterhauser explains how it is our historicity itself that facilitates this insight: "One might say that for Gadamer our historical involvement makes possible a revealing of an aspect of the thing; we never can see the whole truth but only a partial truth or a perspective *but a truth about the thing itself nevertheless*."[22] In this way, Gadamer demonstrates how our historically and linguistically situated perspectives point to the possibility of "finitely grasped truth."[23]

The Historicity of the Good

With respect to Gadamer's conception of the good, it is first worth acknowledging that in light of Gadamer's historicism, his relationship with Heidegger, and the epistemologically relativistic interpretation of Gadamer popularized by Richard Rorty, among others, many have been led to conclude that Gadamer is part of the anti-foundationalist or anti-realist tradition in modern Western philosophy that includes Friedrich Nietzsche, Jacques Derrida, and Rorty himself.[24] However, it is important to recognize that there has also been a persistent, more faithful reading of Gadamer among scholars who have argued, conversely, that he is in fact a hermeneutical thinker who eschews many of the anti-metaphysical assumptions of those who are traditionally identified as "hermeneuticists."[25] In contrast to the Rortian interpretation, therefore, Wachterhauser has demonstrated that Gadamer, far from attempting to undermine the idea of truth, was attempting to "rethink" or "transform," even deepen the metaphysical tradition in Western thought in light of these insights into human historicity.[26] This suggests that if Gadamer is indeed collapsing the metaphysical dualism between the moral and the historical, he is doing so in a way that does not bluntly conflate the two, such that moral judgments are seen as little more than historically particular vantage points from which the world may be understood or interpreted but without any access to what is real. On the contrary, Gadamer's most explicit remarks on morality suggest that his insights into the historical nature of human life can be seen to illuminate and actually further an understanding of the truth of moral reality rather than simply undermining its possibility.

When it comes to his most explicit remarks on the subject of justice in *Truth and Method*, Gadamer draws heavily on Aristotle, whose understanding of the natural law seems attractive and unique to Gadamer, insofar as it appears to indicate an openness to the compatibility between the historical, or particular, and the permanent, or universal. It is in light of this distinctiveness of his thinking about morality that Gadamer observes that "Aristotle's position on the problem of natural law is highly subtle and certainly not to be equated with the later natural-law tradition."[27] What is unusual and truly profound in Aristotle's concept of the natural law is not, Gadamer explains, the simple distinction between the unchangeability of the natural law and the changeability of the positive law, as is often noted.[28] Rather, it is that the natural law itself contains variability, and that this variability is perfectly compatible with it being "natural" in the sense of it being abiding or transcendent.[29] On Gadamer's reading, Aristotle appears to be saying—in a more radical sense than he is typically interpreted—that the laws of nature assert themselves in different ways at different times and places and yet share something enduring among these diverse manifestations. The original insight of Aristotle on the subject of justice, it seems, is that naturalness does not imply fixity any more than variation implies arbitrariness.[30] On the contrary, the historical nature of reality actually seems to *require* variation in order for the particular needs of justice itself to be met.

For Gadamer, justice thus appears to be mutable or subject to change because it in fact emerges within history. What is just, in other words, or morally universal, does not exist outside of history as the later natural law tradition came to believe, but actually depends upon historical enactment or concretization within a particular set of circumstances for its existence. In line with this view, justice must be seen as ethical conduct itself, not a set of abstract or otherworldly principles that are said to inhere in such conduct, but the very conduct that is often thought to be measured by such principles.[31] However, contrary to what many interpreters would infer from this insight, this need not imply that whatever conduct is historically enacted or concretized may be called "just."[32] Rather, it simply means that justice, where it does exist, always takes place within history, and that as we act within a historically particular situation, it is merely *possible* to instantiate justice with right ethical conduct. The good, for Gadamer, only comes to be within the concrete reality of the particular. It is again Aristotle who best captures this dependence on concreteness and historical particularity for the manifestation or enactment of what is just or right. Gadamer thus notes that with regard to the teaching of ethics, Aristotle shows that there are no guiding principles—or, at least, not "principles" in the traditional sense—that may be taught. At most, there is only a "schemata"[33] of ethical conduct grounded in particular, that is, historical, action:

> [The guiding principles of ethics] are concretized only in the concrete situation of the person acting. Thus they are not norms to be found in the stars, nor do they have an unchanging place in a natural moral universe, so that all that would be necessary would be to perceive them. Nor are they mere conventions, but really do correspond to the nature of the thing—except that the latter is always itself determined in each case by the use the moral consciousness makes of them.[34]

For Gadamer and Gadamer's Aristotle, it thus would appear that justice actually comes into being when it is made real or concrete in the action of the moral decision-maker that takes place within his historically particular, and thus novel, situation. Consequently, the moral consciousness actually contributes to what justice is through its novel enactment of moral reality, which is being accumulated or "built" over time, as it were, through a multitude of historical instantiations.[35]

But this would seem to raise a serious difficulty if Gadamer is indeed aiming to further or deepen the metaphysical tradition in Western thought. For, how is it possible for one to know that *justice* is what is being created in each historical instantiation of the moral consciousness without a set of principles or intellectual criteria that distinguish just actions from those that do not qualify as just? And if Gadamer's answer is simply that one looks to previous manifestations as a guide, then why should one look to *these* historical actions over *those* as the source of guidance? While Gadamer does not believe that principles are the ultimate source of moral authority, he does nonetheless appear to believe that there are standards to which our actions must conform in order for an instantiation of justice to have occurred. For Gadamer believes that standards of conduct need not be abstract or intellectual but can actually exist through a commonality of quality that certain concrete actions, each in response to its particular circumstances, exhibit.[36] Still, if the latter is the case, the intellectualist or more traditionally metaphysically minded may further press Gadamer: Can we not then articulate this "quality" in a way that would capture its existence among all such manifestations, so that we may know, intellectually or rationally, what the criterion is for just actions? In other words, if there is truly something in common among all such concrete manifestations of justice, may we not separate out into an articulable form, something that may be called justice as such?

This is the fundamental question that Gadamer is led to confront in *The Idea of the Good in Platonic-Aristotelian Philosophy*.[37] For he argues in this work that while such articulation has been attempted with some—albeit limited—success, as in the case of Plato's philosophy, there is also a danger, as Aristotle shows, in such abstraction from the particularity of justice, insofar as it tends to hypostatize that which has come to be uniquely and concretely, thus neglecting the full extent of justice's variability.[38] In other words, the problem with abstracting from the particular instantiations of justice is that it tends to make the mistake of asserting the particular—one unique instance of justice's concretization—as the universal, and, in the case of ethical conduct, this runs a risk for justice itself. Aristotle thus famously critiques Plato for such abstraction and the dangers associated with his theoretical method, that is, with disconnecting justice from the particularity of concrete circumstance. And the fundamental concern motivating this critique elicits considerable sympathy from Gadamer.

However, while Gadamer shares Aristotle's concern about reification in a general sense, he nonetheless argues that Aristotle obscures the degree to which Plato is, in fact, quite close to Aristotle's own understanding of the immanence and concreteness of justice.[39] For, although Plato does abstract from the particular occasions or instantiations in which justice presents itself and speaks of it as apart or distinct from the concrete world in which we live, he does not view justice as truly "separate" (*chorismos*) from concrete reality, as he sometimes seems to suggest. Such a reading of Plato—of which the Aristotelian tradition has been guilty, according to Gadamer—fails to appreciate the metaphorical sense in which Plato intends his portrayals of the good as existing beyond or separate from the physical world.[40] Instead, Gadamer argues, such portrayals ought to be viewed as the function of the intellect connecting together diverse manifestations of justice in an effort to make a metaphorical argument against the Sophists, who had inferred justice's relativity from its variability. However, according to Gadamer, Plato never intended such separation to be taken literally. It is Aristotle, not Plato, Gadamer contends, who interprets such metaphors as one finds in the *Republic* and the *Phaedo* in their strictest or most literal sense, thus denying the proximity of Plato to Aristotle's own concrete way of thinking about justice.

Gadamer's analysis of the idea of the good in Plato is, therefore, designed to show the dependence of the universal on the particular, of which Plato too demonstrates an incipient awareness. It is with this in mind that Gadamer focuses on Plato's coining of the term *methexis*, so that he may characterize the relationship between the particular and the universal as one of "participation," "coexistence," or "taking part," and precisely not separation.[41] Gadamer claims, "With this word [*methexis*], it seems to me, Plato wants to bring out the logical connection of the many to the one, the thing 'in common,' a connection that was not implied in *mimesis* and in the Pythagorean relationship of number and being."[42] In short, Gadamer reads Plato as striving to articulate the inseparability of the universal and the particular, the sense in which there is no "good" as removed from all concrete, historical reality but only good as a universal characteristic immanent to reality itself. To be sure, Gadamer notes, it is Plato's use of the term *chorismos* that is responsible for the interpretation of him as setting apart completely the realm of the noetic from the world of experience, thus setting the stage for the literalist interpretation of which the Aristotelian tradition has been guilty. Yet, Gadamer contends, "the locution of *chorismos* was never intended to call into question the fact that what is encountered in appearances is always to be thought of in reference to what is invariant *in it*. The complete separation of the world of ideas from the world of appearances would be a crass absurdity."[43] For Gadamer, the oneness of Plato's idea of the good exists within and not beyond the physical world, and it is in fact *through* or *by virtue of* the many itself that such oneness comes to be. In his translator's introduction to this work, P. Christopher Smith explains that, on Gadamer's reading of Plato, "the good is what Hegel calls *ein Moment*, namely, an aspect of something which does not exist separately from it. Thus, when we say that it is *choriston* (separate), we are not denying that it is *in* the thing. We are saying only that it must be distinguished from the thing in our thinking."[44] Such separation, in other words, to the extent that it ever exists, is only the work of the intellect on reality, not reality itself.

Tradition's Authority

What kind of "knowing" is this, then, if one is not able to speak of a set of principles or intellectual criteria that will identify, distinguish, or separate out just from unjust actions? What does it mean, in other words, to have knowledge of the good that is not abstract, but instead is based on concrete, historical experience? Just as the good itself only exists in particular, historical actions, for Gadamer, it appears that knowledge of the good is similarly restricted to certain types of concrete, historical persons and the way in which they "know" how to respond to concrete, historical situations. Thus, it is Aristotle's concept of *phronesis* that ultimately plays a substantial role in Gadamer's understanding of moral knowledge, for this concept seems to express the dependence of the latter on the historical nature of both knower and known.[45] This is to say that *phronesis* seems to capture the situated and responsive nature of moral judgment, always adapting itself to and taking into account circumstantial variety in the discernment of the good, as well as the need for such judgment to be cultivated, developed, and refined within a historically embedded decision-maker. It is this concept, above all, that allows Gadamer to call into question Enlightenment standards of absolute moral knowledge while resisting the relativistic inferences to which epistemological skepticism frequently succumbs.[46] As Aristotle explicitly warns in the *Nicomachean Ethics*, serious limits do present themselves to our knowledge of human affairs, but this acknowledgment certainly does not imply the futility or arbitrariness of such judgments. Rather, it simply recommends humility and caution, always allowing for the possibility of human error, partial knowledge, and revision of understanding. Consequently, Gadamer articulates a hermeneutically informed conception of *phronesis* in order to provide the most appropriate account of moral knowledge in light of the epistemic limitations that man's historicity places on his moral decision-making.

Still, *phronesis* can only be part of the picture with respect to the implications of human historicity for knowledge of the good, since Gadamer rejects the idea of moral precepts or principles that such circumstantial judgment has traditionally been thought to apply. Although there may not be anything like fixed principles at our disposal, Gadamer nonetheless believes we are guided in our phronetic activity by a "sense" of the good that helps us to differentiate particular courses of action within the moment of ethical decision-making. According to Gadamer, this sense of the good is always already involved in any search for the good and must in fact be present from the beginning in the decision-maker. Drawing on Plato's doctrine of *anamnesis* (notwithstanding its more typical, rationalist connotations), Gadamer thus argues that pre-knowledge of the good is present as much in our choice of action or conduct as it is in the dialectic. Consequently, following a discussion of this "prior knowledge which guides all one's seeking and questioning," Gadamer indicates that such recollected knowledge applies to the practical pursuit of virtue (*arête*) as well as the philosophical pursuit of truth.[47] He concludes that "knowledge of the good is always with us in our practical life. Whenever we choose one thing in preference to another, we believe ourselves capable of justifying our choice, and hence knowledge of the good is always already involved."[48] Gadamer thus reaffirms the involvement of such prior knowledge in the operation of practical wisdom when he says that "there can be no doubt that even in the *Meno* Plato intends *anamnesis* to have a much broader sense which should hold for *every sort of real knowing*";[49] that is, it will hold for our practical knowledge in the ethical situation no less than for our theoretical knowledge in philosophy.

Combining Plato's doctrine of *anamnesis* with Aristotle's *phronesis*, Gadamer thus portrays the manner in which moral judgment always proceeds in particular, historically embedded situations, guided wherever it truly exists by a pre-existing knowledge of the good. Such knowledge is strictly a "sense," that is, it is not a script or set of preordained principles, which helps us to navigate our way through novel situations with an orientation toward a just outcome. Although this moral pre-knowledge is within us and can be said to be brought forth or recollected, as with any hermeneutical application and revision of fore-knowledge, Gadamer clarifies that this is not a literal remembering in the sense of "being reminded of something forgotten. Rather, it is a new revelation about something already known."[50] And what is already known, at varying levels of awareness, is the historical concretizations or instantiations of what is right or just, that is, the concrete or immanent good as it has been revealed through prior human conduct and that is continually made manifest through novel moral actions taking place within particular historical circumstances.[51] In other words, with every new circumstance in which just decisions are required and made, the past will be brought to bear or applied in novel and creative ways on the present, such that the source of guidance for future action is continually being enriched and grown in the concrete. In short, this concrete growth can be understood as the latent knowledge within prejudice, that is, the moral resource that is being built up or laid forth within history and that acts as a guide for moral decision-makers in their exercise of *phronesis*.

Seen in this broader context, the well-known section of *Truth and Method* that most explicitly deals with "prejudice" now shows itself to be concerned with more than a phenomenological sense in which the past influences or facilitates understanding in the present. Furthermore, it moves beyond traditional hermeneutics as a way of promoting better understanding of the meanings of historical texts. Gadamer's discussion of prejudice (*Vorurteil*) now appears, as well, to have been concerned with the essential precondition that enables or makes possible our *moral knowledge*, that is, "knowledge of the good [that] is always with us,"[52] which is necessary to guide our seeking and participating in virtue in particular situations. As is indicated above, such pre-knowledge of the good must come to us from the past, insofar as Gadamer sees what guides our phronetic activity as a form of recollection or bringing the past to bear on the present. And, therefore, whatever problematizes or impairs such historical knowledge—as Kantian and post-Kantian epistemology had done—will also put our moral decision-making in jeopardy. Still, it is important to note here that Gadamer does not have in mind any blunt or simplistic attempt to re-instantiate previous concretizations of the good in the present. Rather, he sees prior human experience as a critical guide or model,[53] informing our decision-making in situations whose uniqueness requires the ability to respond (*phronesis*) in new ways and actually seek out what is right. In this manner, the decision-maker is capable of "knowing" in advance how to make moral judgments without "knowing" in advance what particular judgments will be needed. When we ultimately discover right action, its historical particularity then gives us a "new revelation" about the good, supplementing our familiarity with it by showing it to us in a new way.

Viewed in this light, Gadamer's attempt to "rehabilitate"[54] tradition and prejudice may be seen as fundamentally grounded in the notion that the latter contains truth or knowledge—for our present purposes, knowledge of the good that is concretely embodied in history. It is for this reason that Gadamer identifies tradition as an "authority" over us, and he explicitly says that this authority rests on its being a source of superior "insight," "knowledge," and "judgment" over that of the individual left to his own devices.[55] Tradition guides, as it were, in the manner of the teacher, superior, or expert, whose authority is based in sound judgment and the notion that "what the authority says is not irrational and arbitrary but can, in principle, be discovered to be true."[56] Consequently, he argues, the radical Enlightenment rejection of prejudice must be brought into question once it is understood that the prejudices that tradition instills derive their legitimacy not simply from their source—their merely being named or identified as an authority or as authoritative over us[57]—but from their latent knowledge of the good. That is to say, they are authoritative, not simply because of their possessing a title or occupying a position that is recognized as having this status, but due to the fact that what they say is ultimately based in "good reasons."[58] Gadamer thus resists the Enlightenment's blanket disparagement of all prejudice—what he famously refers to as "the prejudice against prejudice"[59]—and it is for this reason that he seeks to restore recognition that there is latent historical knowledge within tradition that such biases against prejudice neglect.

Knowing how to bring the past to bear on the present—the phronetic *anamnesis* of the Platonic-Aristotelian tradition—is thus at the center of Gadamer's moral philosophy, and this returns us to his principal concern in *Truth and Method* with the modern human sciences. When the past no longer makes its claims on the present and is merely perceived as a distantiated object of empirical investigation, there must be a substantial loss in knowledge. This detriment has further ethical implications when philosophical hermeneutics is understood as pertaining to all aspects of human consciousness, as Gadamer indicates, including the moment of practical choice (*prohairesis*). Our "know-how" in the practice of ethics must ultimately be undermined once the past is alienated from us in this way. We are, in short, cut loose from the experience of tradition and its truth claims. However, a restoration can be sought, according to Gadamer, by returning to a relationship with the past in which we let ourselves "be *addressed* by tradition," such that its truth claims are once again heard or become part of a conversation with the present, and the objectifying gaze of historical consciousness is, as a result, overcome.[60]

Prejudice Rehabilitated

In the present chapter, Gadamer's promotion of a "thoughtful mediation and integration" of the past with the present has been interpreted as motivated by a concern that there is human knowledge or truth at stake when we suffer from the distortions of historical consciousness. For Gadamer, this alienation from and relativizing of the past has cut us off from our source of experiential guidance, a phenomenon whose reach encompasses our moral life. Gadamer draws on both Plato's doctrine of *anamnesis* and Aristotle's *phronesis* to show that living virtuously requires a responsive "know how" on the part of ethical actors, which can only come from the fore-knowledge of the good that we owe to our historical life. This prejudice or knowledge belonging to one who is already under way is what Gadamer seeks to "rehabilitate" as a source of authority, one that is ultimately based on the superior insight, sound judgment, or "good reasons" associated with lived experience over time. What has been called Gadamer's phronetic *anamnesis*, his belief that "knowledge of the good is always with us"[61] and helps us to make "new revelation[s] about something that is already known,"[62] thus sheds an important light on the section of *Truth and Method*, "The Rehabilitation of Authority and Tradition," that is devoted to his discussion of the hermeneutical importance of prejudice (*Vorurteil*). It demonstrates that Gadamer views tradition as worthy of status as an authority, that is, as having a legitimate basis, insofar as tradition contains knowledge of the concrete good and thus facilitates the "know how" involved in the pursuit of virtue. Moreover, it results in a claim that we ought to approach our historical life in a certain way, that is, by integrating, mediating, and assimilating tradition into the life of the present, so that we may lean on the superior insight of the past in the moral lives in which we are embedded.

Notes

1. See Hans-Georg Gadamer, *The Idea of the Good in Platonic-Aristotelian Philosophy*, trans. P. Christopher Smith (New Haven, CT: Yale University Press, 1986); *Reason in the Age of Science*, trans. Frederick G. Lawrence (Cambridge, MA: MIT Press, 1982); *Hermeneutics, Religion, and Ethics*, trans. Joel Weinsheimer (New Haven, CT: Yale University Press, 1999).

2. Foreword to the second edition, in Hans-Georg Gadamer, *Truth and Method*, trans. Joel Weinsheimer and Donald G. Marshall, 2nd rev. ed. (New York: Continuum, 2004), xxxiv.

3. Gadamer, *Truth and Method*, 3–171.

4. According to Gadamer, the development of the concept of "genius" in Kant's aesthetic philosophy was what set the stage for this "radical subjectivization of aesthetics" and, ultimately, the relativism of the modern human sciences as a whole. In order to establish the universality of aesthetic experience, Kant believes it necessary to abstract from the particularity of any individual experience of art or nature (e.g., the emotional state evoked in the observer) so as to identify what is truly universal in it. For Kant, it is the a priori subjective consciousness, experiencing the free play of the imagination and the understanding, that alone constitutes the defining aspect of aesthetic experience in which all human beings participate. The genius is the artist whose creativity makes this experience in the observer possible through the work of art that effectively communicates his own free play of imagination and understanding. The universality of aesthetic experience is, therefore, found solely in the ability of the artist to evoke the disinterested pleasure associated with the free play of these mental faculties in all observers. However, Gadamer notes, the content of what may cause such pleasure—and thus qualify as beautiful—under Kant becomes entirely unrestricted and subjective. After Kant, this subjectivization of aesthetics is extended and further radicalized. The genius of the individual artist who creates now corresponds to the genius in every individual interpreter of art. Consequently, neither artist nor interpreter is bound to any criterion of beauty. Moreover, for Romantics such as Schiller, aesthetic experiences are seen as not only radically idiosyncratic, but also immediate and fleeting for the individual himself. According to Gadamer, the life philosophy of nineteenth century Romanticism subsequently turned to this aesthetics as the paradigm for understanding all experience, since its radical subjectivity helped resist the homogenizing tendencies of modern rationalism against which it was protesting. Now, all "experience" (*Erlebnis*) could be seen as confined to the individual subject as well as the historical moment of its occurrence. Ibid., 37–55.

5. Ibid., 188.

6. Ibid. Gadamer explains that for Romantic hermeneutics "every encounter with a text is an encounter of the spirit with itself. Every text is strange enough to present a problem, and yet familiar enough to be fundamentally intelligible even

when we know nothing about it except that it is text, writing, an expression of mind" (233).

7. Ibid., 189.

8. Ibid., 6.

9. I have further explored this concern of Gadamer's with the truth that is lost in the objectivizing of texts through historical consciousness in Ryan Holston, "Anti-Rationalism, Relativism, and the Metaphysical Tradition: Situating Gadamer's Philosophical Hermeneutics," in *Critics of Enlightenment Rationalism*, ed. Gene Callahan and Kenneth B. McIntyre (Cham, Switzerland: Palgrave Macmillan, 2020), 193–209.

10. Gadamer, *Truth and Method*, 233–34. Gadamer summarizes this objectification in Dilthey's historical method: "In Dilthey's grounding of the human sciences hermeneutics is . . . the universal medium of the historical consciousness, for which there no longer exists any knowledge of truth other than the understanding of expression and, through expression, life. . . . Thus Dilthey ultimately conceives inquiring into the historical past *as deciphering and not as historical experience* (*Erfahrung*)" (234). Emphasis in the original.

11. For the same reason, in Gadamer's earlier, corresponding discussion of "aesthetic consciousness," he laments the loss of art's ability to speak to us in this way, and he illustrates this objectivizing view of art by pointing to the advent of the art museum. Ibid., 75.

12. Ibid., 194.

13. Ibid., 157. Emphasis added.

14. This interpretation of Gadamer is echoed by Jean Grondin, whose account of Gadamer's critique of historical consciousness makes reference to "the lost metaphysical experience of the humanities." He explains that "the humanities teach us truths and real-life lessons, in the sense that history used to be seen as a *magistra vitae*." Jean Grondin, "The Metaphysical Dimension of Hermeneutics," in *Hermeneutics and Phenomenology: Figures and Themes*, ed. Saulius Geniusas and Paul Fairfield (New York: Bloomsbury Academic, 2018), 128.

15. To be sure, subsequent to the writing of *Truth and Method*, Gadamer asserts the purely phenomenological or descriptive, rather than normative, purpose that motivated his writing of the text. However, I have argued that this self-interpretation must either be understood in a highly qualified sense, that is, in that Gadamer had been describing *genuine* or *authentic* interpretation, or else be seen as committing a performative contradiction. In other words, Gadamer's self-interpretation claims, in the latter case, that in writing *Truth and Method*, he had been engaged in precisely the sort of distantiated, positivist account of understanding that in this very text he was simultaneously arguing was impossible. See Ryan Holston, "Two Concepts of Prejudice," *History of Political Thought* 35, no. 1 (2014): esp. 177–184. In his review of *Truth and Method*, Alasdair MacIntyre similarly observes the irony of Gadamer's subsequent claim to have been purely descriptive in writing this text, and he says

that this demonstrates the remarkable grip of the views against which Gadamer had written. MacIntyre concludes with the acerbic remark that "Gadamer partially misunderstands his own book." Alasdair MacIntyre, "Contexts of Interpretation: Reflections on Hans-Georg Gadamer's *Truth and Method*," *Boston University Journal* 24, no. 1 (1976): 41–46. Lawrence Hinman argues that Gadamer's claim to have had purely descriptive purposes would render the content of *Truth and Method* entirely irrelevant, since the description of what one inevitably does whenever one understands anything implies the impossibility of acting differently. See Lawrence Hinman, "Quid Facti or Quid Juris? The Fundamental Ambiguity of Gadamer's Understanding of Hermeneutics," *Philosophy and Phenomenological Research* 40, no. 4 (1980): 512–35. Frederick Lawrence echoes the first interpretation I have given in this note, which says that Gadamer was describing genuine or authentic interpretation, when he says that Gadamer's focus on the *quaestio facti* means asking the question, "What are we doing when we are being *authentically* human?" Frederick G. Lawrence, "Hans-Georg Gadamer: Philosopher of Practical Wisdom," *Theoforum* 40, no. 3 (2009): 270. Emphasis added. Indeed, one might say that Gadamer had sought to describe the achievement of human understanding, a normatively positive phenomenon, and that having collapsed the is/ought dichotomy, his later characterization of *Truth and Method* reflects a view of "description" that, unlike the modern social sciences, does not exclude such normative content.

16. Ibid., 161. Emphasis in the original.

17. Ibid., 310.

18. Ibid., 269.

19. This would be one way in which Gadamer might respond to Hinman's criticism alluded to in note 15. In other words, calling attention to the inevitable role of prejudice in all understanding is certainly not irrelevant if it serves as a warning against the detrimental aspiration of removing all of our prejudices. That we are incapable of removing our prejudices is no assurance against the disasterous consequences of such an attempt.

20. Brice R. Wachterhauser, "Gadamer's Realism: The 'Belongingness' of Word and Reality," in *Hermeneutics and Truth*, ed. Brice R. Wachterhauser (Evanston, IL: Northwestern University Press, 1994), 153.

21. Ibid., 154.

22. Ibid., 155. Emphasis in the original.

23. Ibid., 165. It is important to note that what has been said here does not imply Gadamer's possession of a correspondence theory of truth but entails an understanding of truth (*aletheia*) as in-motion or under way, a concept that Gadamer inherits from the early Heidegger, who in turn had recovered it from the ancients. Gadamer rejects the relativistic conclusions regarding truth belonging to Heidegger after the self-described "turn" (*Kehre*) in his thinking. See Robert J. Dostal, "The Experience of Truth for Gadamer and Heidegger: Taking Time and Sudden Lightning," in *Hermeneutics and Truth*, ed. Brice R. Wachterhauser (Evanston, IL: Northwestern University Press, 1994), 47–67; Wachterhauser, *Beyond Being: Gadamer's Post-Platonic*

Hermeneutical Ontology (Chicago: Northwestern University Press, 1999), 166–99.

24. Wachterhauser, "Gadamer's Realism," 148. See Richard Rorty, *Philosophy and the Mirror of Nature* (Princeton, NJ: Princeton University Press, 1979); Gianni Vattimo, *The End of Modernity: Nihilism and Hermeneutics in Postmodern Culture* (Baltimore: Johns Hopkins University Press, 1988). To be sure, Rorty rightly identifies Gadamer's opposition to a hermeneutics that takes the form of a "method" for uncovering truth, modeled along the lines of the natural sciences. However, Rorty neglects entirely Gadamer's aim to recover an older notion of truth, along with the fundamental opposition or tension Gadamer establishes between "truth and method." Rorty's radical historicism ultimately overlooks or at best trivializes the productive role that our prejudices play in providing a standpoint from which reality may be perceived and through which truth or genuine knowledge about reality—albeit from a limited perspective—may emerge. In this way, Rorty's position represents a perpetuation of the Enlightenment's divorce of morality from history, failing to appreciate their compatibility. Its overemphasis on the historicity of morality is the mirror image of the cognitivist conceptions of deliberative democracy.

25. In addition to Wachterhauser, "Gadamer's Realism: The 'Belongingness' of Word and Reality," see also *Beyond Being*, "Getting It Right: Relativism, Realism, and Truth," in *The Cambridge Companion to Gadamer*, ed. Robert J. Dostal (Cambridge: Cambridge University Press, 2002), 52–78; P. Christopher Smith, translator's introduction" to Gadamer, *The Idea of the Good*; P. Christopher Smith, "The Ethical Dimensions of Gadamer's Hermeneutical Theory," *Research in Phenomenology* 18 (1988): 75–91; *Hermeneutics and Human Finitude: Toward a Theory of Ethical Understanding* (New York: Fordham University Press, 1991); Frederick G. Lawrence, translator's introduction to Gadamer, *Reason in the Age of Science*; Frederick G. Lawrence, "Gadamer, the Hermeneutic Revolution, and Theology," in *The Cambridge Companion to Gadamer*, ed. Robert J. Dostal (Cambridge: Cambridge University Press, 2006), 167–200; Grondin, "The Metaphysical Dimension of Hermeneutics," 125–37.

26. Wachterhauser, "Gadamer's Realism," 150–51. Wachterhauser says that Gadamer "has his roots in a metaphysical tradition beginning with Heraclitus and Parmenides, continuing with Plato (especially the later Plato), Aristotle, Neoplatonism, Augustine, and Hegel. In fact, Gadamer claims that his hermeneutical theory refers back to the metaphysical tradition that connects Parmenides to Hegel" (150).

27. Gadamer, *Truth and Method*, 316.

28. Ibid., 316, 518–19.

29. Ibid., 316.

30. Ibid., 317.

31. With respect to the mutability of justice and the compatibility of the universal and the particular, Gadamer's view bears striking affinities with the theory of "value-centered historicism" articulated by Claes G. Ryn. See "Universality and History," *Humanitas* 6, no. 1 (1992): 10–39; *A Common Human Ground: Universality and Particularity in a Multicultural World* (Columbia, MO: University of Missouri

Press, 2003). Also echoing Aristotle, Ryn argues that the standard regarding which conduct qualifies as just and which does not is only known by contact with concrete experience that is ultimately conducive to human flourishing (*eudaimonia*). However, to articulate the latter as principles of the intellect is to begin to fix that which is always in flux (or, in Gadamer's Heideggerian language, "under way") and better "known" as it is concretely lived.

32. This certainly is the inference of Leo Strauss in his interpretation of *Truth and Method* revealed through his correspondence with Gadamer. I have argued the shortcomings of this position in Ryan Holston, "The Poverty of Antihistoricism: Strauss and Gadamer in Dialogue," *Modern Age* 58, no. 2 (2016): 41–53.

33. Gadamer, *Truth and Method*, 318.

34. Ibid.

35. Smith echoes this interpretation of Gadamer in a footnote to his translation of *The Idea of the Good*, in which he discusses Gadamer's understanding of "the existential status of moral rules, and how we can be said to 'know' them when we apply them." For Gadamer, Smith says, "rules in ethics have their reality only in the tradition of their applications, instantiations, or interpretations. And each of these, far from being a diminution of some ideal rule in itself apart from its instantiations, is thus to be viewed as an 'accretion of reality' (Gadamer: *Zuwachs an Sein*) in the rule." Gadamer, *The Idea of the Good*, 164–65n2. Ethical rules, it might be said, are at once created and discovered through each application, instantiation, or interpretation, as the past is continually brought to bear on the present and the tradition of application grows.

36. Ryn has similarly pointed to the existence of concrete standards or the passage of judgment that comes from lived experience itself. Surely, both are indebted to Hegel's thinking to a considerable degree for this insight. However, it is interesting that both have chosen to draw, more deeply and explicitly, on Aristotle's conception of moral experience at this point in their thinking. See Ryn, *A Common Human Ground*, esp. ch. 4. More will be said about the content of this standard of justice in the context of Gadamer's thinking in the following chapter. In his most explicit moments confronting this question, we will see that it is to Aristotle, Hegel, and Kierkegaard that Gadamer turns to flesh out this content.

37. To be sure, this question is anticipated and implied within Gadamer's discussion in "Supplement I" to *Truth and Method*, 518–19, where he echoes his earlier remarks pertaining to Aristotle's understanding of the mutability of justice. Yet here he goes further and begins a preliminary consideration of the relationship between the universal and the particular, or the one and the many, which he ultimately deals with in greater depth in *The Idea of the Good*.

38. Aristotle expresses this concern, according to Gadamer, in terms of the need to keep theoretical and practical knowledge distinct from one another. See Gadamer, *The Idea of the Good*, 159–78. There is a temptation, of which Gadamer and Aristotle both are aware, to neglect the difficult work of *phronesis* and to try "to

grasp the good directly and know it like some *mathēma* (learned insight)." However, Gadamer cautions that, "[The good's] ineffability, its being *arreton* (unsayable) should be interpreted as soberly as possible" (28). The idea that what ought to be done in the practical situation is teachable, like some fixed and relayable insight, is to be seen as the reification associated with abstraction and brings with it the attendant danger of imputing a fixed blueprint to reality without circumstantial knowledge thereof.

39. Gadamer believes this misreading of Plato by Aristotle to have been deliberate and says that it was designed to facilitate Aristotle's own articulation of the concreteness of the good by way of critique. Ibid., 133n6, 144.

40. For Gadamer, the "separation" of the good from reality for which Aristotle critiques Plato more accurately characterizes the thinking of Plotinus, who loses completely the sense of interdependence between the one and the many and distorts Plato's thought along these lines. Ibid., 28n22. Ryn, though sharing this concern about the separation of the good from reality, sees Plato as thoroughly culpable in this regard. See Claes G. Ryn, "The Politics of Transcendence: The Pretentious Passivity of Platonic Idealism," *Humanitas* 12, no. 2 (1999): 4–26.

41. Ibid., 10, 11.

42. Ibid., 11.

43. Ibid., 16. Emphasis added. Still, despite his downplaying of Plato's use of *chorismos* here, Gadamer also resists its dismissal and at one point even reaffirms the importance of this concept—presuming it to be understood metaphorically—for Plato's refutation of Sophism: "True and just human behavior cannot be based on the conventional concepts and standards to which public opinion clings. Rather, such behavior must take as its standard only those norms that transcend any question of public acceptance, and even the question of whether they can be, or are ever found to be, fully realized, and that thereby display themselves to our moral consciousness as incontestably and unalterably true and right. This severance of the noetic from the sensory, of true insight from mere points of view—this *chorismos*, in other words—is the truth of moral consciousness as such" (18). There is, in short, something captured by Plato's attempt to identify true and right behavior as "separate" from all other behavior. We may, correctly, see and describe such behavior as set apart, distinct, and even "severed" from the rest. And yet we need not look beyond the particular things in human life to apprehend this quality and determine that which is truly right and just. Indeed, having a sense of this quality would be impossible without these particular instantiations.

44. Ibid., xxi. Emphasis in the original.

45. More will be said in chapter 5 about Gadamer's use of the early Heidegger's reading of Aristotle and the importance of book 6 of the *Nicomachean Ethics*. But see, in general, the section entitled "The Hermeneutic Relevance of Aristotle" in Gadamer, *Truth and Method*, 310–21. With regard to the importance for Gadamer of Heidegger's teaching and reading of Aristotle, see Holston, "Anti-Rationalism, Relativism, and the Metaphysical Tradition," 198–99.

46. Lawrence has pointed to the substantial influence of Aristotle on Gadamer's thinking and especially the centrality of *phronesis* to his moral philosophy. In particular, Lawrence emphasizes the contrast such situated judgment presents with Habermas's Cartesian demand for absolute certainty for the legitimacy of moral norms and the rejection of judgments or beliefs as mere dogma that are incapable of providing complete or definitive justification. Gadamer finds Habermas's theory lacking insofar as it does not allow for this sort of historically situated, practical wisdom, which he believes is essential for the very critical moral judgment that Habermas himself advocates. See Frederick G. Lawrence, translator's introduction to Gadamer, *Reason in the Age of Science*, xxv.

47. Gadamer, *The Idea of the Good*, 57.

48. Ibid.

49. Ibid., 58–59. Emphasis added.

50. Ibid., 58.

51. Smith similarly interprets Gadamer's *anamnesis* as operating at varying degrees of awareness in the ethical decision-maker. Drawing parallels to Edmund Burke's emphasis on historical precedent and example, Smith describes our more conscious recollection as seeing an "analogousness of what is right and wrong in present circumstances to what was right and wrong in the historical circumstances that have led up to the present." Though at other times, he sees the function of *anamnesis* as more latent, as when he says that "ethical thinking, deliberation (*bouleuesthai*), occurs against the background of what is not thought about at all. Indeed it is grounded in pre-conscious dispositions, or *hexeis*, as Aristotle calls them," which include not only customary ways of acting, but even our linguistic habits, or speech. Smith, *Hermeneutics and Human Finitude*, 217, 229–30.

52. Gadamer, *The Idea of the Good*, 57.

53. Gadamer thus describes tradition as "a model or exemplar" that we do not and cannot objectify as the modern social scientist conceives, but something that we always carry with us. Gadamer, *Truth and Method*, 283. See also his extended remarks indicating the possibility of seeing certain "classical" historical texts as exemplary and authoritative, a possibility that he says seems to reemerge with each new humanist movement (286–91). It is thus no coincidence that one sees such a perspective in the thinking of Irving Babbitt, who is an inspiration for much of Ryn's value-centered historicism and is considered to be the foremost representative of the early twentieth-century school of thought known as the "New Humanism." For Babbitt's views on the importance of teaching "classical" historical texts, see Irving Babbitt, *Literature and the American College: Essays in Defense of the Humanities* (Washington, DC: National Humanities Institute, 1986). For a recent, humanistic appropriation of Babbitt along these lines, see Eric Adler, *The Battle of the Classics: How a Nineteenth-Century Debate Can Save the Humanities Today* (New York: Oxford University Press, 2020).

54. Ibid., 278.

55. Ibid., 281. But how is it, it may be asked, even assuming the existence of standards that are concrete rather than abstract, that tradition comes to embody and convey the latter? Consider Smith's helpful account of Gadamer's distinction between experience (*Erfahrung*) that teaches and the previously mentioned experience (*Erlebnis*) that is momentary or fleeting. Drawing on Aristotle's and Hegel's teleological epistemologies, Smith describes knowledge or insight into universals that can only come about by virtue of "the experience of particular developing things," that is, by virtue of contact with a thing's historical being or being over time, as it is under way rather than as a still life or snapshot in time. On this view, universals are never known abstractly to the reflecting individual but may only be uncovered "*in rebus*" and even "in the *res publica* as we experience it." *Hermeneutics and Human Finitude*, 189–92, 273–74. Tradition, though never fixed, can thus be seen as a repository of knowledge and teacher insofar as it is the locus of the most protracted human experience (*Erfahrung*). See Gadamer's extended discussion of *Erfahrung* in *Truth and Method*, especially where he explicitly identifies "insight" with this view of experience, properly conceived (341–55, esp. 350).

56. Gadamer, *Truth and Method*, 281. Note that Gadamer only believes that the insight of the authority can, *in principle*, be discovered to be true, which is not to say that it must, *in fact*, be shown to be true. Such demand for rational demonstration is more emblematic of the Enlightenment thinking that Gadamer critiques and more closely approximates Habermas's position.

57. This would appear to be the basis of authority in Thomas Hobbes's *Leviathan*, whose sovereign is justified or legitimated based on the need merely for *someone* to be named the recipient of the rights transfer by which all can escape the state of nature and its "warre of every man against every man." See Thomas Hobbes, *Leviathan*, eds. Richard E. Flathman and David Johnston (New York: Norton, 1997), 71. This person, whoever it may be, will possess a monopoly of violence and thus be capable of providing the physical security sought by all individuals. What is important for Hobbes is not *who* is identified as an authority but simply *that* there is an authority. It is the diffusion of authority, in other words, that is problematic for Hobbes. For Gadamer, by contrast, authority is based on the superior knowledge of whoever (or whatever, in the case of tradition) is guiding peoples' behavior.

58. Gadamer, *Truth and Method*, 281.

59. Ibid., 273.

60. Ibid., 283. Emphasis in the original.

61. Gadamer, *The Idea of the Good*, 57.

62. Ibid., 58.

Chapter 5

Tradition's Deliberation

The purpose of the previous chapter was to place Gadamer's famous "rehabilitation of authority and tradition" in *Truth and Method* within the context of his normative concerns regarding prejudice. It is important to note here that the collapse of the dichotomy of morality and historical experience that was attributed to Gadamer in that chapter needs to be seen in the light of the broad intellectual trend discussed in the first three chapters. In other words, it is precisely this tendency of the Enlightenment project to separate or divorce the good from history that Gadamer is fundamentally responding to as he attempts to close the gap or collapse the sharp metaphysical dualism that arises within modernity. To be sure, as was noted in the first chapter, this dualism is ultimately traceable to ancient rationalism and is thus properly viewed as a philosophical tendency that has long been present in the Western intellectual tradition. In light of this, Rousseau and Kant ought to be seen as inheritors of this intellectual lineage and, to reiterate an earlier point, did not as historically situated thinkers themselves emerge from nowhere. Nevertheless, such tendencies have become heightened or accentuated in modernity through a variety of intellectual attitudes and prejudices that have been combined and further developed. The present chapter, whose primary purpose is to articulate an alternative model of deliberation to contemporary democratic theory, builds on Gadamer's moral philosophy, and, in doing so, provides further evidence of the thesis regarding his normative purpose of discrediting such abstract thinking about the good.[1]

Kantianism and Imperative Ethics

It might be argued that Gadamer is fundamentally more ambivalent toward the thinking of Kant than he is toward that of any other thinker.[2] This is attributable to the fact that, while Gadamer agrees with those who charge Kant's deontological approach to ethics with being "unrealistic and transcendental"[3] in its abstraction from the ethical life, he nonetheless makes prominent in his own thinking an explicit recognition of the ethical truth contained within the categorical imperative, which is that one must hold steadfastly to what is right and resist the temptations of "interest and inclination."[4] Gadamer thus sees Kant's formulation of the categorical imperative as an insight into the human propensity to rationalize self-exemption from our duties toward one another, such that we often fall prey to what he terms "the dialectic of the exception."[5] Moreover, while Gadamer agrees with Hegel that our ethical imperatives are fundamentally grounded in *ethos* or *Sittlichkeit*—which is to say, their substantiality or concrete embodiment in institutions such as the family, the church, and the state[6]—he believes that this critique is more appropriately applied to neo-Kantianism than it is to Kant himself.[7] Still, Gadamer ultimately sees Kant's moral philosophy as "unsatisfactory" for its inattention to the "conditionedness" of human experience, which he aims to supplement with a return to Aristotle.[8]

For, though there may be truths to which Kant is sensitive in his isolation and articulation of the will that characterizes the purest fulfillment of ethical duty, there is at the same time a neglect in his thinking of the underlying *ethos* upon which appeals to human reason and choice must always depend, and with respect to which Kant fails to do justice.[9] The imperative character of morality, in Gadamer's estimation, is therefore only one of its dimensions, and what is neglected by Kant and the neo-Kantians in this one-sidedness is "the richness and breadth of moral truth and reality that is to be found in Aristotle."[10] It is in calling attention to the concrete texture and complexity that characterizes the ethical life that one is able to recognize the variety of influences that constitute the very being of the subject whose choices are at issue and always rely on pre-formation within ethical substance. And it is Aristotle, with his focus on the habituation of virtue and the development of ethical character, much more than Plato, with his intellectualist orientation, who provides this needed corrective.[11] For Aristotle, there is no transcendental subject independent of the development of the person in *ethos*, whose choices are to be evaluated as the fulfillment or violation of duty. Rather, it must be understood that the knowledge and habits (*hexeis*) preceding our choices constitute the whole concrete reality of the ethical life in which the latter are embedded: "[Aristotle's] analysis of *phronesis* recognizes that moral knowledge is a way of moral being itself, which therefore cannot be prescinded from the whole concretion of what he calls ethos."[12]

It is in modernity, however, that one witnesses the substantial erosion, for the first time since the Greek *polis*, of a common life of institutions reflecting shared virtues.[13] And, with the attenuation of this *ethos*, Gadamer argues, practical reason—no longer the Christian virtue of *prudentia*—comes to be seen in merely technical or instrumental terms, as the faculty through which one discerns the proper means to obtaining the objects of individual desire.[14] This is certainly not to say that morality becomes inconceivable in this context, but that a vital distinction is now recognized—and reflected, in particular, among Kant and his followers—between practical reason conceived as mere cleverness or calculations regarding desire satisfaction, on the one hand, and the commands of morality, on the other.[15] This is Kant's fundamental opposition between the causality of the material world and the autonomy or freedom of the rational subject, that is, the moral-philosophical dichotomy between "is" and "ought" that informs the epistemology of all post-Kantian scientific inquiry, natural or social.[16] And it is this dualism, the acute separation of the material from the immaterial realm within modern thought, that Gadamer seeks to confront in his engagement with the Kantian legacy of thinking about morality: "The opposition of Is and Ought has certainly always been an aspect of morality. But only in modernity has it found its formulation. *For only now is it the case that 'is' (or today 'the facts') lacks all relation to the good.*"[17] As a result, characteristic of imperative ethics is what Gadamer calls a "narrowness,"[18] by which he means a tendency to consider only the truncated or circumscribed moral status of individuals outside or apart from *ethos*, where it is difficult to recognize anything more than the abstract rights of the subject. Aristotle's much broader orientation toward "the whole of the moral-political world" is said to bind us through the much thicker, shared experience of the good conceived as what is "necessary" and "obligatory" in contradistinction to the mere "should" associated with the "duty" of any single individual.[19] This return to Aristotle is thus a way of reconnecting us to what Gadamer refers to as "the humanly good" in all its concreteness, in contrast to the theoretical or intellectual "idea of the good," which, he says, "can afford no genuine satisfaction to human life."[20]

This bindingness to which Gadamer alludes, which is made available only within the concrete substantiality of shared experience and custom

(*Sittlichkeit*), is succinctly captured by Ronald Beiner when he refers to the preeminent place Gadamer ascribes to the latter in all moral knowledge as "the primacy of *ethos*."[21] What Gadamer shares with Alasdair MacIntyre, according to Beiner, is the fundamental conviction that what comes first in moral knowledge and understanding, prior to any reasoning or theoretical ordering of reality, are these concrete ways of living.[22] The implication, therefore, is that with respect to practical philosophy, all that can really be hoped for is the successful clarification and conceptualization of the already lived and shared ethical life of a society, and, similarly with respect to moral argument, one must make appeals to what resonates with or corresponds to what is already known to be true at an experiential level of reality in order to be persuasive.[23] It is having been under way within *ethos*, in other words, that alone can supply what is essential to the convincingness or normative pull of any argument. And no theoretical brilliance can compensate for the latter's absence: "Good theory is no substitute for good socialization, and even the best theory is utterly helpless in the face of bad socialization."[24] The character and habituation that any Aristotelian would contend is essential preparation for choosing rightly and living a life of virtue (*arête*) is here understood, in similar fashion, as a precondition that is decisive with regard to successful moral persuasion.

The Localization of Truth

Given the pervasive role that Gadamer sees with respect to "socialization" or acculturation in moral understanding, it may be worth reconsidering whether he sees morality as so deeply embedded in tradition that his thinking ultimately devolves into moral relativism, as some have contended. In other words, in collapsing the dichotomy between the moral and the historical in this manner, it might be asked, are not Gadamer and his followers—such as Beiner, Smith, and the present author—simply adopting a form of ethical particularism, such that the effort to collapse the metaphysical dualism of the Enlightenment has resulted in the sacrifice of the good to history, or anything worthy of being called morality? This is certainly the claim of two of Gadamer's most prominent interlocutors—Habermas, on the left, and Strauss, on the right—both of whom argue that Gadamer's epistemological position effectively precludes distantiation from tradition and, along with it, truth claims that transcend the historical particularity of one's horizon of understanding.[25] Without access to moral standards independent of one's tradition, both thinkers contend, one necessarily obviates the possibility of critiquing or judging one's tradition to be morally deficient.

However, as Beiner insightfully observes, with respect to the role of tradition and moral knowledge, the dichotomy of truth versus relativity is a false one that leaves us with only the extreme epistemological alternatives of the absolute knowing of a god, on the one hand, and radical moral skepticism, on the other, which clearly is not adequate for depicting the nature of human knowledge within history. As an alternative way of conceptualizing such disputes between Gadamer and his rationalist critics, Beiner helpfully reframes the positions that are adopted in terms that may be seen as fairer to Gadamer, positing the dichotomy instead as "truth at the level of abstract principles versus truth embedded in particular circumstances."[26] As is similarly the case with Aristotle, Beiner argues, Gadamer's insistence on the centrality of *phronesis* in moral knowledge does nothing to undermine the existence of truth, but instead emphasizes the "local encounter" with what is knowable within the particularity of the situations in which human beings always find themselves.[27] This "localization" of ethical knowledge, in calling attention to the locus of truth as "inside" as opposed to "outside" of experience,[28] reveals that it is the implicit identification of truth with an external vantage point—the forgetfulness of being—that inclines philosophers such as Habermas and Strauss to think in such Manichean categories of all or nothing with regard to knowledge of reality. And it is noteworthy, particularly in light of the discussion of Kantian and post-Kantian epistemology earlier in this chapter, that the external vantage point is precisely that which is privileged in the model of the scientific observer, which in modernity has been so influential in all of our conceptions of knowing and understanding.

Gadamer's own response to such rationalistic critiques of his thinking typically takes the form of calling into question the fundamental premises of what is required for "knowledge" of reality, thus depicting them in one way or another as utopian with regard to their aspirations for the human intellect.[29] Moreover, with respect to the human sciences (*Geisteswissenschaften*), such approaches fail to heed the cautionary remark issued at the outset of Aristotle's *Nicomachean Ethics*, which is that we must "look for precision in each class of things just so far as the nature of the subject admits."[30] For example, Aristotle tells us that one cannot treat rhetoric with the same standards of exactitude as mathematics, or vice versa.[31] And it would, for this same reason, be inappropriate to demand for knowledge of moral truth the clarity of the intellect that we would expect for the apprehension of a mathematical or scientific law, which would require liberation from the formative influence on our thinking of any particular tradition.[32] For Gadamer, it is precisely this sort of category error—the demand for scientific certainty in areas of life in which such knowledge is inappropriate—that arises in the modern human sciences when one associates the "truth" of social reality with the application of the "method" of the natural sciences.[33] For this is to treat what is part of the social world in which we are internal participants and from which we can never extricate ourselves as if it were an object of study, of which we were merely external observers.

Such confusions are also the source of Gadamer's interest in book 6 of the *Ethics*, where Aristotle not only devotes an extended discussion of *phronesis*, but also provides a schematic of different types of knowledge or understanding and what characterizes the operation of each. Such a schematic, for Gadamer, may be helpful in resisting the scientism of modernity, which identifies all knowledge exclusively with the scientific method at the expense of all other forms. For Gadamer, as for Aristotle, what distinguishes *phronesis* from many other forms of knowing is its practical "application" of acquired experience or know-how within an unpredictable set of circumstances,[34] situations in which human beings are no mere observers of social phenomena but find themselves continually confronted with the call to action or choice (*prohairesis*). By contrast, the theoretical understanding of science (*episteme*) is knowledge of things that are immutable and objectively provable.[35] However, Aristotle shows that the variability of the ethical situation precludes the possibility, and indeed the luxury, of such precision, as one is afforded in the study of fixed entities and as one finds in the paradigmatic case of mathematical inquiry.[36] In the case of *phronesis*, one is aiming, as it were, at a (historically) moving target.

But in addition to this distinction from theoretical knowledge, Aristotle shows that *phronesis* also may be seen to differ decisively from the knowledge of a craft (*techne*), which is practical knowledge of particular things that are produced.[37] Although similar, insofar as *techne* and *phronesis* both concern themselves with knowledge pertaining to practical action, *techne* is a skill that can be learned and then forgotten or given up, whereas withdrawal from the ethical situation for a human being is never an option.[38] As Gadamer explains, "The human being always already stands within the realm of what is at stake in *phronesis*."[39] It is for this reason, therefore, that it is possible to "take up" carpentry or to "begin" a medical residency, but we can neither choose to participate nor cease to find ourselves within the situation of having to exercise the practical reasonableness involved in ethical decision-making. Moreover, in contrast with a *techne*, there is always an incompleteness of knowledge among those who engage in *phronesis*—training, therefore, is not possible in the manner one would associate with the master-apprentice relationship, as in the case of a particular craft.[40] To be sure, ethical actors do have historical exemplars or models to serve as their guides, but the development of *phronesis* is not "teachable" in the same, explicit manner as a *techne*, for there is no object-at-hand or "thing" on which one works—only the actions themselves, which are the goal of this activity, are that which is "made." But, as a person who engages in practical reason, "I cannot deal with myself as if I were an object. What is clearly missing here is the detachment that makes it possible to look at myself in the way one looks at an object."[41] In the end, there simply is no such external perspective, or view from the outside, as one finds in the producer of a thing, when speaking about the action that is the object of choice, which is part of who I am as an ethical being.[42]

In contrast to these other forms of knowing, therefore, the knowledge that characterizes *phronesis* is not merely something that is "possessed" but is "participat[ion] in shared norms by which one is antecedently shaped."[43] For I am within the world in which I act, neither a scientist who learns *about* the world, nor a producer who acts *upon* it—both of which imply separation or distance. Only *phronesis* closes this gap and adequately reflects the involvement of the ethical actor in or with the world that is always "there." This critique of "knowing from a distance"[44] or "ethics at a distance"[45] in Gadamer's thinking has its origins in the philosophy of Kierkegaard, whose attack on all "understanding from a distance," Gadamer says, was aimed at both the speculative philosophy and the church theology of his own day.[46] Gadamer's appropriation of Aristotle's practical philosophy, although in the contemporary context of neo-Kantianism and imperative ethics, is thus aimed at discrediting this same illusion.[47] For Gadamer, *phronesis* emphasizes a relationship to what is known that is precisely the opposite of being "at a distance"—which is to say, it implies being up close, intimately familiar, and a part of that with which one is working. The "application" at the heart of phronetic know-how is thus not that which we might associate with "applying" polish to a shoe, but is an inarticulable responsiveness captured when one has a "feel" for what to do.[48] It requires something like the knowledge that one may be said to have at one's fingertips, rather than what is held explicitly in one's mind.[49] To be sure, tacit knowledge is also an aspect of any *techne*. However, Smith emphasizes the key difference: "In bringing forth his product . . . [the craftsman] adheres to the fixed idea, the *eidos* or form, as best he can. In the realm of *phronesis*, however, the realm of ethical choices, there is precisely nothing fixed in this way to go by. As Aristotle puts it, there is no 'idea of the good.'"[50] To reiterate, this is not to say that there is *no such thing* as the good, but that the good *is not a thing* that we know at a distance, as in discussions of "principles" or "reasons" that all can accept. That is to say, the good is not intellectual or ideational, for it is bound up in the substantiality that contributes to who we are, or more precisely, who we have become over time.

Philia and Forbearance

The charge of relativism has thus far been rejected based on the reframing of the debate between Gadamer and his rationalist critics as different conceptions of the locus of moral truth—it has been claimed that, for Gadamer, the vantage point that gives us access to or knowledge of what is right has been "localized," such that he identifies the latter with the embeddedness of the ethical decision-maker in his particular situation, as opposed to the point of view of a distanced observer. Still, it is worth asking what the grounding of this claim is, since it is possible to conceive of a community that defends questionable moral practices with the argument that such judgment has been exercised by individuals who are a part of that tradition and from within the particularity of the situations that arise therein. Meanwhile, moral criticism of these practices might be dismissed as "external" or "from a distance." But surely, one might respond, not all such moral criticisms can be rejected out of hand as merely the product of post-Kantian, scientist epistemology. And if such communities and their decision-makers were forever capable of falling back on claims of having an epistemologically superior or privileged position, one would never have access to a vantage point from which they might be judged, resulting in the complete insulation of all such traditions from moral criticism. As a result, there would appear to be few limits to what might be defended as "right," in light of this localized or particularized conception of ethical truth. Such a challenge to Gadamer's position would thus demand to know *why* one ought to trust the assertion that the locus of moral truth must be exclusively identified with this internal perspective.

To begin, it ought to be made clear that the Gadamerian understanding of an ethical tradition or community, as it is articulated by both Gadamer and Smith, would appear to be less capacious than might be assumed by such a persistent rationalist critic. Certainly, we are not given a strict set of rules or principles to which any concrete community that exists over time must conform in order to qualify as a genuine "community." For, this would clearly belie the dissatisfaction that Gadamer expresses with Kantian formalism. However, to say that Gadamer gives no such formalistic rules or criteria does not imply that he tells us nothing about the nature of genuine community—as one finds in Aristotle's *Ethics*, here we are given a sketch, not a blueprint. What does it mean, then, for a person to become capable of living in community among other human beings, or to become civilized so that, in Aristotle's famous formulation, he may live as neither a beast nor a god but in enduring association with others?[51] What is perhaps the most basic element of ethical substance, the foundation for any such association of human beings, is what Smith, elaborating on Gadamer in *Truth and Method*, refers to as the individual " 'cancelling his physical aspect insofar as the world into which he grows is a human world shaped by language and custom' (WM 11 . . .) . . . for the 'physical aspect' is egoistic and 'mine' now, the world of language and custom, however, precisely not 'mine' now but 'ours' through time."[52] It is only through such "disciplining" and "training" of the egoistic and antisocial appetites that, on the Gadamerian account, genuine community can ever be said to exist—one must instill limits, in other words, of moderation on natural impulse so that self-control becomes not merely a choice but part of who one is as a matter of predisposition (*hexis*).[53] It is upon this foundation, and indeed, in this spirit, that the whole complex of institutions that comprise *ethos* or *Sittlichkeit* are built, a fact that is recognized not only by Aristotle but even the more intellectualist Plato, since both seek to build up those dispositions and character—through *paideia* (upbringing) and especially Aristotle's *hexeis*—which rein in urges otherwise prone to limitless excess.[54]

That ethical knowledge is epistemologically "internal," to the situation is thus grounded in the fact that we live continuously within and among particular people, which gives rise to the forbearance and restraint that is owed *to them* in order that we might live together in community. To illustrate the emergence of such obligations, Smith points to institutions in which we are continually required to overcome or transcend natural impulse or physical desire and enter into less fleeting, more permanent forms of association. Such is the case, he says, borrowing Hegel's illustration, with the physical love of man and woman that is ultimately transformed into something spiritual—a partnership in trust, faith, and confidence—when it develops and matures into the "ethical love" of marriage.[55] Hegel's word for marriage (*Trauung*), Smith explains, is used with deliberate intent for its connotation of "entrusting," which takes place among close or familiar partners in such a relationship, and Smith shows it to be linguistically close to the Greek *philia*, which means not only friendship, as is commonly understood, but also family.[56]

In both the German and the Greek, Smith further argues, one sees that the trust that another will fulfill his or her obligations to behave unegoistically is of the same type among members of the family as it is among friends.[57] Such "ethical love" ultimately has its origins in the development or maturation of a particular, concrete relationship, which begins with physical wants or needs but is transcended, and it is known best to those who have participated and lived within it. One "knows" the nature of these obligations because they are part of one's history, the experiences (*Erfahrungen*) that define who one is. This is a knowledge that is not a priori but pertains to particular people and develops up close, over time. Consequently, one sees that the epistemological claim to the superiority of the local vantage point is grounded in this embeddedness within, and the attendant understanding of, these foundational relationships, which is the source of our obligations. Such an understanding and qualification of what characterizes genuine community would thus rule out any who would claim moral rightness or justice while using the latter as cover for mere egoistic indulgence or advantage.

At the same time, what is central to the thinking of both Gadamer and Smith is that such self-regulation of impulse would not be conceivable if left up to each individual to exercise merely out of a calculated desire to avoid conflicts or collisions with the interests of others.[58] In other words, the forbearance that one finds essential to living with others is made possible by virtue of the fact that historically formed and inherited patterns of behavior serve this Platonic-Aristotelian function of socializing or civilizing individuals. This is not to say that *phronesis* or practical reasonableness, on the Gadamerian conception, means blindly following patterns of behavior that have been passed down and thus lacks any willful choosing. Indeed, Gadamer would see such an assumed antithesis between freedom and tradition, whereby these are conceived as occupying mutually exclusive space in the lives of individuals, as ultimately mistaken. Instead of seeing freedom as antithetical to tradition, as is so often assumed within contemporary, analytic philosophy, Smith explains that "in making ethical choices I am elaborating . . . a tradition that I myself am, and always already was, a part of."[59] Because the ethical actor is within, and not apart from, tradition, his actions constitute the tradition, just as it does him. And because the good has been instilled in one's character, recollection (*anamnesis*) actually gives meaning to present choices, as one continually applies this fore-knowledge to new situations. Thus, one is always choosing *with* the past when one cleaves to what is right: "I remember, recall, what I already know, namely the tradition of which I have always *been* a part and which is constitutive of my character."[60] This relationship to the authority of the past is therefore not blind determination, but is more accurately described as a codetermination with the tradition in which, Gadamer says, one is "answerable," in the manner one would be toward a father.[61] Indeed, Smith shows how on Gadamer's reading of Plato's *Crito*, it is in deference and fidelity to the laws and customs of Athens, "the 'parent' polis with its . . . *nomoi*," that Socrates exemplifies this answerability of the individual to the community. Such deference is precisely not blind but is actively *chosen* by Socrates as an ethical decision, as what is right in light of his opportunity to evade punishment.[62] The authority of tradition is thus binding on us, as the Laws of Athens make clear in their hypothetical speech, in the sense that we are indebted to them for making possible the life that is lived in community with others.

The Self and the *Sensus Communis*

The obligations that are built upon this foundation, however, cannot be described as "principles," understood in the abstract sense of contemporary democratic theory. Rather, they are the product of a relationship of "right," which has its roots in historical experience: "Aristotle rightly says that the 'principle' to begin with in all deliberation about the good is the 'that' (*das 'Daß'*), the recognition of the force of the norm."[63] Gadamer thus points to our norms' bases in custom (*Sittlichkeit*) and the idea that our "state of being arising from training" is the "fundamental ground of ethics."[64] Understood in this way, the normative consciousness that makes judgments of right and wrong is not to be thought of as apprehending a separate realm of being—as if "principles" existed in some noetic reality all their own—but as the intimate connection between, or the interpenetration of, that consciousness with such concrete, historical experience within the community.[65] As a result of this connection, a collective normative consciousness may be seen to emerge, which is the sense or awareness of the concrete patterns of behavior that have developed over time, what Gadamer calls the *sensus communis*.[66] As the raising to consciousness of this concrete sense of right, the *sensus communis* is ultimately given expression and preserved in a language (*logos*). This is the meeting place where ethical conduct, the *ergon*, that is constitutive of ethical substance (*ethos*) is capable of being transformed into the articulation of right (*logos*). Smith explains, "Ethical understanding is . . . a function not just of mind but also of who we are. There is no *logos* without *ergon*, which is to say, no reason and reasoning without deed."[67] Such a shared sense pertains to what is suitable or appropriate within a concrete pattern of obligations,[68] a collective awareness or judgment of what is fitting and proper within *these* particular relationships.[69]

Consequently, insofar as this interpenetration exists between word (*logos*) and deed (*ergon*), any such articulation or conceptualization will be meaningful that corresponds to a shared set of experiences among interlocutors. Conversely, insofar as language diverges or separates from this experience, one is left increasingly with empty abstractions, which lack such a grounding in concrete reality.[70] It is for this reason that socialization plays the important role Beiner alludes to above with respect to all communication and understanding. For, the *ergon* (deed) tethers deliberation, as it were, to specific experiences within a community, thus orienting or inclining interlocutors toward particular kinds of justifications that are perceived as sound or right—resonating, in other words, with who we already are. One of Gadamer's most prominent illustrations of this relationship between *logos* and *ergon* is in his essay on Plato's *Lysis*, in which Socrates's dialogue with two young men on the subject of friendship (*philia*) ultimately ends in an impasse (*aporia*). The reason for this, Gadamer explains, is that these boys do not, at an experiential level, which is to say, at the level of *ergon*, truly know what friendship is. Instead, what they know at this level is "that naive comradeship of boasting and outdoing one another," which will not suffice for the more mature Socrates who "has no ear" for that sort of experience.[71] It is for this reason, Gadamer argues, that Plato ends the dialogue with the youth confused and with Socrates saying that he wants to look for older (and thus more experienced or mature) interlocutors.[72] Such shared experience thus grounds *logos* and, when it may be lacking in this way, has the potential to disrupt communication, even among members of the same community.

Smith thus echoes Beiner when he says that character (*ēthos*), ethical custom (*ethos*), and reason (*logos*) are "inseparable" when it comes to the resonance of some arguments over others.[73] But he further elaborates on this connection when he adds that "ethical thinking, deliberation (*bouleuesthai*) occurs against the background of what is not thought about at all. Indeed, it is grounded in preconscious dispositions, or *hexeis*, as Aristotle calls them. We have seen that the individual cannot be said to invent autonomously the content of the custom that guides deliberation and choice and sustains the justification given for it."[74] Consequently, though it is true that the *sensus communis* is the raising to consciousness of a community's concrete sense of right, this does not imply that the experience underpinning this awareness can be made fully explicit, or ever completely articulated. Rather, Smith says that "what informs conscious deliberation and choice, which remains inexplicit and unconscious, is a blend of what one thinks and does without thinking."[75] While word (*logos*) and deed (*ergon*) are thus linked in this fundamental way and are the basis of all successful communication within a community, our inability to stand outside of *ethos* ultimately precludes any comprehensive conceptualization.

But still more must be said about this intimate connection between *logos* and *ergon* as a precondition for mutual understanding and agreement. The pursuit of ethical truth among interlocutors, Gadamer believes, points not only to the existence of a shared sense of right, but also the sense in which the very use of *logos* is, itself, a cultural achievement, the product of individuals having been civilized into a unique kind of relationship or attitude toward one other, such that beyond the restraints each puts on desire, they are impelled by the bond of *philia* to use language in order to reason and seek agreement on the good. Where this relationship exists, therefore, we see a change in the nature of communication, which becomes a collaborative endeavor, a dialectical engagement in which interlocutors seek after what is good or right, rather than an antagonistic struggle grounded in their physical nature that, conversely, draws them apart, isolating them from one another. Smith observes the usefulness to Gadamer's thinking of Aristotle, who sees that "right understanding of ethical truth" is in fact a matter of developing a "mental habit" or "right pattern or predisposition (*hexis*) in one's thinking."[76] For Gadamer, this means that custom must "raise [individuals] out of their initial physicality"[77] so that they become "trained to maintain (*sōzein*) reasonableness (*phronesis*) when buffeted by passions and desires."[78] What is essential about *ethos* to ethical thinking and reasoning, then, among participants in such a dialogue is not only the concrete sense of right that furnishes the *sensus communis* that is articulated, but also the ethical predisposition that habituates and motivates individuals into the practice of seeking agreement through the use of reason. The *logos*, it may be said, is thus shaped by the *ergon* not only in the substance or content of what is articulated, but actually as an attitude and behavior that emerges when one enters into specific patterns of linguistic practice and relationship with others.

On more than one occasion, Gadamer thus alludes to this predisposition (*hexis*) toward others that is essential to such a collaborative search for the good. One sees it on display, in particular, in those instances in which he discusses the confrontations between Socrates and the Sophists in the Platonic dialogues, especially Callicles and Thrasymachus, who lack precisely this "mental habit" needed to maintain ethical reasonableness (*phronesis*) in the face of inundation by passions and desires.[79] Indeed, Gadamer makes it clear that the interlocutors in Plato's dialogues are more than just "speakers," but in fact are embodied characters whose predispositions (*hexeis*) toward others tend to open up or close off the cooperative search of the dialectic.[80] Gadamer thus refers to the Sophists as "questionable *personalities* for whom justice is nothing more than a word to be used in duping the dim-witted."[81] And he uses them to illustrate the impossibility of reasoning together if one's interlocutor is intransigent or altogether unwilling to listen, as would appear to be the case with their respective behavior in *Gorgias* and the *Republic*.[82]

What is particularly interesting, in light of what has been said regarding the disposition that supports this collaborative search, is the Sophists' backgrounds and their relationship to Socrates and the Athenians. For, it is worth noting—as Plato himself indicates—that the Sophists were not, in fact, members of the Athenian community, who entered the dialogues with a preexisting bond of *philia* toward the other discussants. Rather, it is clear that the Sophists were not only foreigners to Athens, but that they lived the lives of itinerants, seemingly lacking any such relationship of "ethical love" and the attendant desire to seek agreement with others about the good.[83] The Sophists, deracinated and cut off from all community, had essentially severed the bonds with any and all interlocutors needed for such a collaborative search. Consequently, Gadamer shows that, for Plato, *logos* is more than "reasoning," but should be seen as a linguistic practice or behavior, an *ergon*, that can only emerge when relationships defined by *philia* already orient members toward the search for the good.

Bouleuesthai (Deliberation)

What is distinctive about the Greek concept of *bouleuesthai* (deliberation) is that unlike other uses to which *logos* may be put (e.g., moral philosophy), its implied purpose is to arrive at a concrete decision regarding a particular ethical choice—individual or collective—that arises in the world in which one is always situated. This key concept at the center of Gadamer's practical philosophy once again assumes that "we are already shaped by normative conceptions [*Vorstellungen*] in the light of which we have been brought up and that lie at the basis of the order of our entire social life."[84] Therefore, there is no question here of the ideal of a "non-participating observer" inherited from the natural sciences.[85] Rather, one is engaged in the same process described earlier in this chapter—reflective awareness on the concrete sense of right, the *sensus communis*, along with the "mental habit" that sustains ethical reasonableness (*phronesis*)—only here, one is aiming at problems that pertain to individual or collective choices (*prohaireseis*) that issue in concrete action or conduct. And, Gadamer says, it is being bound together in a community that is key to this task, insofar as this particular context provides both a shared framework of ethical meanings and an orientation toward the other that facilitates the collaborative search for what is right.[86]

The virtue that Gadamer believes is central to such practical deliberation is known in Aristotelian ethics as *synesis*.[87] And what is captured by this word in the Greek is what Gadamer calls the "act of understanding" or "being habitually understanding toward others," suggesting a disposition much like the ethical reasonableness of *phronesis*—and the words are semantically related—but that pertains to insightful judgment regarding the situations *of others*.[88] Therefore, this "being understanding"[89] is a disposition that implies more than merely the pursuit of agreement regarding what is good or right— itself a cultural achievement—but entails "a kind of communality in virtue of which the reciprocal taking of counsel, the giving and taking of advice is meaningful."[90] In other words, by "counsel" and "advice" here, Gadamer is pointing to the involvement, sharing in, or concern for the particular life of a specific person, precisely not "from a distance," but up close, among those with the intimacy and familiarity entailed in relationships of *philia*. And the semantic proximity of *synesis* to *phronesis* implies its similar focus on more than the material interest or advantage of that person but their good character or moral excellence (*arête*). But in the case of *synesis*, Smith says, one seeks such excellence with regard to the concrete choice that such a person has to make, as opposed to oneself. And yet, in spite of this shift in focus from oneself to another, one is at the same time not altogether extricated from the concrete situation, as in the ideal of an impartial or distantiated observer, but remains involved in a continuous relationship with the other, seeking "not just understanding *of* a situation, but also understanding *for* the view of someone else as he judges that situation."[91]

It is for this reason, Smith suggests, that for Gadamer the understanding involved in *synesis* is, in a sense, more foundational even than *phronesis* with respect to the disclosure of reality, or truth, that comes to light in all understanding. This is not, of course, to detract from the prominent role that *phronesis* plays in Gadamer's illustration of interpretation in his philosophical hermeneutics, which is alluded to here and in the preceding chapter. However, there is in the concept of *phronesis* the somewhat illusory implication that one could consider or reflect upon a concrete choice by oneself, when, in fact, even in the case of deliberating over one's own ethical situation, such decision-making always takes place against the background of a community of language and thought, in which one is always conversant and thus in an ongoing "conversation." For Gadamer, this means that even in solitary deliberation over ethical choices, a "taking counsel with ourselves" occurs, which is ultimately a consultation with the *sensus communis* that informs our thinking and constitutes who we already are.[92] Echoing this, while emphasizing the giving instead of the taking of counsel, Smith says that "the process is one of 'advising myself' concerning what is right."[93]

The actual giving and taking of counsel that takes place between us in the *res publica* then is only more overt or explicit than what is occurring by oneself, in that one considers a situation that is not one's own, or at least not exclusively one's own, and an understanding is reached in actual dialogue with others. What is shared, in such discussion, is both a subject matter upon which individuals seek an agreed upon ethical resolution and a concern that the latter is what is right for those who receive counsel.[94] Here one thinks through a predicament with another that, though less one's own, is taken up as a shared problem, in which one becomes invested.[95] Gadamer explains:

> Both the person asking for advice and the person giving it assume that they are bound together in friendship. Only friends can advise each other or, to put it another way, only a piece of advice that is meant in a friendly way has meaning for the person advised. Once again we discover that the person who is understanding does not know and judge as one who stands apart and unaffected but rather he thinks along with the other from the perspective of a specific bond of belonging, as if he too were affected.[96]

It is this "understanding for someone else" (*synesis*) that is thus primary in all genuine deliberation, and Gadamer believes at its origin to have been developed by living in community with others. It is, in other words, only in the community that is characterized by *philia* that one's being bound to others in this manner forces the individual outside of the horizon of his natural, physical self, with its myopic preoccupation with desire-satisfaction. And it is here, therefore, that we come to see the origins of any true or genuine deliberation (*bouleuesthai*).

As Smith makes clear, Gadamer's appropriation of Aristotle in *Truth and Method* on this subject is intended to emphasize precisely the sense in which ethical deliberation requires attachment to *particular* people as a precondition of its occurrence. And it is for this reason, Smith explains, that Gadamer calls our attention not only to *synesis* here but also *gnome* (considerateness), *sugnome* (forbearance), and *epieikeia* (fairness), all of which pertain to "put[ting] oneself in the fully concrete position in which the other person has to act."[97] In other words, true consideration and concern for what is right will not—contrary to the thinking of so much contemporary, analytic philosophy, particularly the ideal of "the moral point of view"—be impartial but will involve relating to the situation of another whose moral excellence (*arête*) is at stake and in which one has become invested.[98] It is only in friendship (*philia*), Gadamer argues, that such giving and taking of counsel (*sumbouleuesthai*) is conceivable.[99] It is only when one is bound to another in this way that one is engaged in the sort of committed and involved, indeed partial, judgment—the judgment by and for the *philos* (dear, beloved friend)—that can be seen to facilitate genuine deliberation about a choice of action.

Understood in this way, the structure of public deliberation, that is, deliberation on matters collective or political, that Gadamer and Smith's practical philosophy points toward begins to come more clearly into focus. One does not, as an individual with thoughts formed privately and in isolation from others, come together in public with other individuals, whose thoughts have also been formed in private, in order to exchange ideas, and ultimately to arrive at an understanding or perspective on some particular question. Rather, "what is commonly held to be appropriate and inappropriate" is brought to bear, in a collaborative effort, on a particular situation, through the merging or fusion of horizons among the members of an existing community.[100] This is because an individual's understanding of a political situation, even prior to such collaboration, is never simply one's "own" thought or idea, as if that could be articulated or expressed to others in some manner of communication freed from this communal and historical context.[101] Furthermore, the outcome of any communication, Gadamer believes, is more accurately viewed as something that must be "reached" through a dialogue, whose contours are always already shaped by *logos* and the *sensus communis* upon which it draws, and the right thing to do is then held in common, "on the basis of the understanding I have for the other and he or she has for me."[102] Through *synesis* and *gnome*, in particular, Gadamer says, the distinct members of a given community come to understand perspectives outside themselves, seeing the world "in one another's shoes," as we often say, and, consequently, by these individuals transcending their own "self-referentiality," they deliberate over the concrete ethical choices confronted together with the other members of the community.[103]

For concrete beings, however, "putting oneself in another's shoes" is never a process of seeing the world exactly as they see it. Horizons of understanding can only be merged or fused, which is to say, there can be no swapping of vantage points or jumping out of one's skin in order to adopt the perspective of another whose history and experiences, even when part of a shared tradition, are incapable of being acquired as one's own. To be habitually understanding, therefore, in the sense of *synesis*, entails the use of analogical thinking, in the sense of both recognizing likenesses in another's experience to our own and assimilating each into the broader context of the tradition of historical experience. The individual and collective history in which all understanding is embedded thus provides the framework for the process of assimilating new experience into old, and thus making sense of whatever happens. Understood in this way, there are, in fact, no insights in the giving and taking of counsel that are, strictly speaking, "mine" or "yours," but only "ours," since knowledge is furnished through this process of assimilating likenesses in experience, which are never exclusively one's own. Just as one deliberates with other individuals in this way, so one can essentially be seen to deliberate with tradition itself, gaining insight by relating experience to this store of precedents and examples, so much that Smith compares such analogical thinking in Gadamer again to the thinking of Burke, who speaks of a type of reason that is guided by the "spirit of philosophic analogy."[104] Both thinkers, Smith indicates, are influenced by medieval Aristotelian philosophy and the concept of *analogia entis* (analogy of being), the idea that qualities such as "good" come to be known through the concrete experience of such similarities, so that these qualities are seen, not as residing in abstract forms or ideas, but only their particular instantiations.[105]

As we engage in such deliberations, therefore, Smith and Gadamer believe we are essentially furnishing one another with, and reasoning to and from, particular cases[106]—whether in the case of one's consultation with the tradition or an actual giving and taking of advice among existing members of the community. Smith explains that "in ethical reasoning . . . one reasons from within one's situation in relationship to what has preceded it, or, as Burke says here, in relationship to precedent and example. For there is no abstract right or wrong independent of our historical experience . . . but only an analogousness of what is right and wrong in the present circumstances to what was right and wrong in the historical circumstances that have led up to the present."[107] To reason from within a tradition, according to Gadamer, is to interpret and be interpreted in the manner of *dikaste phronesis* (jurisprudence). One is always comparing cases to one's own, which are compared, in turn, by others, in a process that resembles common law decision-making. Analogical reasoning, it might be said, is thus a giving and taking of counsel (*sumbouleuesthai*), in which the concrete experience of another—whether person or tradition—lends itself either implicitly or explicitly to the concrete choice of a member of the community. Our deliberations are, in this way, a part of the tradition as much as they draw on the tradition, such that it is not "we" as individual agents who deliberate but the tradition that deliberates through us, as the conversation comprised of such analogical reasoning extends itself over time.[108]

Chapters 4 and 5 have argued that Gadamer's theory of philosophical hermeneutics, connected as it is to his moral philosophy, demonstrates the impossibility of genuine deliberation (collectively, but individually as well) about the good without relying on the shared meanings and acculturated dispositions of a historical community or tradition. To assume the persuasiveness of moral reasoning outside of shared historical experiences is to neglect the importance of a *sensus communis*—the substantive sense of right—informed by the concrete practices of a community of speech and action. Moreover, the willingness to enter into deliberative engagements with others relies upon bonds that similarly develop up-close over time and cannot be assumed among individuals who lack any such relationship to their interlocutors. The following chapter takes this analysis further, aiming to place these problematic assumptions of contemporary democratic theory within the context of Enlightenment thinking vis-à-vis questions of philosophical anthropology. Additionally, it argues that the appeal to a particular historical narrative regarding "modernity" is responsible, at least in part, for obscuring and undermining the normative priority of tradition for genuine or authentic deliberation.

Notes

1. Although the fullest development of Gadamer's moral philosophy does not emerge until the publication of *The Idea of the Good* in 1986, it is worth noting that such concerns regarding the ethical life were present from his earliest years as a scholar. Donatella Di Cesare observes that well before even his work on hermeneutics, Gadamer's interest in ethics had been cultivated by his contact with the Marburg School, the value ethics of Max Scheler and Nicolai Hartmann, and the famous seminar of Heidegger on book 6 of Aristotle's *Nicomachean Ethics*. See Donatella Di Cesare, *Gadamer: A Philosophical Portrait*, trans. Niall Keane (Bloomington: Indiana University Press, 2013), 109. Gadamer's habilitation thesis, which was completed under the supervision of Heidegger in 1929 and later published as *Plato's Dialectical Ethics: Phenomenological Interpretations Relating to the Philebus*, trans. Robert M. Wallace (New Haven, CT: Yale University Press, 2009 [1991]), similarly reflects his early ethical concerns. While serving as an investigation of Plato's *Philebus*, the thesis was originally intended to foreground a study of Aristotelian ethics, a subject to which Gadamer returns repeatedly throughout his career. Richard Palmer brings this insight of Jean Grondin's to bear in his prefatory remarks to Gadamer's essay, "On the Possibility of a Philosophical Ethics," in *The Gadamer Reader: A Bouquet of the Later Writings*, ed. Richard E. Palmer (Evanston, IL: Northwestern University Press, 2007), 274. For Grondin's authoritative intellectual biography which traces the path of Gadamer's philosophical interests, see Jean Grondin, *Hans-Georg Gadamer: A Biography* (New Haven: Yale University Press, 2003).

2. Gadamer's most explicit engagements with Kant's moral philosophy may be found primarily in two essays. The first of these, "On the Possibility of a Philosophical Ethics," was written in 1963 and has attracted the most attention. He demonstrates a sustained concern with the critical themes of this essay by returning to its principal subject matter in another piece written in 1989 entitled "Aristotle and Imperative Ethics." Gadamer's remarks on problems in Kantian and neo-Kantian moral philosophy are also scattered elsewhere throughout his life's work. Additionally, it is worth noting that his lengthy treatment of Kant in *Truth and Method*, though primarily dealing with epistemological issues related to the interpretation of art, examines the phenomenon of "aesthetic differentiation," which similarly deals with the Kantian and neo-Kantian neglect of the *ethos* in which all understanding is embedded. See Hans-Georg Gadamer, *Truth and Method*, trans. Joel Weinsheimer and Donald G. Marshall, 2nd rev. ed. (New York: Continuum, 2004), esp. 27–87.

3. See, once again, Palmer's introductory remarks to Gadamer, "On the Possibility of a Philosophical Ethics," 275.

4. Gadamer, "On the Possibility of a Philosophical Ethics," 280.

5. Ibid. See also Gadamer, "Aristotle and Imperative Ethics," in *Hermeneutics, Religion, and Ethics*, trans. Joel Weinsheimer (New Haven: Yale University Press, 1999), 158.

6. Gadamer, "On the Possibility of a Philosophical Ethics," 282.

7. See Gadamer's remarks about the grounding of the categorical imperative in "Aristotle and Imperative Ethics," 150, along with his later remark that "Kant's concern was to define the essence of moral reason on which all obligation was founded. We have already seen that he did not undertake to found the whole of moral self-determination upon the omnipotence and authority of subjectivity—as preeminently Fichte understood him to do, as well as Schiller, probably even Reinhold, and at any rate the whole of the post-Kantian tradition" (157). In *Truth and Method*, Gadamer similarly attributes the problem of aesthetic consciousness to those in the Romantic tradition who later appropriate Kant's epistemology, such as Schiller (again) and Schleiermacher.

8. Gadamer, "On the Possibility of a Philosophical Ethics," 282. Gadamer is clear about the "questionableness of law-based ethics" for its neglect of situational contingency and the fact that Aristotle's account of ethical decision-making furnishes that which Kant neglects: "the concreteness with which conscience, sensitivity to equity, and loving reconciliation are answerable to the situation" (279).

9. Ibid., 288.

10. Gadamer, "Aristotle and Imperative Ethics," 142.

11. Gadamer, "On the Possibility of a Philosophical Ethics," 284. In spite of Gadamer's substantial indebtedness to Plato's philosophy discussed in the previous chapter, Smith makes a compelling case for Gadamer's ambivalence toward certain elements in Plato's thinking, which he sees as problematically abstract. See Smith, "Plato as Impulse and Obstacle in Gadamer's Development of a Hermeneutical Theory," in *Gadamer and Hermeneutics: Science, Culture, Literature*, ed. Silverman (New York: Routledge, 1991), 23–41. In light of this, one might conceivably dispute the claim at the outset of this chapter that Gadamer is more ambivalent toward Kant than any other thinker and that it is Plato who deserves this attribution. However, the centrality of Plato to Gadamer's philosophical hermeneutics in *Truth and Method*, his practical philosophy in *The Idea of the Good*, and works devoted exclusively to the study of Platonic dialogues, such as *Plato's Dialectical Ethics* and *Dialogue and Dialectic*, renders any such ambivalence insubstantial. See also Gadamer's unequivocal remark in his interview with Ernest Fortin that, "I am a Platonist." Ernest Fortin, "Gadamer on Strauss: An Interview," *Interpretation* 12 no. 1 (1984): 10. It may, notwithstanding this self-characterization, be more accurate to describe Gadamer as a Platonic-Aristotelian. Regardless, the contribution of Plato to his thinking was profound.

12. Gadamer, "On the Possibility of a Philosophical Ethics," 284.

13. Gadamer, "Aristotle and Imperative Ethics," 144.

14. Ibid.

15. Ibid.

16. Ibid.

17. Ibid., 146. Emphasis added.

18. Ibid.

19. Ibid.

20. Ibid., 148.

21. Ronald Beiner, "Do We Need a Philosophical Ethics?" *Philosophical Forum* 20, no. 3 (1989): 230–43.

22. Ibid., 235.

23. Ibid., 235. Regarding what is "already known," see the discussion of *anamnesis* in chapter 4.

24. Ibid., 237.

25. For a thoughtful examination of Gadamer's practical philosophy, which frames the latter through these critiques of Strauss and Habermas, see Matthew Foster, *Gadamer and Practical Philosophy: the Hermeneutics of Moral Confidence* (Atlanta: Scholars Press, 1991). Beiner provides an incisive defense of Gadamer against such criticisms of Habermas in "Do We Need a Philosophical Ethics?"

26. Beiner, "Do We Need a Philosophical Ethics?," 236.

27. Ibid., 237.

28. Ibid.

29. Beiner thus says that Gadamer essentially finds Habermas guilty of "rationalistic utopianism" and "sociological naivete." Ibid., 239. In his correspondence with Strauss, Gadamer makes the point as follows: "What I believe to have understood through Heidegger (and what I can testify to from my protestant background) is, above all, that philosophy must learn to do without the idea of an infinite intellect." Leo Strauss and Hans-Georg Gadamer, "Correspondence concerning *Wahrheit und Methode*," *Independent Journal of Philosophy* 2 (1978): 10.

30. Aristotle, *Nicomachean Ethics*, trans. David Ross (New York: Oxford University Press, 2009), 4.

31. Ibid.

32. Strauss makes the same claim with regard to historical truth, that we must achieve complete liberation from our tradition so that we may "understand the thinkers of the past exactly as they understood themselves." Leo Strauss, *What Is Political Philosophy?* (Chicago: University of Chicago Press, 1959), 67. Beiner is critical of Strauss's utopianism here when he refers to this as Strauss's "stunningly ambitious thesis" that "one could in effect set aside millennia of intellectual and moral history and see the ethical world exactly as Plato and Aristotle saw it." Ronald Beiner, "Gadamer's Philosophy of Dialogue and Its Relation to the Postmodernism of Nietzsche, Heidegger, Derrida, and Strauss," in *Gadamer's Repercussions: Reconsidering Philosophical Hermeneutics*, ed. Bruce Kajewski (Berkeley: University of California Press, 2004), 149.

33. Di Cesare, *Gadamer*, 112.

34. Ibid. As noted in the previous chapter, the pertinent text here is "The Hermeneutic Relevance of Aristotle," in Gadamer, *Truth and Method*, 310–21. Di Cesare says that this section, which "signals the rebirth of practical philosophy in the

twentieth century, outlines in just a few pages at least four key ideas: the autonomy and particularity of practical actions; the value of phrónesis, which Gadamer translates as 'reasonableness' and which guides human behavior; the necessity of taking ethós into consideration, in particular the context in which ethico-political relations orient action; and finally his view of a necessarily dialectical path for ethics, in which the theoretical search for the good, which is articulated in the dialogue with the other, is already in itself a realization of the practical good." Di Cesare, *Gadamer*, 112.

35. Gadamer, *Truth and Method*, 312; Di Cesare, *Gadamer*, 112.

36. Gadamer, *Truth and Method*, 312; Di Cesare, *Gadamer*, 112.

37. Gadamer, *Truth and Method*, 313–14; Di Cesare, *Gadamer*, 113.

38. Di Cesare, *Gadamer*, 113; Gadamer, *Truth and Method*, 315.

39. Gadamer, in his *Gesammelte Werke*, quoted in Di Cesare, *Gadamer*, 113.

40. Gadamer, *Truth and Method*, 314, 318; Di Cesare, *Gadamer*, 113.

41. Di Cesare, *Gadamer*, 114.

42. Ibid., 113–14; Gadamer, *Truth and Method*, 314.

43. Beiner, "Do We Need a Philosophical Ethics?," 234.

44. Gadamer, "The Ethics of Value and Practical Philosophy," in *Hermeneutics, Religion, and Ethics*, trans. Joel Weinsheimer (New Haven, CT: Yale University Press, 1999), 109.

45. Di Cesare, *Gadamer*, 111.

46. Ibid., 108. See also Smith's helpful discussion in which he relates this to Hegel's analysis of the abstraction in *Raisonnieren* and the ways in which MacIntyre does and does not overcome these difficulties in *After Virtue* and *Whose Justice? Which Rationality?* See also the similar sympathetic critique of neo-Aristotelian philosophy (including that of MacIntyre) in Holston, "Deliberation in Context: Reexamining the Confrontation between the Discourse Ethics and Neo-Aristotelianism," *Telos* 181 (2017): 151–75.

47. Beiner, "Do We Need a Philosophical Ethics?," 234.

48. P. Christopher Smith, "The Ethical Dimensions of Gadamer's Hermeneutical Theory," *Research in Phenomenology* 18 (1988): 77.

49. Ibid. The German *Fingerspitzengefühl*, Smith argues, invokes a "pre-conscious delicacy of touch and discretion in knowing properly how to size things up" (78).

50. Ibid.

51. Aristotle, *Politics*, trans. Carnes Lord (University of Chicago Press), 11–13 (1253a).

52. Smith, "The Ethical Dimensions of Gadamer's Hermeneutical Theory," 82, quoting Gadamer.

53. Ibid., 83–86.

54. Ibid., 86.

55. P. Christopher Smith, *Hermeneutics and Human Finitude: Toward a Theory of Ethical Understanding* (New York: Fordham University Press, 1991), 27. Elsewhere, Smith shows that in Kierkegaard, marriage is seen in a similar light,

insofar as it represents the culmination of the ethical stage of life's way after having passed through the aesthetic stage. While the latter, epitomized in Kierkegaard's aesthete, is characterized by the pure immediacy of impulse and is self-consumed and self-indulgent, the ethical stage of life transcends these self-destructive tendencies, and instead achieves "integrity" and "continuity" both within ourselves and with others. One sees here, once again, Kierkegaard's influence on Gadamer, insofar as this critique of subjectivity appears to have informed Gadamer's own critique of aesthetic consciousness. The fleeting and impressionistic experience (*Erlebnis*) of art as a "subjective event," is thus similarly seen by Gadamer as a distortion precluding true understanding, in contrast to the truth in the experience (*Erfahrung*) of a work of art from the past in continuity and conversation with the horizon of the present. See Smith, "The Ethical Dimensions of Gadamer's Hermeneutical Theory," 76, 80–83.

56. Smith, *Hermeneutics and Human Finitude*, 29.

57. Ibid.

58. More will follow on this point in the subsequent chapter, which deals, in part, with social contract theory.

59. Ibid., 79.

60. Ibid. Emphasis in the original.

61. Gadamer, "Aristotle and Imperative Ethics," 153.

62. Smith, *Hermeneutics and Human Finitude*, 219. Smith notes that, on Gadamer's reading of the *Crito*, Socrates is ultimately making a choice between "his *Zugehörigkeit*, his belonging to the historical traditional community, and the free thinking of 'wise' (*sophoi*) individuals who in severing themselves from the tradition, forgetting it, reason out on their own what is advantageous" (219). The sophists, as it were, represent radical freedom from tradition and community.

63. Gadamer, "The Ethics of Value and Practical Philosophy," 108.

64. Ibid., 108–9.

65. Ibid., 108.

66. Gadamer, *Truth and Method*, 17–27. See Smith's discussion of this concept in *Hermeneutics and Human Finitude*, 201, 205, 208. See also Beiner, "Do We Need a Philosophical Ethics?," 234.

67. Smith, *Hermeneutics and Human Finitude*, 231.

68. Ibid., 201.

69. Ibid., 205.

70. Gadamer's grounding of *logos* in custom (*Sittlichkeit*) echoes the argument made by Ludwig Wittgenstein that the context of a particular language game is essential to the meaning of words and thus the utterances of any speaker. As a result, Gadamer may be said to concur with Wittgenstein that when language is severed from its context in the manner indicated here, the resulting abstraction may be seen as language "on holiday," such that mutual understanding becomes problematic. See Wittgenstein, *Philosophical Investigations*, trans. G. E. M. Anscombe (1953; Upper

Saddle River, NJ: Blackwell, 1958), sec. 38. Smith notes this affinity as well in a translator's notation to Hans-Georg Gadamer, "*Logos* and *Ergon* in Plato's Lysis," in *Dialogue and Dialectic: Eight Hermeneutical Studies on Plato*, ed. P. Christopher Smith (New Haven, CT: Yale University Press, 1980), 2n2. Elsewhere, he further observes that Gadamer is nonetheless more sanguine than Wittgenstein about the prospects of philosophical discourse to avoid such abstraction and remain bound to *ethos*. See Gadamer, "Dialectic and Sophism in Plato's Seventh Letter," in *Dialogue and Dialectic: Eight Hermeneutical Studies on Plato*, trans. P. Christopher Smith (New Haven, CT: Yale University Press, 1980), 114n33.

71. Gadamer, "*Logos* and *Ergon* in Plato's Lysis," 6–7.

72. Ibid., 6, 8. Smith notes that it is for this same reason that Aristotle demands a mature, experienced readership for his ethics (8n3).

73. Smith, *Hermeneutics and Human Finitude*, 263.

74. Ibid., 229.

75. Ibid.

76. Smith, "The Ethical Dimensions of Gadamer's Hermeneutical Theory," 89.

77. Ibid.

78. Ibid., 90.

79. See, for example, in the *Republic*, where Thrasymachus is so infuriated by the *elenchus* of Socrates that he becomes incapable of refraining from interrupting the discussion and ultimately bursts into it "like a wild beast," that is, in an undisciplined and uncivilized manner. Plato, *The Republic*, trans. Desmond Lee (New York: Penguin Classics, 2007), 16 (336b5–6). Furthermore, one certainly does not get the sense, at the conclusion of Socrates's questioning of Thrasymachus, that he has been open to persuasion and thus convinced by Socrates's reasoning, and it is telling that it is left to the more even-tempered Glaucon to explore with Socrates the nature of justice as it is depicted in Kallipolis.

80. Gadamer's discussion of "openness" as a predisposition essential to understanding pertains not only to the understanding of texts but, he indicates, to interlocutors as well. According to Gadamer, openness entails "listening" to what another—whether person or text—has to say. The Socratic dialectic, for Gadamer, is considered to be paradigmatic with regard to the logical structure of such openness. See Gadamer, *Truth and Method*, 355–56. It therefore comes as no surprise that the foils in these dialogues are prime examples for Gadamer of personalities that are closed off to this cooperative search.

81. Gadamer, "Dialectic and Sophism in Plato's Seventh Letter," 116. Emphasis added. Echoing this view, Gadamer further argues, is Aristotle's discussion in the *Metaphysics* of the distinction between dialectic and sophism, which he says is ultimately rooted in a "choice or commitment in life . . . i.e., only in that the dialectician takes seriously those things which the sophist uses solely as the material for his game of winning arguments and proving himself right." Gadamer, "*Logos* and *Ergon* in Plato's Lysis," 6.

82. Ibid. See additionally Smith's extended discussion of the *Gorgias* in *Hermeneutics and Human Finitude*, 158–71.

83. Plato notes their habit of "wandering from city to city and having no settled home of their own." Plato, *Timaeus* (19e), quoted in W. K. C. Guthrie, *The Sophists*, vol. 3 (New York: Cambridge University Press, 1971), 40. It is interesting, in this regard, the role that Polus plays in the *Gorgias*. Although an outsider to Athens and lacking any community of his own, he speaks Attic Greek, which Smith says binds him to some degree to Socrates, who is therefore able to draw out of him at least a limited sense of communal obligation. See Smith, *Hermeneutics and Human Finitude*, 159, 165.

84. "Hermeneutics as Theoretical and Practical Task," in Hans-Georg Gadamer, *The Gadamer Reader: A Bouquet of the Later Writings*, ed. Richard E. Palmer (Evanston, IL: Northwestern University Press, 2007), 263.

85. Ibid.

86. Ibid.

87. Ibid., 261.

88. Ibid. See also Gadamer, "Aristotle and Imperative Ethics," 156.

89. Ibid.

90. Ibid.

91. Smith, *Hermeneutics and Human Finitude*, 86.

92. P. Christopher Smith, "The I-Thou Encounter (*Begegnung*) in Gadamer's Reception of Heidegger," in *The Philosophy of Hans-Georg Gadamer*, ed. Lewis Hahn (Chicago: Open Court, 1997), 519. Smith argues that even when we say that *phronesis* guides a personal deliberation (*bouleuesthai*), this originates in "*our* sum*bouleuesthai, our* taking counsel *with* others." P. Christopher Smith, "*Phronesis*, the Individual, and the Community: Divergent Appropriations of Aristotle's Ethical Discernment in Heidegger's and Gadamer's Hermeneutics," in *Gadamer verstehen = Understanding Gadamer*, ed. Mirko Wischke and Michael Hofer (Darmstadt: Wissenschaftliche Buchgesellschaft, 2003), 179. Emphasis in the original. Elsewhere, Smith points to the fact that, for Plato as well, ethical deliberation by an individual takes a dialectical form, and is the "discussion of the soul with itself." Smith, "The Ethical Dimensions of Gadamer's Hermeneutical Theory," 90n7.

93. Smith, *Hermeneutics and Human Finitude*, 87.

94. P. Christopher Smith, "The I-Thou Encounter (*Begegnung*) in Gadamer's Reception of Heidegger," 518–19.

95. Ibid., 519.

96. Gadamer, *Truth and Method*, 320.

97. Gadamer, quoted in Smith, "*Phronesis*, the Individual, and the Community," 180.

98. Ibid.

99. Walhof sees Gadamer's conception of friendship not itself as a basis for political life but only as a foundation from which "solidarity" can emerge. In other words, through friendship, he says we become attuned to the ways our lives are

intertwined with neighbors, coworkers, and fellow citizens beyond these intimate relations. Friendship, on this account, has instrumental value, since it facilitates an awareness of "mutual interdependence beyond our circle of friends." The "reciprocal co-perception" of solidarity, which Walhof sees existing at a level between friendship and citizenship, thus brings to awareness the ways our lives are intertwined with "strangers who are also co-inhabitants of a shared world." Darren Walhof, *The Democratic Theory of Hans-Georg Gadamer* (Cham, Switzerland: Palgrave Macmillan, 2017), 114. Such recognition, however useful it may be for identifying affinities with others beyond our sphere of friends, would be incapable of sustaining the genuine or authentic deliberation (*sumbouleuesthai*) that Gadamer believes is involved in the giving and taking of counsel. In other words, if such solidarity among strangers is all that can be hoped for in contemporary political life, or all that is ever meant by a "shared world" that underpins our deliberation, then genuine deliberation must be inconceivable as part of our modern moral and political landscape. However, I do not take this to be the case, nor do I believe that it is for Gadamer, who sees the bonds of friendship as a prerequisite to authentic deliberation. See Smith, "The Uses of Aristotle in Gadamer's Recovery of Consultative Reasoning: *Sunesis, Sungnome, Epieikeia,* and *Sumbouleuesthai,*" *Chicago-Kent Law Review* 76 (2000): 731–50. Walhof omits entirely these Aristotelian dimensions of Gadamer's understanding of deliberation, and nowhere in his book is there any mention of Gadamer's appropriation of Aristotle's concept of *bouleuesthai* (deliberation). It is interesting in this regard that Walhof's principal illustration of political deliberation involves an ideological position among strangers—the Occupy Wall Street movement—rather than questions among those whose "shared world" would consist of concrete experiences (*Erfahrungen*) lived together. See Walhof, *The Democratic Theory of Hans-Georg Gadamer,* 119–25.

100. Smith, *Hermeneutics and Human Finitude,* 86–87.

101. This is the implication of the famous heuristic device belonging to Wittgenstein, the concept of a "private language," which he uses to show the performative and intersubjective origin of all linguistic meaning. See Wittgenstein, *Philosophical Investigations,* sec. 269. See also Smith's discussion of Gadamer's affinities with Wittgenstein in this regard, along with his account of Gadamer's more historically informed and embedded conception of the speaker who always finds himself "within" language. Smith, *Hermeneutics and Human Finitude,* 107–31.

102. Smith, *Hermeneutics and Human Finitude,* 87.

103. Ibid., 86, 87.

104. Smith quoting Burke in ibid., 216.

105. Ibid., 216.

106. Ibid., 55–56.

107. Ibid., 217.

108. Drawing on Heidegger, Gadamer says that "it is quite literally more correct to say that language speaks us than that we speak it." Gadamer, quoted in ibid., 121–22.

Chapter 6

Deliberation and Modernity

While the previous chapter aimed to make use of the theory of deliberation whose principal contours were first articulated by Gadamer and then further elaborated by his interpreters, such as Smith and Beiner, the present chapter aims to supplement concerns voiced by Smith regarding the philosophical anthropology necessary for a proper conception of sound deliberation. In contemporary analytic philosophy, Smith calls attention to a problem within argumentation theory that he describes as a "concealment and distortion" of the conditions of reasoning, as well as a devolution of the idea of reason into an adversarial encounter in which interlocutors each try not just to "state" but to "stake" their claim and defend it against other individuals.[1] Smith believes this to be the application to argumentation theory of the philosophical anthropology that C. B. McPherson terms "possessive individualism," whose roots lie in the social contract tradition of Thomas Hobbes and John Locke. For them and other thinkers in Anglo-American political philosophy, these fundamental assumptions support a view of communication that sees private individuals as attempting to "vanquish and dominate" their adversaries in what amounts to a verbal promotion of self-interest.[2] According to Smith, this competitive view of reasoning, which finds its most extreme form in the model of advocacy and litigation, in fact abstracts from and obscures the communal origins—in Heideggerian terms, the "original phenomena"—of all communication.[3]

In what follows, it will be argued that Smith's Gadamerian understanding of deliberation, along with his critique of such individualist accounts of reasoning, is fundamentally correct. However, his analysis is incomplete for the purposes of the present study, insofar as it does not touch upon the parallel danger of conceptually expanding the scope or scale of human association within which deliberation takes place. This, it will be contended, is the error of contemporary democratic theory whose demand for universal justification tacitly or effectively posits what has been called a community without limits. Such is the legacy of the Enlightenment's abstract thinking about the good, insofar as it neglects both the concrete sense of right, or *sensus communis*, to which interlocutors must appeal for their arguments to have real resonance, and the essential predispositions, that is, those "habits of thought," that facilitate a cooperative search for the good, as opposed to mere conflict and manipulation.

The chapter begins with a brief overview of Smith's critique of Hobbes and Locke, which demonstrates the problem of abstraction at the level of the individual. Building on the difficulties that Smith identifies in the theory of possessive individualism, the chapter then extends his analysis to a parallel critique of deliberative democracy's recent turn to Rousseau and the autonomy tradition, showing a strikingly similar problem that emerges regarding the neglect of the concrete origins of language, even when collective agreement or consensus is the focus of such thinking. The argument concludes that only the conditions that cultivate the bonds of *philia*—namely, concrete communities that exist over time—can furnish the essential support for a *sensus communis* and a predisposition toward a cooperative search for the common good. The chapter ends with a reflection upon the appeal to "modernity" as, essentially, a justification for perpetually neglecting the value of such concrete communities. Echoing a recurring theme within Gadamer's work regarding the ongoing nature of dialogue, I argue that such historical narratives or argumentative moves are attempts to remove from future discussion the possibility of choosing the promotion of concrete, historical communities over individual autonomy. However, such appeals to the impossibility of cultivating the institutions of the ethical life represent, somewhat ironically, an attenuation of the very freedom that deliberative democrats aim to promote.

Abstract Individualism

According to Smith, individualist accounts of reasoning under Hobbes and Locke have accentuated an abstractionist tendency that was present in a more latent form in the ancient world under Plato. That tendency is identified as a turn found in Plato's later writing, in dialogues such as the *Philebus* and the *Sophist*, where one sees a shift in emphasis or "turn[ing] away from communicative, acoustical orality to privately read, interiorized writing."[4] What had formerly been an understanding of dialectic or *dialegesthai* as a "talking things through" among interlocutors, who learn from others in the community through the speaking and hearing of questions and answers, was now conceived as the visual "sorting things out" through *gene* (classes) and *eide* (forms), which were understood to be private perceptions of the mind by itself. There is, in other words, an abstracting or turning away from the language community toward an understanding of communication that sees words, names, and signs as the soul's way of memorializing individual knowledge for its own purposes.[5] With this turn in the dialogues, according to Smith, one observes a shift in the conception of reason from the dialogical "talking things through" of the community to the "monological demonstration" or "'sorting things out' by genus and species" within the mind.[6] Monologue therefore replaces dialogue at the center of the idea of reason with this interiorizing of thought in Plato: "Speech is thought to begin with what individuals see for themselves, not with what they hear from others in their community."[7]

This abstraction from the original community of speakers, Smith further contends, is exacerbated or "amplified" in the English-speaking tradition in the thinking of Hobbes and Locke, whose individualistic understanding of human nature makes it receptive to a conception of reason as a private or solitary event.[8] In Hobbes, one sees this clearly in *De Cive* where he gives an account of internal thinking or ratiocination that occurs prior to, and thus independently of, the names that are spoken by the community in reference to such thoughts. This differs substantially from the Gadamerian conception, which comprehends language as disclosing the world to us, such that there is ultimately no meaningful distinction between word and idea. This is to say, I do not see a structure outside of my study window whose name is "shed"; rather, what I see is simply understood by me as "the shed." Language, in other words, does not give names to a reality we antecedently experience but is the experience of reality itself, insofar as it defines the manner in which consciousness furnishes the world with meaning for us.[9] However, in contradistinction to this, Hobbes sees our ideas about the world as based on experience that is known to us prior to the process of naming that imposes a mark on it, the purpose of which is to preserve experience in memory, in the first place, and to enable it to be expressed to others, in the second place.[10] In short, Hobbes sees words as tools for the signification of private or individual experience, not the communal meanings that themselves give shape and significance to—indeed, facilitate or make possible—our very consciousness of the world.[11]

In Locke, one similarly sees the twofold use of language as the preservation or recording of ideas, in the first place, and the communication of such ideas to others, in the second place.[12] Following Hobbes, Locke believes in the insignificance of the choice of sound that may record a thought,[13] and that the assignment of any particular, fixed meaning is only for the practical purpose of mutual understanding regarding individual experiences.[14] What is important, for Smith, is the abstraction from the community of speakers and listeners that is implied by the independence of our thoughts from the speech that signifies them. He summarizes his purpose here, which is to establish,

> how [Locke], like Plato and Hobbes before him, has reversed the actual sequence in knowing for oneself what something is and hearing and having a name for it. It is clear that in Locke's, just as in these other thinkers' misunderstanding of reasoning, private individuals are assumed to think for themselves without having first heard the words for things from others, and only then do they import audible words into their thinking. . . . But in fact we never think in wordless ideas, but only in the words we have first heard from others and then hear again in our thinking.[15]

The individualist conception of reason, therefore, can be seen to distort the original phenomenon of language by reversing the relationship between knowing and naming. It is the linguistic community, in other words, that exists prior to the individual that first provides language as a framework for understanding, and only then does the individual come to know the reality that emerges through the play of a particular language game. However, in seeing names as arbitrary designations that memorialize and communicate private experience, Hobbes and Locke neglect this role of the linguistic community in facilitating our understanding of the world, thereby obscuring the dependence of reason on a shared historical life or tradition.

In this Enlightenment perpetuation of the later Plato's earlier distortion of reason, it is interesting to note, it makes no difference that Hobbes and Locke, unlike Plato, understand such private knowledge in "empirical" terms. For, in light of Smith's charge that all three thinkers are guilty of abstraction, it is worth considering the potential objection that, although Plato's *eide* are thought to be knowable prior to experience, this is a rationalist move that

Hobbes and Locke explicitly reject. Thus, it might be argued that although there may be an affinity among these three thinkers, insofar as they all conceive of language as a tool for the communication of privately acquired knowledge, there is also an important difference between them. For the later Plato alone, such individual knowledge can be described as an abstract perception of the intellect or "prior mental vision,"[16] whereas Hobbes and Locke, it might be argued, understand "sense impressions" or "sense perceptions" to be the source of the private knowledge that is to be communicated. Therefore, one might see it as unfair, in light of this empirical foundation they give to such knowledge, to accuse Hobbes and Locke of the sort of abstraction of which the rationalist Plato alone is thought to be guilty.

However, even in light of this acknowledgment of their "empiricism," such epistemological distance from Plato does not save Hobbes and Locke from the charge of abstraction. Recalling Gadamer's distinction between *Erlebnis* and *Erfahrung*,[17] it is important to note that the concrete or experiential aspect of human life can be conceived in very different ways. And the "empirical" understanding of experience in Hobbes and Locke can, in its own way, be seen as one that in fact distorts or is not faithful to human reality as it is experienced in human consciousness. Therefore, it is important to recognize that it is not simply the intellect's flight from our materiality that qualifies as "abstraction," but its flight from life as it is actually lived and experienced by human beings in the world. While asserting the empirical foundations of knowledge, however, Hobbes and Locke develop a conception of "experience" that can be seen as severed or alienated from the reality within which human consciousness is embedded. For, in identifying "experience" with mere sense impressions, modern empiricists undertake an atomization or "chopping up" of lived reality into discrete or isolated moments that are theoretically postulated but never actually encountered by human beings. Such individual "experience" (*Erlebnis*) is, contrary to the claims of empiricism, an imagined subunit or fracturing of what are really coherent and meaningful wholes, which are actually encountered as the experience (*Erfahrung*) *of something*, that is, an event with some meaning or significance in the context of a particular historical life. The integration of new moments within this coherent whole is performed by the historically and linguistically pre-formed consciousness, hermeneutically fusing together would-be "sense impressions," so that a person has an experience (*Erfahrung*) with meaning, as opposed to discrete moments of sensory "data."

The individualist abstraction from the linguistic community is thus a conceptual distortion of which all three thinkers—the later Plato, Hobbes, and Locke—are guilty. For, in Plato's case, the intellect falsely dissects or individuates that which is ultimately inseparable: the solitary individual philosopher from the community that is antecedent to his existence and without which life would be incomprehensible. This atomization of *society* in all three thinkers, which imagines individuals possessing something like a "private language," independent of a linguistic community, can thus be seen to resemble the atomization of *experience* exclusively articulated by Hobbes and Locke, whose discrete or isolated moments are torn by the intellect from the seamless whole of consciousness and create a distorted view of experience as "sense impressions" or "sense perceptions." It is worth noting, therefore, that among the three philosophers discussed, only Hobbes and Locke, the social contract thinkers, engage in both of these abstractions—the fragmentation of society into discrete individuals *and* the chopping up of experience into discrete moments—which points to the accentuation of this tendency in the Enlightenment.

The philosophical anthropology underpinning the thinking of Hobbes and Locke has implications for the two thinkers' political philosophies that echo those belonging to their language theories. Similar to his abstraction from the communal conditions of reason, Locke's *Two Treatises of Government* sees the tacit political agreement among solitary individuals with natural rights as the essential precondition for entering into social relationships in which they can more effectively or efficiently exchange their property with that of others.[18] But this, Smith convincingly argues, makes the same mistake as Locke's theory of language, essentially reversing the relationship between the individual and the community of which he is a part. Smith explicitly connects these two problems in Locke's thinking: "No more are we originally thinkers without a common language than are we originally private persons without a community that raises us and endows us with the language and material goods that then allow us, secondarily, to think on our own and to appropriate private property for ourselves."[19] The mistake in Locke's language theory can thus be seen as mirroring that in his political theory, which is viewing the community as derivative of the activity of private individuals.[20]

The implication of these individualist abstractions, Smith demonstrates, is disastrous for a theory of political discourse. For, under the assumptions of possessive individualism, both words and institutions are seen as no more than instruments of self-interest, such that discourse forsakes entirely its "consultative dimension and becomes the adversarial contention of contestants."[21] Political deliberation, the public communication that employs language and reason, based on this model becomes "corrupted," insofar as possessive individualism transforms all political activity, so that it facilitates "transactional exchanges of private property in accord with legal contracts," which is seen as the fundamental purpose of social and political order.[22] As this view of political deliberation has taken hold in the English-speaking world, Smith notes, commercial metaphors have likewise emerged with respect to the idea of reason, such as the "marketplace of ideas."[23] Elsewhere, he demonstrates the adversarial view of reason even in the philosophy of MacIntyre, who, despite what is at times a richly historical and communal orientation, similarly sees the rationality of tradition as established through a competition among rival frameworks of moral enquiry—sometimes approximating a marketplace of ideas, though other times resembling conflict and war—in which some are vindicated over others through their superior responses to dialectical questioning.[24]

Possessive individualism, as a social and political ideal, thus undermines the "customary communal values of fairness and decency" by encouraging the withdrawal of individuals from genuine community. Furthermore, the ideal for organizing such behavior then becomes one in which institutions actually facilitate the sort of competitive, self-regarding behavior that weakens the bonds of *philia*. Under these circumstances, it is no wonder that public deliberation becomes impossible. For the institutions themselves actually promote the evisceration of the preconditions of genuine deliberation. They do so, in the first place, by undermining the *sensus communis* upon which interlocutors must draw in order for their arguments to resonate with one another and, in the second place, by failing to prioritize the cultivation of those habits of thought that are needed in order for interlocutors to engage in a cooperative search for the good with one another.

Abstract Community

From Smith's incisive analysis of modern social contract theory, as articulated in the thinking of Hobbes and Locke, one comes to appreciate the problems attendant to abstract individualism, or the conceptual contraction of both the original phenomenon of communication and just political institutions. These problems have been shown to play out in argumentation theory and in political theory in ways that ultimately devalue or fail to appreciate the vital role of historical communities to the formation of political reasoners, both with respect to the *sensus communis* on which citizens must draw for mutual persuasion and the habits of thought essential to their deliberating the common good. But this analysis must now be taken further, since a parallel abstraction can be seen to characterize the understanding of community—even when collective agreement or consensus, rather than the individual, is made the central focus of political theory—as one witnesses in the Enlightenment's autonomy tradition and, more recently, in the deliberative democrats who inherit its way of thinking about morality.

As thinkers of the Enlightenment, Rousseau and Kant's influence on the contemporary theory of deliberative democracy can be seen to parallel the influence of Hobbes and Locke on the theory of possessive individualism. Each of these pairs of Enlightenment philosophers may be said to prescind from the original community of interlocutors, though in opposing ways. Therefore, instead of "narrowing or contracting the social sphere" down to the level of the individual and his or her "sense impressions" to the point of obviating the concept of community, deliberative democrats conversely extend or expand the sphere of would-be interlocutors to the point of the latter's unrecognizability as a "community" of political decision-makers. That is to say, instead of atomization, which philosophers such as Smith have rightly observed as inappropriately dividing or dissecting human life into discrete parts, one sees in theories of deliberative democracy an exaggerated tendency toward abstract synthesis or combination, a holism in which the importance of concrete particularity is either diminished or altogether neglected. Rather than cutting the individual off from the community by truncating their social or relational existence, as in the case of possessive individualism, one sees here a parallel attempt in the autonomy tradition to unite individuals into infinitely extensive moral or political entities tied to no particular temporal horizon. As a result, the theory of deliberative democracy elides concrete differences among diverse interlocutors, which contribute in essential ways to the operation of both the content and form of deliberation. However, it is concrete communities existing over time that alone are capable of furnishing the *sensus communis* from which shared meanings emerge, as well as the sound habits of thought that orient individuals toward a collective pursuit of the common good.

The autonomy tradition thus represents the corresponding danger within Enlightenment thinking that is the counterpart to the extreme tendencies of possessive individualism. In their justifications to "all," deliberative democrats neglect or overlook important differences in the meaning of language within large and diverse populations, differences that point toward the reliance of reason (*logos*) upon shared historical experience or *praxis*. However, the metaphysical dualism inherited from the autonomy tradition precludes recognition of reason's particularity and its limited nature, insisting instead that emancipation from ethical substance (*ethos, Sittlichkeit*) entails an escape from the latter resulting in a universalization of moral language and the reasoners that use it. This divorce from the concrete context and meanings of *ergon* (deed), however, renders the universality upon which such theories draw illusory. Both the procedural and constitutional strains of thinking within deliberative democracy thus entail an elision of historical particularity, which results in the postulation of an abstract unity that is relied upon to claim universal justification. However, the elimination or neglect of particularity for the sake of this alleged unity comes with a price. Whereas Habermas's "universal exchange of roles," which informs his legitimating procedure, blithely neglects the essential connection between particularity and meaning, or the concrete, existential nature of moral language, Rawls's overlapping consensus trades on the noncontroversial character of abstract principles, whose severance from particular contexts renders any such principles normatively hollow and politically indeterminate. Positing unity where there is in fact lived diversity or historical particularity, both thinkers create hypothetical conditions for political legitimacy that, similar to possessive individualism, take for granted the collective goods they seek to promote—in this case, deliberation among the members of society.

This leads to the central concern regarding the cost of deliberative democracy as a theory of justice, which is that it not only fails to recognize the essential role of historical communities or tradition as a precondition of deliberation, but it actively undermines the normative import or priority of the latter's cultivation. While it may not, like possessive individualism, actually endorse institutions that facilitate competitive, self-regarding behavior, deliberative democracy as an ideal nonetheless promotes a weakening of the bonds of *philia*, further contributing to the deracination of modern social and political life. It does so, principally, by sustaining the false belief in political legitimacy amid the deep and wide pluralism of large-scale democracies, sustaining the illusion of moral unity among hundreds of millions of citizens, facilitated by the alleged individual autonomy they promote. The political and legal systems of democratic societies are thus perceived as redeeming the autonomy tradition's original demand for self-determination or universal authorship of the laws and policies that govern citizens, as a result of their endorsement of the moral basis upon which those laws and policies are justified. In essence, they claim to have vindicated Rousseau's original aspiration of leaving us as free as before we entered political society.

In chapter 2, it was mentioned that Kant sought to demonstrate how pure practical reason, through the application of the categorical imperative,

might serve as a more reliable basis for realizing the fundamental moral purposes—respecting all individuals as free agents or moral ends—that he had
learned from Rousseau regarding the dignity of human nature. Rousseau's
anticipations of Kant in his articulation of the general will, it was argued,
established insight into the impartial standpoint later known as the moral
point of view, which Habermas argues all cognitivist or rationalist theories
of morality must retain at their core. That impartial perspective entails as
its central moral intuition a reciprocity or reversibility of perspectives if
political choices are to meet the demands of the public, discursive testing of
norms. Although Rousseau had argued in the *Second Discourse* that reason
becomes distorted or perverted in the society of *amour propre*,[25] elsewhere in
his work, he speculates as to how reason might be built on a foundation of
pure sentiment or conscience. In particular, it is the sentiment of empathy
(*pitié*) or feeling for the plight of others, which anticipates the reversibility
and reciprocity of perspective that is later developed by Kant and others
into the idea of the moral point of view. Rousseau's abstraction from the
preconditions of reason thus begins this aspiration of identifying with the
perspective of "all," which later becomes synonymous with the adoption of a
"moral" perspective, one that is thought to escape all temporal limitations.[26]

Examining this unity of reason and sentiment in a recent study, David
James has demonstrated that there is in Rousseau's account of reason and
its role in the general will a kind of "Hegelian" quality, which characterizes
Rousseau's understanding of the movement or development of the individual's faculties as they grow from sentiment into reason.[27] In other words,
empathy (*pitié*) exhibits a kind of transformation in *Emile* and demonstrates
how human beings might arrive at such a sensibility in which the impartial
or universal standpoint can be adopted.[28] Reason is vindicated, as it were,
when it emerges from a foundation of benevolence. James explains: "As we
shall see, the preservation of sentiment in the course of the ascent to a more
rational standpoint means that, even at a relatively late stage in the system
of education outlined in *Emile*, Rousseau is at pains to prevent his pupil's
reason from becoming detached from his emotional life. He in fact views
the development of moral reasoning, which involves adopting the standpoint
of others as one's own, as depending on the development of the particular
sentiment of pity."[29] While reason certainly can exist without sentiment, as
Rousseau believes it does in the exploitative institutions of Western society,
or for that matter in the undeveloped pupil, Emile, sentiment is seen as
the proper foundation for the "production" of rational judgments regarding
what is morally good and bad, right and wrong.[30]

What is key to the cultivation of empathy (*pitié*) as this foundation for reason, according to Rousseau, is for Emile to come to an understanding and appreciation of human suffering. In other words, "it is, for Rousseau, the awareness of the evils that human beings suffer, or can suffer, that is most fundamental when it comes to the development of the sentiment of pity. It is therefore by making the pupil aware of the common evils afflicting humankind that the sentiment of pity is aroused in him, leading him to enter a moral order in which he recognizes the existence of relations uniting him to his fellow human beings."[31] The tutor's job in the development or education for such virtue is then "instilling in his pupil an awareness of the fact that it is the miseries and evils of life, and not happiness, that constitute the common lot of humankind."[32] With happiness, in other words, there appears to be no possibility for Rousseau of developing an understanding of others, whereas with misery, the other's lot can be understood and appreciated by the evocation of empathy. To make the child social, therefore, the tutor is actually required to elicit empathetic responses with regard to visceral sights and sounds of others' suffering.[33]

In short, the imagination must be wakened, ultimately developing into a kind of awareness or reflection through which comparative judgments are made with others, such that the individual is effectively "transported outside of himself"[34] and his self-love (*amour de soi*) may essentially be transposed onto others. In this way, James explains, the affective element in moral reasoning can be supplied by empathy, while our capacity to adopt the standpoint of others becomes not only imaginatively cultivated but capable of articulation through generalizations or conceptualizations of the rational intellect. Moral ideas become possible, on Rousseau's account, only when imagination, imbued in such a manner with affect, informs the judgments of reason, so that one learns "to generalize his individual notions of his identity with others under the abstract idea of humanity."[35] James continues, "This process of generalization consists in an ever greater, in the sense of more expansive, ability to combine and compare which finally gives rise to ideas that appear to be independent of sensation altogether."[36] Abstraction as the very goal of reason is thought to be dependent on an affective, imaginative flight from one's individual horizon of understanding.

What is interesting and noteworthy about Rousseau's account of the development of the imagination and our capacity to identify with others is the focus on society-wide or top-down institutions as the source of what is common and unifying among society's members. In other words, in basing the imaginative perspective on a shared idea of human suffering, Rousseau overcomes (or, more precisely, circumvents) the problem of human beings actually relating to one another, notwithstanding the innumerable differences that may exist among their historical backgrounds or experiences. Ostensibly united in suffering, all are conceived as seeing the world from a universal perspective of human impotence and anguish in the face of institutional oppression. One's "humanity" is thus identified with this shared source of regard for self and regard for other, or to put it in the more spiritual terms with which Rousseau conceives the emotions, the soul's love of self (*amour de soi*) and its love of all others. The generalization of reason based on this benevolence or universal love is thus the logical development or extension of natural emotion (*sentiment*), combined with an awareness of the a priori of universal human suffering.

As a result, James is in a sense correct in his identification of a "Hegelian" quality that he believes characterizes this progression from affect to reason, culminating in "the abstract idea of humanity." However, what is important to note about this "development" is that it is a logical unfolding, not in actual human beings who must reason with one another, but *within the thinking of Rousseau himself.*[37] That is to say, such development must be distinguished from the real, gradual historical development that Gadamer sees as attendant to concrete, social interactions, or the building up of patterns of living slowly over time among situated human beings. Like his state of nature in the *Second Discourse*, Rousseau's conceptualization of "humanity" here ultimately creates no more than a hypothetical conjecture—an ideal that proceeds from the development out of pure sentiment or conscience, to an imaginative vision of abstract others, to the rational extrapolation of universal moral principles. Consequently, Rousseau's foundational epistemology of the moral point of view occupies a position that is at once solipsistic and expansive. One identifies with the whole of humanity without ever having contact with any other person.

However, no more are we the isolated individuals of possessive individualism, who without a shared language or existing society are nonetheless capable of deliberating and choosing our governing institutions, than are we, as the autonomy tradition presupposes, noumenal selves capable of identifying with the whole of society in the adoption of a reversible, reciprocal perspective, sharing in principles that are said to establish the moral basis of our collective choices. To be sure, it is obviously possible to entertain such imaginative conceptualizations regarding "humanity" or "all" members of society, based on broad generalizations of benevolent feeling toward others. However, the correspondence of the latter to comparable perspectives in the other members of society is an illusion rather than something that is grounded in a mutual experience of reality. In other words, such conceptualizations are ultimately no more than theoretical speculation about a *hypothetical* general will rather than having a basis in that which is historically real, a coming together or growth of mutual understanding based on actual experience and interaction. Indeed, when ascriptions of such a common will or universally held "reasons" nevertheless results in intense disagreements on moral or political matters, the cognitive dissonance that ensues seems to betray the speculative nature of such suppositions.[38]

The alleged universality of the moral point of view, though it appears as an enlargement of the individual's perspective, actually prescinds from or truncates our experiential encounters, which alone have the ability to expand or enlarge our imaginative horizons while remaining connected to reality. In other words, it is only through encounters with flesh and blood human beings, through interactions that are prefigured by existing patterns of behavior and hermeneutic understanding, that one's horizon of understanding may be *gradually* enlarged by new experiences to the point of achieving mutual understanding (though never absolute or complete) with other members of a particular community. Consequently, bridging the gap to understanding others' points of view is never, in reality, an imaginative leap, culminating in universal understanding, as in Rousseau's account, but always entails a partial assimilation of new encounters, which are at once underpinned by common practices and subject to both individual and collective interpretation. That is to say, meaning occurs for each member of a community at the nexus of common *praxis* and *logos*, when new concrete experiences are folded into old horizons of experience and interpretation, which has already been acquired and understood in the word (*logos*) or language of an existing *sensus communis*. The idea of universal justification, therefore, ultimately fails to locate meaning in precisely the light of what has previously—which is to say, historically—been both individually and collectively experienced and understood.

What is interesting, not to mention troubling, about the epistemological orientation of the autonomy tradition is that it actually bears a certain theoretical similarity with possessive individualism, even if their respective emphases on the individual and the community exist in a more obvious or overt tension with one another. For its requirement of a consensus to underwrite political legitimacy, though certainly more onerous than the minimal demands on public life put forth by possessive individualism, does not encumber citizens with the sort of thick obligations traditionally associated with *ethos* or *Sittlichkeit*. Rather, the autonomy tradition uses such claims of legitimacy for the purpose of securing freedom from historical obligation for individuals. In other words, both the autonomy tradition and possessive individualism, which are the inheritors of different sides of the social contract tradition, share an underlying commitment to the idea of society as a voluntary or freely entered agreement between self-deter-mining agents. In that sense, although deliberative democracy synthesizes or unifies individual citizens into a theoretical collectivity, it shares with possessive individualism a fundamental aversion to the unchosen inheritance of tradition, or concrete communities that exist over time. Each of these competing strains of Enlightenment thinking thus serves to reinforce the shared liberal premise that a society of free choosers is the basis of political legitimacy, and the aversion of each—though more explicit in Rousseau's anti-historical outlook—to tradition as a moral ground for deliberation and political decision-making is based on the threat that the latter poses to the priority of individual liberty.

Therefore, although one of these contemporary descendants of social contract theory, the autonomy tradition, emphasizes collective agreement or consensus, both are, at bottom, individualistic. At its base, deliberative democracy inherits the individualism that underpins Rousseau's theory of the social contract and the concept of the general will, which is grounded in the idea of submitting to the law while remaining as free as before. It is in light of this important feature—its normative commitment to retaining individual liberty or self-determination, understood as autonomy—that deliberative democracy may also be seen as contributing to the deracination of modern society. For, it reinforces the basic premise of the social contract conception of justice, which says that institutions are legitimate insofar as they resemble an agreement that allows for the pursuit of one's private, individual good, abstracting from the shared life with others that, in reality, precedes any such good.

However, when no longer understood in the Manichean terms of "morality" and "history" or "reason" and "experience," an alternative, more realistic conception of deliberation emerges, in which reason operates, not in the absence but precisely *in the light of* the historical particularity of *logos*. On this Gadamerian conception, reason is more than merely the narrow expression of egoistic drives aimed at securing private interests, while also less than a God's eye view or Archimedean vantage point that speaks from the perspective of an all-inclusive or boundless community of reasoners. Instead, this conception recognizes the situated and thus limited nature of human reason, which only emerges, wherever it does, in concrete communities that exist over time, with common practices and a corresponding *sensus communis*, as well the imperative of orienting members toward discussion about the common good. Such recognition or acknowledgment, in turn, points to the normative import, or moral priority, of cultivating these preconditions, so that reason may flourish and genuine political deliberation can become more realistic.

Modernity as Historical Narrative

The utopian promise of autonomy and its assertion of the legitimacy of large-scale, pluralistic democracies still does not, however, capture the full extent of deliberative democracy's undermining of communities that exist over time and its previously mentioned contribution to the deracination of modern life. An additional cost is incurred as a result of the historical narrative put forth by many deliberative democrats, which says that political legitimacy must be grounded in universal justificatory procedures, since it is no longer possible, under the conditions of modernity, for citizens in a democracy to appeal to shared values inherited from a particular *ethos*. In other words, there is an onto-historical claim on the part of many deliberative democrats, which says that while there have been times during which such shared meanings and values may have been possible as a basis for politics—as, for example, in the ancient Greek polis or within medieval Christendom—the fragmentation of worldviews that has taken place since then has made this model obsolete. In short, the nature of social life and the kinds of appeals that can ground political legitimacy have changed. One must recognize the "fact of pluralism," which is the diversity of worldviews or "comprehensive moral doctrines" that exist within modern democratic societies, none of which has the right to rule over the others. It is by virtue of this historical narrative regarding the nature of social relations in modernity that one arrives at the conclusion that *only* justifications that can meet with the consent of all, regardless of one's particular ethical orientation, can support the legitimacy of the modern political order.

It should be noted that with these claims of deliberative democrats, there is not merely an acceptance or willingness to live with the fact of pluralism as a feature of modern political life. There is the attendant claim that a refusal to recognize this feature and an obstinate commitment to the "ancient" or "Aristotelian" model of politics, in which small communities of inherited values provide a common ground for political legitimacy, represents a quixotic attempt to live in the past, at best, or an intolerant moral imposition vis-à-vis minority moral outlooks, at worst. In other words, the onto-historical argument regarding the nature of modern politics insists that what has been called "genuine deliberation" in the present work is entirely out of the question, simply because its time has passed, and it is no longer a realistic model of political legitimacy, in light of existing moral diversity. In short, the arrival of modernity is said to close off any possibility of politics smaller than large-scale nation-states that would attempt to rely on the sharing of values within a particular ethical community.

However, such claims regarding the impossibility of smaller-scale politics based on shared values ultimately misconstrue the choices with which we are confronted in modern political life. To be sure, it will not be disputed that there exist conditions within modern society that create substantial challenges for justification and deliberation grounded in a shared *ethos*. However, there is more at work in the claims of deliberative democrats regarding the advent of "modernity" than this admittedly important acknowledgment. In what follows, it will be argued that, among the early, influential expositors of deliberative democracy that have been discussed, the idea of "modernity" is understood and invoked in terms that are absolute and, as a result, it obviates any possibility of qualifying the normative claims that they attach to the "fact of pluralism." After brief sketches of the historical narratives of modernity in Habermas and Rawls, two such features of their accounts will be highlighted: (1) the implication that there exists a strict division or distinction between "premodern" and "modern" societies and (2) the idea that the historical development that has led to "modernity" is unidirectional.

Habermas's idea of modernity takes its bearings predominantly from the social theory of Max Weber and the philosophy of history belonging to Hegel, and the central idea that, since the late eighteenth century, traditional sources of social—particularly religious—authority have been subjected to processes of "rationalization" and the self-reflectiveness of historical consciousness, resulting in the weakening of the "quasi-natural" status of such authority.[39] For Weber, social modernization is a process defined by massive expansion of the administrative state, together with the capitalist economy, whose mutual reinforcement and proliferation results in the increasing differentiation of social life into diverse "value spheres," such as science, law, morality, art, and so on. According to this account, the internal rationality of each of these spheres eventually becomes detached from the religious orientation (e.g., the "Protestant ethic") that once provided the motivational basis for its creation. Such detachment ultimately results in a loss of meaning or what Weber famously described as the "disenchantment" of the traditional world view from which it emerged.[40]

At the same time, Habermas sees these functional pressures on the lifeworld described by Weber as accompanied by a new historical consciousness, or consciousness of the present as standing apart from and even in opposition to the past, as expressed in the distinction between the "modern" and the "old" world.[41] Within Hegel's philosophy, Habermas says, the Enlightenment signifies a new openness of the future in the "modern" world and the self-consciousness of this freedom and the break with the past that it represents.[42] What is of central importance to modernity's "grasping its own time" and "awaken[ing] to consciousness of itself" is therefore its relationship to tradition.[43] According to Habermas, "Modernity can and will no longer borrow the criteria by which it takes its orientation from the models supplied by another epoch; it has to create normativity out of itself. Modernity sees itself cast back upon itself without any possibility of escape."[44] Consequently, in addition to the functional pressures identified by Weber, Hegel describes a new sense of freedom within the consciousness of the modern subject, which Habermas sees further disintegrating the unity and authority of the lifeworld, or traditional ethical life (*Sittlichkeit*).

The legacy of modernity, however, is not merely negative for Habermas but ultimately serves as a source of ambivalence for him, due to the potential he sees built into the newfound freedom of the individual subject, emancipated from these older sources of authority.[45] For it is in modern society that Habermas believes a new form of social integration becomes possible, which is no longer based upon the blind acceptance of traditional authority that he believes once characterized the normative structures of the lifeworld; it is here, in other words, that Habermas thinks normativity can be created "out of itself." Consequently, alongside the "instrumental rationality" that Weber and others see as "colonizing" the traditional lifeworld, Habermas notes the new possibility of "communicative rationality"—the reflective form of discourse that becomes possible among modern subjects by virtue of the same detachment or distantiation from tradition that is responsible for their social deracination. Drawing on the empirical research on cognitive development by the psychologist Lawrence Kohlberg, Habermas thus argues that individuals in modern societies develop a critical, rational attitude toward conventional norms that opens the door to intersubjective will-formation. At the "post-conventional" level of moral development, cognition is said to break free from the concrete ethical substance of tradition, and as the individual acquires an abstract self-identity, along with individual life-projects, his or her capacity for autonomous self-regulation grows. Collectively speaking, social integration now becomes less reliant on tradition, according to Habermas, and more reliant on institutions and procedures aimed at reaching consensus, such as the deliberative bodies—both formal and informal—of constitutional governments.[46]

The basis for Rawls's conception of modernity is found neither in the early systems theory of Weber, nor in the philosophy of consciousness of Hegel, but in what he refers to as the "common sense" knowledge of "our shared history and the evident features and aspects of our political culture and present circumstances."[47] Such awareness, Rawls contends, may be said to characterize "the common sense political sociology of democratic societies."[48] Following the European Wars of Religion of the sixteenth and seventeenth centuries, along with the growth of constitutional government and industrial market economies, Rawls claims that there emerged a new set of circumstances within the shared political culture of Western democracies that would "profoundly affect" what could be hoped for regarding a "workable" and "practicable" conception of justice. Most prominently, he says, these conditions entailed: "(1) the fact of pluralism; (2) the fact of the permanence of pluralism, given democratic institutions; (3) the fact that agreement on a single comprehensive doctrine presupposes the oppressive use of state power."[49] According to Rawls, the consequences of the Reformation should therefore be seen as including not merely the bloodshed often associated with the Wars of Religion, but also the increasing recognition and ultimately the settled realization that the only alternative to such "mortal conflict" when it comes to the political relations of "salvationist" and "creedal" religions is peaceful toleration.[50]

As a result of this realization, Rawls sees the "fact of pluralism" in post-Reformation democracies as giving birth to a fundamentally novel orientation toward political justice, which no longer pursues the highest good, as it did under the sectarianism of the Wars of Religion, but now merely seeks "fair terms of cooperation" between citizens divided by deep doctrinal commitments.[51] Most significantly, citizens within these circumstances no longer concern themselves with the *truth* of their principles in regard to questions of justice, but instead make arguments referring only to what is *reasonable*, or what other citizens can reasonably be expected to endorse.[52]

The emergence of this "reasonable pluralism" is not, for Rawls, to be derived from "social theory"—as it is for Habermas—but should be seen as one of the "virtual truisms" to be gleaned from the collective history of Western society.[53] For this new perspective, "pluralism is not seen as a disaster but rather as the natural outcome of the activities of human reason under enduring free institutions," a view that Rawls believes stands in marked contrast to the "centuries-long practice of intolerance" and the belief that such intolerance was necessary as "a condition of social order and stability."[54] For Rawls, reasonable pluralism thus appears to be a "quintessentially modern" or "uniquely modern"[55] phenomenon, in light of its break with previous practice and what has become the predominant outlook in Western society. The achievement of liberal constitutional government, according to Rawls, should be seen as "the discovery of a new social possibility."[56]

For both Habermas and Rawls, the transition to "modern" society is thus understood to be monumental, an awakening of the subject to new social possibilities created by the emancipation from dogmatic belief in older sources of authority. In both theories, one sees an attitude toward tradition that has radically changed, an epistemic transformation of the subject vis-à-vis the past that is wholesale rather than partial. Following Hegel, Habermas sees the loss of *Sittlichkeit* in the West in absolute terms, establishing the fundamental distinction between "ancient" and "modern" societies. Hegel identifies the loss of *Sittlichkeit* with the passing of Greek antiquity, and, anticipating Weber, he points in particular to liberal economic policies and behavior, resulting in the cultivation of private life at the expense of the public.[57] Here, Hegel establishes a strict duality, which does not admit the possibility of conceiving the attenuation of ethical community in terms of degrees, but instead posits an either/or framework that is used to distinguish ancient and modern ways of life. It is with this feature in mind separating the ancient and modern worlds that Hegel presents a series of contrasts, in which he juxtaposes *Moralität* and *Sittlichkeit*, particular and universal, *bourgeois* and *citoyen*, civil society and state, and *Gesellschaft* and *Gemeinschaft*.[58] For Habermas, Hegel is thus the first to provide a "conceptual framework" that distinguishes "modern society" from the "Aristotelian tradition," which comprehended a single sphere encompassing politics and civil society.[59] Following Hegel, Habermas instead sees modern societies as defined by the radical detachment of civil from political life, a development that has "put too great a strain upon the classical doctrine of politics."[60] Though he disagrees with Hegel's "tendentious solution"[61] of constitutional monarchy as a way of restoring the "ethical whole" that was lost, Habermas adopts

Hegel's fundamental premise that *Sittlichkeit* was not merely attenuated in the transition to modern society but that it has been entirely lost or "shattered."[62]

For Rawls, there is a similarly thoroughgoing transformation of the world view of the modern subject. In post-Reformation society, Rawls believes there is an important change with regard to the political conception of justice, such that comprehensive moral doctrines are now no longer seen as providing a valid source of justification among morally diverse populations regarding law or policy. In recognition of the fact of pluralism, he argues, only two perspectives are conceivable: the members of a society are either "modern" and share in the belief of the democratic tradition, which denies that comprehensive moral doctrines are the proper basis for governance, or they are willing to use the state as a means of coercing or "oppress[ing]" other citizens, who must accept comprehensive doctrines that are not their own.[63] There exists, in other words, a similar Manichean division in Rawls's thinking between "premodern" and "modern" societies. Those societies whose citizens seek only "fair terms of cooperation" are thus modern, for Rawls, in a manner comparable to those in Habermas's thinking whose citizens achieve sufficient moral maturity to make them capable of communicative rationality. The cognitive leap into modernity, in both cases, changes the outlook of the subject toward political life in toto. It may therefore be said that Rawls, in similar fashion to Habermas,[64] does not conceive of the defining attributes of "modern societies" in terms of tendencies or degrees, but that he sees this ascription as an all-or-nothing transformation that has played out at the historical or sociological level.

That Habermas believes modernity to be unidirectional is evidenced by the fact that he describes the shift in the modern subject's perspective toward the lifeworld in terms of a "disintegration" of their preexisting cognitive framework, which has the character, following Weber, of an ultimate disillusionment or grand revelation regarding the ethical life. Consequently, this change in the outlook of the subject, on his account, is seen as part of a permanent development, marked by a keener awareness of the allegedly arbitrary normative authority of tradition that, once learned, cannot be unlearned or forgotten. To be sure, it might be argued that to assert the acquisition of such knowledge does not, theoretically, rule out the possibility that a society could, over time, lose sight of the allegedly contingent authority of tradition. However, Habermas frequently characterizes such awareness in terms of growth or maturity, a passage beyond the credulity of a society's youth, and it is for this reason that his theory of social evolution lends itself to comparison with the cognitive development of children, who do not (typically) vacillate randomly between stages of development throughout their lives, but follow a more predictable *progression* from one stage to the next. In the similar development of modern societies, Habermas argues that the loss of *Sittlichkeit* at the hands of critical reason implies an *"ever*-widening" horizon of choices for the present, even if one finds this present *"ever-more* disturbed" by this fact.[65] In light of this alleged growth in freedom from traditional authority, whose status as "quasi-natural" has now been "shattered," it would be inconceivable, on Habermas's view, for societies merely to slough off such historical consciousness, once it has been obtained. With the perspective that *ethos* is contingent and the binding authority associated with its givenness of a questionable basis, the individuals in Habermas's modern societies would appear unable to resume their former, more naive outlooks. Rather, Habermas sees this historical consciousness as a mature perspective, the foundations of an older worldview having been made "transparent" and "shaken" and the medium of reason as "incapable of regenerating the unifying force" that once existed.[66]

As is evident from the second condition Rawls identifies with modern democracies earlier in this chapter, the "permanence"[67] of pluralism explicitly points to a single direction of change among the institutions of Western society. On his account, the religious diversity that fragmented the unity of the Middle Ages led to the broader pluralism of "comprehensive moral doctrines," which he describes as "a permanent feature of culture by the end of the eighteenth century."[68] Rawls's repeated emphasis on this permanence leaves unambiguous the unidirectionality he ascribes to modernity. As Russell Hittinger argues, Rawls builds into his account "certain suppositions about the historical direction of society" culminating in an overlapping consensus of reasonable doctrines, which he believes to be an "irreversible achievement."[69] Interestingly, Hittinger also observes that, for Rawls, this achievement of reasonable pluralism is not merely a "fact," but a *"natural* outcome" and the *"inevitable* long term result" of human reason in free institutions, which points toward a latent teleology informing the historical narrative within Rawls's thinking.[70] The rather "vaguely reported"[71] and "highly stylized"[72] history that Rawls sketches may be seen as created with this trajectory in mind. In other words, the sparse account of this history that Rawls invokes, with its attention to such a selective set of facts, is attributable to the fact that he is guided by his own normative ideal, which he imputes to the nature of modern societies.[73] As a result, Rawls sees modernity not only as bringing a novel approach to the question of political justice, but one that represents a purposeful rejection of the intolerance of the preceding political order. This would appear as no mere historical accident, on Rawls's account, but a deliberate progression beyond an unsustainable state of affairs from which Western societies have matured or learned.

The historical narrative surrounding "modernity" put forth by Habermas and Rawls has gone a long way to undermine the argument for politics on any sort of smaller scale, grounded in a shared ethical orientation. Although this narrative claims merely to characterize or describe the present historical situation, it has in significant ways framed the discussion regarding the place of the ethical life in the contemporary conversation about deliberation and justification in democratic societies. However, the dualistic framework of Habermas and Rawls, which divides societies into the categories of "premodern" and "modern," or "conventional" and "post-conventional," has effectively created a straw man argument, which says that calls for the cultivation of concrete, shared ways of living (*ethos, Sittlichkeit*) are by their very nature inappropriate for modern society, since they represent an attempt to return to a "premodern" model of politics whose time has passed. To ignore the "fact of pluralism," which defines modern life, is to be not merely insensitive to contemporary circumstances, but to engage in a kind of reactionary politics, whose fundamental inappropriateness for the present renders it romantic utopianism, oppressive intolerance, or both. Consequently, there is a normative claim attached to the historical narrative of modernity, which attempts to foreclose any such arguments—a claim whose rejection of "Aristotelian" politics is itself absolutist, due to the Manichean framework upon which it rests. Normative arguments that would promote a shared ethical life as a basis for politics—specifically, here, for the purposes of political deliberation—are characterized as denying the fact of pluralism, refusing to accommodate the moral diversity of modern life in any way. Such arguments are viewed as anachronistic reversions to the medieval or ancient political order, whose rejection of "modernity" then amounts to a denial of the autonomy of persons.

When confronted with the choice between a repugnant moral intolerance that violates individual autonomy and obstinately ignores present circumstances, and a humane openness to diversity that respects individual autonomy and is sensitive to the conditions of modern life, it is obvious which most will choose. However, such clear choices between absolute alternatives rarely present themselves in political life, which is more typically characterized by arduous attempts to balance or prudently weigh competing moral priorities that continually come into tension with one another. The choice, in other words, between what Hegel called the Condition of Right or abstract right, on the one hand, and *Sittlichkeit* or ethical substance, on the other, does indeed vary among societies and across human history. However, the outcome of historical choice is never a foregone conclusion based on the recognition of radically new facts that forever alter the nature of social life, thus demanding that one of these values must be chosen over the other *in perpetuum*. Rather, there is always a tension between these polarities or antinomies of political association, which continually need to be weighed against one another within *particular* circumstances, each of which represents some degree of change vis-à-vis its immediate past.[74]

Consequently, it is an illegitimate or unfair turn in such arguments to claim that recommendations for the cultivation of the ethical life are per se invalid and will be so forever more. For this is to deny that there exist degrees of diversity or plurality in every society—not only under the unique conditions of "modernity"—and that the latter is always in tension with the bonds of historical community or tradition. While pluralism is undeniably a feature of contemporary political life and its increase may be a prominent and perhaps even a defining characteristic of modern society, the choice between its continued promotion or the cultivation of historically rooted, shared ways of living does not represent an all-or-nothing state of affairs. Rather, there is always a decision to be made with regard to the degree to which *ethos*, the institutions of ethical substance, are to be cultivated or not. Certainly, the sharing of meanings and values within an ethical life and the common ground this creates for justification and deliberation for the members of a community must be considered among the benefits of its cultivation. Conversely, it must be admitted that the individual freedom and diversity of perspective that is enabled when these bonds weaken can, in certain respects if not others, be seen as a benefit that is not to be dismissed or taken lightly. However, what must be acknowledged is that the choice between these values is, in the first place, not a Manichean one between absolute alternatives, but always that of degrees—one moves the needle, so to speak, in one direction or the other within a broad continuum of possibilities. And, in the second place, the nature of our historical moment must not be seen as part of an irreversible trajectory, which would render inappropriate any choices that cut in the opposite direction of the trend that has immediately preceded it. Instead, each society must be seen as confronted with these competing values, which are to be weighed according to the particular circumstances it encounters and the possibilities these present for human flourishing.

Consequently, the historical narrative that says that we find ourselves within "modernity"—understood as a radically new historical moment, which is incapable per se of sustaining the ethical life—must be seen as an unwarranted attempt to answer the question of this tension once and for all. This narrative interprets all arguments in favor of promoting historically rooted communities as beyond serious consideration, in light of historical developments over the last several centuries. Furthermore, the rhetorical symbols of medieval Christendom and Greek antiquity are thus employed to create a misleading depiction or aesthetic representation of such arguments as profoundly anachronistic, subsuming any such alternatives under the rubric of only the thickest and most historically remote ethical communities.[75] Of course, it is important to admit not only that modern democracies exhibit a broad diversity of moral outlooks, but that this reality should indeed inform the political choices that are to be made in this context. The present argument, in other words, is not that, contrary to deliberative democrats, all choices must be considered "on the table" in our present situation. On the contrary, prudent decision-making must certainly exclude the impossible or unrealistic, which would necessarily mean the aim of instituting anything resembling ancient or medieval communities.

However, recognition of the "fact of pluralism" also must not be taken as ruling out ipso facto all arguments that favor the promotion of traditional ethical community or the normative import of combatting the deracination of modern life. Indeed, this would appear to be an ironic turn, in which deliberative democrats—like the intellectual predecessors Rousseau once criticized—try to justify the perpetuation of existing political institutions with reference to their de facto historical development. What had troubled Rousseau, it will be recalled, about the claims of the Western philosophical tradition, largely (though not exclusively) influenced by the belief in original sin was, in effect, a built-in bias in favor of status quo historical institutions, which had ascribed a naturalness or a necessity to them, thereby catering to and ultimately promoting human selfishness and hierarchy. For, according to Rousseau, this deprived human beings of the freedom by virtue of which they could, in their collective capacity, become self-determining, changing their institutions and themselves and thus exercising what he believed to be the noblest feature of humanity. This appeal to existing institutions, it would appear, ironically anticipates the argument of deliberative democrats, whose invocations of the onto-historical narrative of "modernity" and "the fact of pluralism" aims to rule out the suggestion that we might choose social arrangements that depart from the pluralization and weakening of traditional community that characterizes the last several centuries. In doing so, however, they limit the fundamental freedom to choose our own destiny, a concern that was at the very heart of Rousseau's *Second Discourse* and his *Social Contract.* Denying the possibility of ethical community in modern life, deliberative democrats would appear to decide in advance, in the name of this recent history, one of the central questions that our society, along with every other society, must confront.

The upshot of the present analysis is not—to be perfectly clear—that only a return to something like the medieval "fishing village"[76] will satisfy the political or associational needs of human beings, in light of the emphasis of the Gadamerian conception of deliberation and practical reason, which shows the dependence of the latter upon tradition, or concrete communities that exist over time. To be sure, the point has indeed been made in the present work that there is a tradition-dependency with regard to genuine delibera- tion, since only historically rooted communities can facilitate the form and substance of the latter, that is, an orientation of individuals toward pursuit of the common good, as well as a shared context of concrete meanings through which moral language takes on its deep resonance or persuasive power. However, as this section has attempted to make clear, these fruits of concrete, historical community must be conceived as existing along a continuum, not as an all-or-nothing state of affairs related to our living in "modernity" or "premodernity," "conventional" or "post-conventional" soci- eties. Trade-offs always occur, and while we may gain in individual freedom as a result of the weakening of these bonds, it must be acknowledged that there will be a corresponding loss in our capacity to deliberate the common good. If we are properly to assess the normative import of such rootedness, it must be understood that the latter plays this vital role in the very choice of our moral and political existence.

Notes

1. P. Christopher Smith, "The Uses of Aristotle in Gadamer's Recovery of Consultative Reasoning: *Sunesis, Sungnome, Epieikeia,* and *Sumbouleuesthai,*" *Chica- go-Kent Law Review* 76 (2000): 731–32.

2. Ibid.

3. See ibid., 732; P. Christopher Smith, "Toward a Discursive Logic: Gadamer and Toulmin on Inquiry and Argument," in *The Specter of Relativism: Truth, Dialogue, and "Phronesis" in Philosophical Argument,* ed. Lawrence K. Schmidt (Evanston, IL: Northwestern University Press, 1995), 174; "Not Doctrine but 'Placing in Question':

The 'Thrasymachus' (Rep. I) as an *Erotesis* of Commercialization," in *Who Speaks for Plato? Studies in Platonic Anonymity*, ed. Gerald A. Press (Lanham, MD: Rowman and Littlefield, 2000), 115.

4. Smith, "The Uses of Aristotle in Gadamer's Recovery of Consultative Reasoning," 733. Here, Smith departs from Gadamer's interpretation of Plato in a slightly or moderately Heideggerian direction. That is to say that he recognizes a subjectivist bent in the dialogues of the later Plato that Gadamer does not. Still, it is important to bear in mind that, unlike Heidegger, he sees these as countervailing tendencies within Plato's philosophy and that Smith's normative and political purposes are decidedly Gadamerian.

5. Ibid., 734.

6. Ibid., 743.

7. Ibid., 739.

8. Ibid., 738–39.

9. This is among the central claims in part 3 of *Truth and Method*, which has been encapsulated in Gadamer's now famous and rather pithy statement that "being that can be understood is language." In close proximity to this remark, he likewise explicitly rejects the Hobbesian view when he says, "That which comes into language is not something that is pregiven before language; rather, the word gives it its own determination." *Truth and Method*, 470.

10. Smith, "The Uses of Aristotle in Gadamer's Recovery of Consultative Reasoning," 739.

11. Heidegger's term for this tendency of thought is seeing things as "present-at-hand" (*Vorhandenheit*), essentially comprehending the world as made up of independent objects.

12. Smith, "The Uses of Aristotle in Gadamer's Recovery of Consultative Reasoning," 740.

13. Ibid.

14. Ibid.

15. Ibid., 740–41.

16. Ibid., 734.

17. See chapter 4 and Gadamer's extended treatment of these concepts in *Truth and Method* at 56–61, 341–55. See also the helpful discussion by Joel Weinsheimer in the translator's preface to *Truth and Method*, xiii–xiv.

18. Smith, "The Uses of Aristotle in Gadamer's Recovery of Consultative Reasoning," 734. Locke famously describes this agreement as necessary for overcoming the "inconveniences" of property disputes in the state of nature. See John Locke, *Two Treatises of Government*, ed. Lee Ward (Indianapolis: Hackett, 2016), 127.

19. Ibid.

20. Ibid., 743.

21. Ibid.

22. Ibid.

23. Ibid., 743n54. Smith mistakenly attributes the phrase to J. S. Mill, who does not use the term. See Jill Gordon, "John Stuart Mill and the Marketplace of Ideas," *Social Theory and Practice* 23, no. 2 (1997), 235. This obviously has no bearing on his point regarding reason and the use of commercial metaphors.

24. P. Christopher Smith, *Hermeneutics and Human Finitude: Toward a Theory of Ethical Understanding* (New York: Fordham University Press, 1991), 65. In this section, Smith argues explicitly that MacIntyre, in spite of an often keen historical sense, is an intellectual heir of Mill and the Enlightenment project (66–67). Smith draws on *Whose Justice? Which Rationality?* (Notre Dame, IN: University of Notre Dame Press, 1988), but see also *Three Rival Versions of Moral Enquiry* (Notre Dame, IN: University of Notre Dame Press, 1994), which was published after Smith's study but further supports his interpretation. MacIntyre is indebted to the Scottish Enlightenment here, as Smith rightly observes, but also to the thinking of Thomas Kuhn regarding the superiority and rationality of particular paradigms within scientific inquiry. See Thomas Kuhn, *The Structure of Scientific Revolutions*, 3rd ed. (Chicago: University of Chicago Press, 1996).

25. Rousseau in fact contrasts the "state of nature" with the "state of reasoning" in modern society: "Reason is what engenders egocentrism, and reflection strengthens it. Reason is what turns man in upon himself. Reason is what separates him from all that troubles him and afflicts him. Philosophy is what isolates him and what moves him to say in secret, at the sight of a suffering man, 'Perish if you will; I am safe and sound.' No longer can anything but danger to the entire society trouble the tranquil slumber of the philosopher and yank him from his bed. His fellow man can be killed with impunity underneath his window. He has merely to place his hands over his ears and argue with himself a little in order to prevent nature, which rebels within him, from identifying him with the man being assassinated. Savage man does not have this admirable talent, and for lack of wisdom and reason he is always seen thoughtlessly giving in to the first sentiment of humanity." Jean-Jacques Rousseau, *Discourse on the Origin of Inequality*, trans. Donald A. Cress, introduced by James Miller (Indianapolis: Hackett, 1992), 37–38.

26. See David James, "Rousseau on Needs, Language, and Pity: The Limits of 'Public Reason,' " *European Journal of Political Theory* 10, no. 3 (2011): 372–93.

27. Ibid., 383.

28. Notwithstanding their respective abstractions from the ethical life, one ultimately sees theories of speculative historical development in the thinking of the four major thinkers in democratic theory discussed in the present work—Rousseau, Kant, Habermas, and Rawls—when it comes to our capacity to adopt the impartial or moral point of view. Examination of how Habermas and Rawls connect the latter with the idea of "modernity" will be the purpose of the section that immediately follows.

29. David James, "Rousseau on Needs, Language, and Pity," 383.

30. Ibid., 385.

31. Ibid.

32. Ibid.

33. Ibid.

34. Ibid.

35. Ibid.

36. Ibid., 387.

37. It is characteristic of the thinking of the autonomy tradition, in which the moral point of view may be seen as the central or defining feature of the conception of morality, that philosophical speculation with regard to reciprocity of perspective is ultimately substituted for or conflated with actual concrete relationships among human beings. As Beiner has recently indicated in an understated yet incisive observation, notwithstanding Habermas's repeated assertion that he, unlike Rawls, "affirms dialogical rather than monological reason," *both* contemporary inheritors of the autonomy tradition may be said to rely on "postulated hypothetical 'dialogue' between deliberating parties." Ronald Beiner, *Political Philosophy: What It Is and Why It Matters* (New York: Cambridge University Press, 2014), 200n4. In this regard, it is worth noting that Habermas's (D) principle identifies valid norms as those "that meet (*or could meet*) with the approval of all affected." Jürgen Habermas, "Discourse Ethics," in *Moral Consciousness and Communicative Action*, trans. Christian Lenhardt and Shierry Weber Nicholsen (Cambridge, MA: MIT Press, 1990), 66. Emphasis added. In other words, even the "actual discourses" that Habermas repeatedly emphasizes differentiate his position from that of political constructivists, such as Rawls, leave substantial room for theoretical speculation.

38. To illustrate, Amy Gutmann and Dennis Thompson, in *Democracy and Disagreement* (Cambridge, MA: Harvard University Press, 1996), point to universally acceptable reasons as the basis for what they call a "deliberative disagreement"—citizens coming to differences of opinion on a political issue but achieving political legitimacy by virtue of their reciprocal appeal to such shared reasons. The "paradigm" for such deliberative disagreements, they argue, is contemporary debates surrounding abortion policy:

> Both pro-life and pro-choice advocates argue from fundamentally different but plausible premises to conflicting public policies. Both make generalizable claims that are also recognizably reciprocal in their moral and empirical content. . . . Pro-life and pro-choice advocates can agree that innocent people should not be killed, and that women have a basic liberty to live their own lives and control their own bodies. But they arrive at radically different conclusions about abortion because they cannot agree on whether the fetus is a full-fledged constitutional person, whether a woman's right to control her body takes priority over any claims the dependent fetus may have, and what responsibility a woman

has to realize the human potential of a fetus that lacks consciousness and sentience. The claims on both sides of all these disagreements fall within the range of what reciprocity respects. (74)

However, rather than supporting political legitimacy, these radically different conclusions can easily be interpreted as contributing to exasperation, anger, and even feelings of mutual distrust among citizens and public officials. How, it might be thought, could a rational person conceivably arrive at *that* conclusion based on *these* moral principles? What such responses suggest is that the assertion of mutually acceptable principles that "all" members of society allegedly embrace is more aspiration or wishful thinking than reality. Such an agreement or consensus cannot deliver the universal authorship of policies it promises because, as abstraction, its principles lack the real normative force they would possess within a community of shared experience. Abstract principles instead point in ambiguous directions with regard to policy choices and are ultimately indeterminate until concrete human beings with historically informed backgrounds interpret them.

39. The following account draws primarily from Jürgen Habermas, *The Philosophical Discourse of Modernity*, trans. Frederick Lawrence (Cambridge, MA: MIT Press, 1987), and "Conceptions of Modernity: A Look Back at Two Traditions," in Jürgen Habermas, *The Postnational Constellation: Political Essays*, trans. and ed. Max Pensky (Cambridge, MA: MIT Press, 2001). But see also "Modernity: An Unfinished Project," in Jürgen Habermas, *Habermas and the Unfinished Project of Modernity*, ed. Maurizio Passerin d'Entrèves and Seyla Benhabib (Cambridge, MA: MIT Press, 1997), 38–55, and his more extensive treatment of Weber's theory of modernization in *Theory of Communicative Action*, vol. 1 (Boston: Beacon, 1984), 143–243.

40. Habermas, *The Postmodern Constellation*, 138–41. This destabilization of meaning resulting from the functional modernization of society is the source of value pluralism, on Weber's account. For Habermas, the fact of pluralism that results further contributes to the "shattering" of the religious tradition or *ethos* of Christian community. See James Gordon Finlayson, "Modernity and Morality in Habermas' Discourse Ethics," *Inquiry* 43, no. 3 (2000): 321, 334.

41. Habermas, *The Postmodern Constellation*, 132.

42. Habermas, *The Philosophical Discourse of Modernity*, 6–7.

43. Ibid., 16.

44. Ibid., 7.

45. Finlayson, "Modernity and Morality in Habermas' Discourse Ethics," 322.

46. Habermas, *The Postnational Constellation*, 152. It is important to note that the use that is made of Kohlberg's empirical research here is an attempt by Habermas to lay out a developmental *logic*, or conceptually distinct stages of moral learning, which could, *theoretically*, correspond to stages of social evolution. In other words, there are no empirical grounds for assuming that the cognitive development observed by Kohlberg in studies of children can be extrapolated to societies (ascending from

the "ontogenetic" to the "phylogenetic" level) in order to substantiate the various stages of moral development—preconventional, conventional, and post-conventional—postulated in Habermas's theory of social evolution. See Thomas McCarthy, *The Critical Theory of Jürgen Habermas* (Cambridge, MA: MIT Press, 1985), 245–61. The cognitive capacities that Habermas describes in "post-conventional" societies, in which communicative rationality is said to be the only appropriate or realistic model of discourse, are thus far from empirically grounded, but instead should be seen as highly speculative.

47. John Rawls, "The Idea of an Overlapping Consensus," *Oxford Journal of Legal Studies* 7, no. 1 (1987): 4–5n7.

48. Ibid.

49. Ibid. Four less prominent, though not insignificant, conditions that Rawls appends to the list above include, "(4) the fact that an enduring and stable democratic regime, one not divided into contending factions and hostile classes, must be willingly and freely supported by a substantial majority of at least its politically active citizens; (5) the fact that a comprehensive doctrine, whenever widely, if not universally shared in society, tends to become oppressive and stifling; (6) the fact that reasonably favourable conditions (administrative, economic, technological and the like), which make democracy possible, exist; and finally, (7) the fact that the political culture of a society with a democratic tradition implicitly contains certain fundamental intuitive ideas from which it is possible to work up a political conception of justice suitable for a constitutional regime." Ibid.

50. John Rawls, *Political Liberalism* (New York: Columbia University Press, 1993), xxv–xxviii. See also his *Lectures on the History of Moral Philosophy*, ed. Barbara Herman (Cambridge, MA: Harvard University Press, 2007), 5–8.

51. Rawls, *Political Liberalism*, xvii.

52. Ibid., xxii.

53. John Rawls, *The Law of Peoples* (Cambridge, MA: Harvard University Press, 1999), 124.

54. Ibid., xxvi.

55. Jan-Werner Müller, "Rawls, Historian: Remarks on Political Liberalism's 'Historicism,'" *Revue internationale de philosophie* 3, no. 237 (2006): 330.

56. Rawls, *Political Liberalism*, xxvii.

57. Lawrence Dickey and H. B. Nisbet, "General Introduction," in *G.W.F. Hegel: Political Writings*, eds. Dickey and Nisbet (New York: Cambridge University Press, 1999), xxviii–xxix.

58. Ibid., xxx.

59. Habermas, *The Philosophical Discourse of Modernity*, 37.

60. Ibid.

61. Ibid.

62. Jürgen Habermas, "On the Cognitive Content of Morality," *Proceedings of the Aristotelian Society* 96 (1996): 352.

63. Rawls, "The Idea of an Overlapping Consensus," 4.

64. To be sure, it might be argued that Habermas's "stages" of cognitive development, appropriated from Kohlberg, do represent degrees of moral maturity. However, it is clear from Habermas's sharp differentiation between "conventional" and "post-conventional" societies, which he applies to those stages, that the authority of convention either is or is not binding on the consciousness of the subject. For this reason, societies do not "partially" or "to some extent" engage in communicative rationality in Habermas's thinking. It is thus inconceivable, on Habermas's account, for a society to be "more" post-conventional or to straddle the fence, so to speak, between the premodern and modern world view.

65. Habermas, "Conceptions of Modernity," 134. Emphasis added.

66. Ibid., 135.

67. Rawls, "The Idea of an Overlapping Consensus," 4n7.

68. Rawls, *Political Liberalism*, xxiv.

69. Russell Hittinger, "John Rawls, *Political Liberalism*," *Review of Metaphysics* 47, no. 3 (1994): 590.

70. Ibid., 589–90.

71. Ibid., 589.

72. Jan-Werner Müller, "Rawls, Historian: Remarks on Political Liberalism's 'Historicism,' " 331.

73. Ibid.

74. See Smith, *Hermeneutics and Human Finitude*, 14–17.

75. As was noted in the previous chapter, Walhof resists the assimilation of Gadamer's concept of friendship into his model of democratic politics. In his book's section on solidarity, it becomes clear that this is because Walhof accepts the premise that the pluralism of modernity is incompatible with community, an older idea of association with which the Aristotelian idea of friendship is often connected. Walhof misconstrues a statement of Gadamer's, making it sound as if Gadamer too rules out such forms of association in the modern world when he writes, "Gadamer recognizes that 'the romantic image of friendship and a general love of one's neighbor' cannot be the basis of modern society." Darren Walhof, *The Democratic Theory of Hans-Georg Gadamer* (Cham, Switzerland: Palgrave Macmillan, 2017), 108. However, Gadamer's purpose here is in fact to show the *appropriateness* of the idea of friendship for the situation of modern society. The fuller, original passage from Hans-Georg Gadamer, "Citizens of Two Worlds," in *Hans-Georg Gadamer on Education, Poetry, and History*, ed. Dieter Misgeld and Graeme Nicholson (Albany: State University of New York Press, 1992), reads as follows:

> The Greek concept of the friend articulated the complete life of society. Among friends everything was held in common, that was the old Pythagorean tradition in Greek thought. Here in the extreme form of the ideal, the tacit presupposition is expressed under which it is at

all possible to have something like the peaceful regulation of human communal life, a legal order. As could be demonstrated, the efficiency of the modern legal system still depends on the same presupposition. No one wants to assert that the romantic image of friendship and a general love of one's neighbor are the supporting basis for either the ancient polis or the modern technocratic metropolis. However, it appears to me that the important presuppositions for solving the modern world's problems are none other than the ones formulated in the Greek experience of thought. In any case the progress of science and its rational application to social life will not create so totally different a situation that "friendship" would not be required, that is a sustaining solidarity which alone makes possible the organized structure of human coexistence. (218–19)

It is worth noting here that Gadamer, at a minimum, puts considerably less conceptual distance between "friendship" and "solidarity" than Walhof contends. But, more to the point, Gadamer's purpose in this passage is not to distinguish the situations of the ancient and the modern world, but to separate a specifically romantic ideal of friendship from both and, furthermore, to emphasize the applicability of friendship to both. Walhof concludes with the remark that "even if this [romantic image of friendship] were true of the ancient polis, nostalgia for a mythic past in which citizens were friends will not get us far in complex, anonymous societies." He thus employs the familiar straw man argument upon which deliberative democrats rely, which says that since the only alternative to modernity is something like the ancient polis or medieval village—each of which are romantic impossibilities—reasonable people will rule out as unrealistic anything other than a full embrace of modernity's pluralism. Walhof, *The Democratic Theory of Hans-Georg Gadamer*, 108–9.

76. The reference here is to MacIntyre and the unfortunate illustration to which he adverts, which leaves one with the impression that only the communities of preindustrial society would be satisfactory to fulfill his neo-Aristotelian demands for human flourishing. In other words, there is a romanticism that characterizes his thinking, which itself creates Manichean alternatives between the premodern and modern world that, in effect, is the mirror image of the modernist perspective of deliberative democrats. See Alasdair MacIntyre, "A Partial Response to My Critics," in *After MacIntyre: Critical Perspectives on the Work of Alasdair MacIntyre*, ed. John Horton and Susan Mendus (Cambridge: Polity, 1994), 283–304.

Conclusion

Beyond Autonomy

Since the late eighteenth century, critics of democratic theory have tended to focus their arguments on the totalitarian potential of broad assertions of "the will of the people," in light of the absolutist nature of such claims of political authority. The fear is that invoking the collective will of society in this way might be a pretext for imposing a particular ideal in the name of "the people," while suppressing dissent. Habermas, in particular, has been accused of possessing such tendencies in his thinking, insofar as his appeal to a universal rationality is thought to bear echoes of Rousseau's general will. Critics of the tradition of positive liberty have seen such aspirations to universal agreement or consensus as utopian, insofar as they refuse to accommodate human fallibility, disagreement, and other unfortunate realities of political life. In this regard, Rousseau's theory of the social contract might be seen as quintessentially utopian. For it imagines that each citizen might become the author of all the laws that are to govern him, obeying only himself and remaining as free as one who is subject to no laws whatsoever. As Spaemann observes, the utopian goal of "the abolition of authority" lies behind Rousseau's idea of the general will, and those such as Habermas who share in this aspiration to universal agreement are likewise prone to forcing those who dissent to be "free."

The present study might be seen as examining a problem associated with such utopian thinking that is somewhat less conspicuous, which is to say, it focuses on the ordinary institutions whose value is undermined by such democratic idealism. In other words, along with the threat of political tyranny more commonly identified with such utopianism, there is also a tendency to devalue concrete, ethical community or tradition (*ethos, Sittlichkeit*) and the fundamental norms of citizens that sustain critical aspects of their social lives. Although less egregious than political tyranny, undermining the normative priority of communities of shared practice and meaning is no minor transgression. For here the very ground of moral and political reasoning among the members of society is at stake. Without the ability to genuinely reason, persuade, and deliberate with one another, we are left with the kind of political discourse one witnesses in America today—highly acrimonious, fractured, distrustful, and often lacking in the very willfulness that is essential to coming together in a shared pursuit of the common good.

Notwithstanding the normative import of ethical community that has been asserted, it should be clear by this point that the present argument is *not* that a single tradition should therefore be promoted for a society such as the United States, which is comprised of hundreds of millions of citizens. Rather, the argument is that this precondition of deliberation is subject to temporal constraints, and that deliberative democrats are thus looking to the whole of such large societies for that which they cannot provide. What has been called true, genuine, or authentic deliberation is more appropriately suited to smaller-scale politics, one aligned more closely with the boundaries of historically rooted communities. To be sure, this is not an argument for the devolution of *all* political decision-making down to the local level, where such communities might be seen as more homogeneous bodies of interlocutors in which agreement is assumed to be easy—such aspirations would, themselves, be utopian. By their very nature, certain areas of policy—national security is only the most obvious—could not realistically be conducted at such a level. However, the argument here *does* maintain the need to reclaim some decision-making authority at a level more proximal to the boundaries of citizens' shared ethical lives, lest all political decisions increasingly be made at a level where what is shared among individuals is, ethically speaking, minimal. Certainly, there are no clear or fixed lines that define the point at which such concrete patterns of living become sufficiently different among citizens that shared meanings and conceptions of the good become problematic. Yet there is undoubtedly an attenuation of shared ways of living as the composition of the body of interlocutors is widened and becomes increasingly diverse. At these broader, more encompassing levels of discourse and political decision-making what must increasingly be relied upon is the more pragmatic, interest-based politics of compromise, bargaining, and trade-offs. However, deliberation, justification, and moral reasoning require shared experience to support both the substance of moral language—a *sensus communis*—among its members and the willful pursuit through discussion of one another's good.

The fundamental problem with the aspiration to universal justification, which is assumed to be possible among hundreds of millions of citizens, is that it looks at the "morality" that is to do the work of persuasion as if it were merely the words that are spoken, which must ultimately be assembled in the right order, as Habermas's thinking tends to suggest, or self-regulated, as Rawls suggests, in order to justify one's position to one's fellow citizens. Having disconnected word (*logos*) and deed (*ergon*), or what interlocutors *say* from who they *are*, realistic, temporal limitations are neglected with regard to justification and agreement. It is the "forgetfulness of being," therefore, that makes the impossible seem possible for deliberative democrats, as it was for the early exponents of the autonomy tradition. Once the good has been divorced from the historical life, or the noumenal is no longer seen as informed by the phenomenal, temporal constraints on persuasion are no longer conceived as significant or problematic. However, Gadamer's thinking reminds us that historical particularity is the concrete condition that at once facilitates and limits all understanding. The concrete vantage point from which we view reality gives us the lens through which we are able to "see" the world, while also ensuring that there is a limited perspective from which we may "see" it. Our prejudices allow us to come together in mutual understanding and persuasion with those who share our historical patterns of living and whose linguistic practices illuminate the world in a similar manner to the way ours does for us.

Coming to understand our moral language as actually *a part of* or *embedded within* the concrete vantage point from which we speak and hear its words and through which we apprehend reality necessarily changes the way we think about moral and political deliberation. One does not "have" a comprehensive moral doctrine, as Rawls often suggests, which is at one's disposal and may be appealed to strictly in part, as if one's moral beliefs could be neatly segmented into constituent elements, like tracts of land or financial accounts. Rather, our moral comprehension of the world is better understood as who we, the deliberators, *already are* in our historical being. In other words, it is not possible to get back *behind* such fundamental values—as if one were talking about an object or thing we might see in plain view before us and about which we might make "reasonable" choices. Whether we are members of thick communities with long memories or deracinated cosmopolitans with few attachments, we *always already exist* as concrete, moral deliberators and decision-makers with particular histories. As Gadamer says in the context of his discussion of *phronesis*, our being ethical decision-makers never ceases but is always ongoing and something we necessarily carry with us—indeed, it *is us*—in every deliberative engagement. Our normative judgments and our ethical reasonableness (*phronesis*) are thus bound up with our comprehension and interpretation of the world, in contrast to a *techne*, which one may from time to time choose to pursue or "take up." The ethical life (*ethos, Sittlichkeit*) is therefore more fundamental to our being in the world than a mere hobby or even a profession, but informs the way our language discloses the world to us and how we engage with it.

This constitutive lens through which we make sense of the world is always engaged in interpretation as we encounter others in dialogue. Although there is never a complete lack of comprehension when we encounter others from different ethical backgrounds, the translation between horizons of understanding is increasingly taxed as the concrete ways of living informing these horizons of understanding come to differ in their enactment or practice. The most compelling forms of mutual persuasion will thus take place within a *sensus communis*, among persons of shared historical experience. The promotion of what gives rise to these shared horizons of understanding, that is, concrete communities that exist over time, must for this reason be a normative priority, lest we are willing to live with attenuated comprehension, reasoning, and ultimately persuasion of our fellow citizens. Certainly, sound deliberation is not the only political value. Indeed, there may be historical moments, as surely there have been in the history of Western civilization, when the latter has been deemed worth sacrificing or compromising in favor of the liberty of the individual citizen. Rawls may be correct, historically speaking, that the fallout of the Wars of Religion in the sixteenth and seventeenth centuries represented one such moment in the West. However, it must likewise be recognized that, as the coherence, integrity, or thickness of community becomes attenuated, for whatever reason, it is precisely the resonance of our mutual appeals that will suffer. And, therefore, there will be occasions, such as the present historical moment, when this normative priority will be worth emphasizing over other political values against which it must inevitably be weighed.

Our Present Historical Moment

Is there not, however, something contradictory about the current argument, which has asserted the normative priority of tradition as the basis for sound deliberation, and yet claims to do so under circumstances in which traditional ethical communities—the very ground of its own arguments' receptivity—are said to have become attenuated? For there would appear to be an epistemological difficulty here, which may simply be stated as follows: For whom, in the end, might the present argument hope to resonate if the preconditions of the latter have in fact been undermined as has been conceded? In short, does the argument of this book find itself in a catch-22, whereby its success in persuading others of its rightness would seem to point to the denial of its premises regarding our inability to persuade one another, whereas the reality of its key premise, an attenuated ethical life and mutually problematic persuasion, would seem to entail the impossibility of its argument's success? Here again, it is important to remember that the situation and the choices with which we are confronted are not an all-or-nothing state of affairs. As one often discovers in real dialogues, the outcomes of such discussions are not defined exclusively by Manichean alternatives of persuading or not persuading, arguments that are found to be wholly compelling or entirely incomprehensible. As is the case with most dialectical encounters, the more likely response to the present argument will be somewhere in between these extreme possibilities, a point along a continuum constituted by these two polarities that, hopefully, lies closer to real persuasiveness than to falling on deaf ears.

At the same time, it must be admitted that there is something paradoxical about our present historical moment (and perhaps any other) with respect to our capacity for sound deliberation. To acknowledge this—while avoiding Manichean conceptualization—one might say it is undeniable that the more it is *necessary* to persuade others of the need to promote concrete, ethical community or tradition, the more *difficult* such persuasion will be, precisely because of the deterioration or attenuation of the latter's status. Likewise, the more such arguments *resonate* and are successful, the less likely there is of such a *need*, since the presence or absence of the preconditions that allow these arguments to resonate are the same ones that point to its need or lack thereof. Still, the fact that there is a paradox here that is problematic, practically speaking, does nothing to impugn the soundness of the argument being made. It merely points to the difficulty that we confront. There is, in other words, no logical inconsistency in asserting or admitting this paradoxical relationship between the need for ethical community and one's receptivity to arguments that promote it. Interlocutors who are the most predisposed to "hear" such arguments may indeed be the least in need of hearing it, and those who are the most in need of being convinced of these arguments may indeed be the least predisposed to being persuaded by them. Certainly, this paradox can make such advocacy for ethical community practically challenging or problematic. But the fact remains.

Still, it might be argued, the difficulty of the present argument's success is even more acute than has been stated in the preceding paragraphs. For persuasiveness has been tied not merely to acculturation within an ethical community but to the *sharing* of a *sensus communis* among interlocutors. Consequently, those who encounter the present argument, in light of the temporal constraints and limitations of participation in an ethical community that lie at the heart of it, are also unlikely to share a particular ethical orientation with the author. To some extent, this must obviously be admitted. The validity and indeed the seriousness of the present difficulty must, once again, simply be acknowledged, and the failure of what has been said to resonate with readers may be attributed, with unavoidable irony, to the conditions that occlude mutual persuasion and understanding while bolstering the normative exigency of shared communities of practice and meaning. However, it is also important to bear in mind Gadamer's qualification of failures to understand one another—the latter is never complete. Some comprehension of the present argument will inevitably persist, even under the most infelicitous of circumstances. Moreover, it might ultimately be contended that *some degree* of failure to comprehend others beyond the bounds of one's concrete ethical community is simply to be expected, precisely in light of the temporal constraints on the sharing of a *sensus communis* that have been argued. Lowering expectations for persuasion under the conditions of modernity, defined as it is by the ethos and reality of individual freedom may, therefore, be an appropriate response to our present historical circumstances.

But even among those who deny the persuasiveness of what has been said, it is also worth considering that real persuasion, which is to say, persuasion as one finds it in actual historical experience, often does not take place upon hearing an argument articulated for the first time and becoming immediately convinced of the rightness of another person's position. Although such apodictic recognition of the rightness of another's argument cannot be ruled out as a possibility, it is worth noting that the nature of actual persuasion is, rather, more often that of a subtle shift or alteration of understanding. Such changes take place in conversation with numerous interlocutors speaking or writing in a discourse that takes place over time, in which assertions are made, reiterated, and often rearticulated in a variety of ways. As a result, the immediate "failure" of any argument intended to persuade may not necessarily be the end of the story. The nature of *logos* is such that reasons and assertions work on us and sometimes convince people of their truth not immediately but over time, after protracted periods in which we "hear" the echoes of words that were spoken or written and reflect on them, as we continue to go about our lives and apply them to diverse concrete circumstances, which they slowly begin to illuminate.[1] Sometimes particular articulations become more meaningful or salient when we "hear" echoes of them in others' different articulations of what is essentially the same or similar idea. In other words, becoming convinced or persuaded by what another is saying is rarely a complete or instantaneous acceptance of arguments as we engage in such dialectical encounters.

As Gadamer describes understanding itself, we are continually revising prior expectations or anticipations of reality, as we encounter new evidence and undergo new experiences. Being shown that we are mistaken, or that our understanding is incomplete, whether through our own novel experiences or through exposure to the experiential insights of others, the "pain" of such encounters with unanticipated experience, which is in conflict with what preceded it, will ultimately develop new insights into reality.[2] It is the historical nature of knowing and our folding new experience into memory that reveals such insights to be—wherever they exist—new revelations regarding what is already known.[3] Such an expansion or growth of a horizon of understanding is typically not something that happens all at once, but takes place slowly over time. Insight is gained or acquired, a mind is "changed," as we say, when the mind that is open encounters experience that defies expectation and is then folded into a new, historically informed comprehension of reality, such that we are prepared for future experience in a gradual process of growth.

Our present historical moment, it is also worth remembering, is not defined by a predisposition to hearing arguments for the normative priority of tradition, a phenomenon with which Gadamer himself was certainly familiar. In this sense, his magnum opus and its recovery or "rehabilitation" of tradition ought therefore to be seen as arguing against the predominant prejudice of our time, the "prejudice against prejudice," which is one of the principal legacies of Enlightenment thinking. It is doubtful, in light of this, that Gadamer anticipated any immediate success or receptivity of his own arguments with respect to this rehabilitation. However, seeing dialogue as taking place historically would seem to entail not a solitary, discrete mind or consciousness that once-and-for-all becomes convinced of others' arguments, but broad contributions to a larger discussion, which is never a single "moment" in time, nor even a series of such moments, but a continuing and developing body of ideas. One's arguments or assertions, in this way, may be seen as successful in moving or carrying forward the existing conversation in a particular direction, rather than completely resolving the questions that are under consideration. The arguments of any true dialogue are thus rarely dispositive or definitively convincing, but always further developed through what is said by the various interlocutors.

Such is the ultimate hope for the argument of this book. It aims modestly to move the present discussion regarding deliberation in democratic politics in a more historical direction. The foregoing limitations, however, would preclude any greater aspirations. To be realistic, which is to say, to think and choose and act in the world not as we wish it were but as we find it, means recognizing its facticity and all the limitations that those conditions entail. The universality of hermeneutic understanding does not afford us with an Archimedean position from which we may demonstrate to others the absolute certainty of our position. However, this does not leave us at a loss, without any means of communication or mutual understanding at our disposal. It simply means that we must adjust or revise our expectations, seeking only what is possible, and convince others where we may. This would appear to be the appropriate manner of approaching this ongoing discussion under existing historical circumstances, which is more prudent than suffering the folly that is attendant, as Gadamer reminds us, to the utopian pursuit of the "infinite intellect."[4]

Notes

1. Or as Wittgenstein says, echoing this rather Platonist formulation, "Light dawns gradually over the whole." Ludwig Wittgenstein, *On Certainty*, ed. G. E. M. Anscombe and G. H. von Wright, trans. Denis Paul and G. E. M. Anscombe (New York: Harper and Row, 1972), 21e.

2. Hans-Georg Gadamer, *Truth and Method*, trans. Joel Weinsheimer and Donald G. Marshall, 2nd rev. ed. (New York: Continuum, 2004), 350.

3. Gadamer explains, "Experience . . . inevitably involves many disappointments of one's expectations and only thus is experience acquired. That experience refers chiefly to painful and disagreeable experiences does not mean that we are being especially pessimistic, but can be seen directly from its nature. Only through negative instances do we acquire new experiences, as Bacon saw. Every experience worthy of the name thwarts an expectation. Thus the historical nature of man essentially implies a fundamental negativity that emerges in relation between experience and

insight. . . . [Insight] always involves an escape from something that had deceived us and held us captive." Ibid.

    4. Leo Strauss and Hans-Georg Gadamer, "Correspondence concerning *Wahrheit und Methode,*" *Independent Journal of Philosophy* 2 (1978): 10.

Bibliography

Adler, Eric. *The Battle of the Classics: How a Nineteenth-Century Debate Can Save the Humanities Today*. New York: Oxford University Press, 2020.

Aristotle. *Nicomachean Ethics*. Translated by David Ross. New York: Oxford University Press, 2009.

———. *Politics*. Translated by Carnes Lord. Chicago: University of Chicago Press, 2013.

Arrow, Kenneth. *Social Choice and Individual Values*. 2nd ed. New York: Wiley, 1963.

Augustine, St. *The Confessions*. Translated by Garry Wills. New York: Penguin, 2008.

Babbitt, Irving. *Democracy and Leadership*. Indianapolis: Liberty Fund, 1979.

———. *Literature and the American College: Essays in Defense of the Humanities*. Washington, DC: National Humanities Institute, 1986.

Bächtiger, André, John S. Dryzek, Jane Mansbridge, and Mark E. Warren, eds. *The Oxford Handbook of Deliberative Democracy*. New York: Oxford University Press, 2018.

Beck, Lewis White. "Kant's Two Conceptions of the Will in Their Political Context." In *Kant and Political Philosophy*, edited by Ronald Beiner and William James Booth. New Haven, CT: Yale University Press, 1993.

Beiner, Ronald. "Do We Need a Philosophical Ethics?" *Philosophical Forum* 20, no. 3 (1989): 230–43.

———. "Gadamer's Philosophy of Dialogue and Its Relation to the Postmodernism of Nietzsche, Heidegger, Derrida, and Strauss." In *Gadamer's Repercussions: Reconsidering Philosophical Hermeneutics*, edited by Bruce Kajewski, 145–57. Berkeley: University of California Press, 2004.

———. *Political Philosophy: What It Is and Why It Matters*. New York: Cambridge University Press, 2014.

Benhabib, Seyla. "In the Shadow of Aristotle and Hegel: Communicative Ethics and Current Controversies in Practical Philosophy." *Philosophical Forum* 21, no. 1 (1989): 1–31.

Berlin, Isaiah. *Four Essays on Liberty*. Oxford: Oxford University Press, 1969.

Bertram, Christopher. "Rousseau on Public Reason." In *Public Reason in Political Philosophy: Classical Sources and Contemporary Commentaries,* edited by Piers Norris Turner and Gerald Glaus, 248–63. New York: Routledge, 2017.

———. "Rousseau's Legacy in Two Conceptions of the General Will: Democratic and Transcendent." *Review of Politics* 74, no. 3 (2012): 403–19.

Bessette, Joseph M. "Deliberative Democracy: The Majority Principle in Republican Government." In *How Democratic Is the Constitution?,* edited by Robert A. Goldwin and William A. Schambra, 102–16. Washington, DC: American Enterprise Institute, 1980.

———. *The Mild Voice of Reason: Deliberative Democracy and American National Government.* Chicago: University of Chicago Press, 1994.

Bohman, James, and Henry S. Richardson. "Liberalism, Deliberative Democracy, and 'Reasons That All Can Accept.'" *Journal of Political Philosophy* 17, no. 3 (2009): 253–74.

Burke, Edmund. *Reflections on the Revolution in France.* Indianapolis: Hackett, 1987.

Cassirer, Ernst. *The Question of Jean-Jacques Rousseau.* New York: Columbia University Press, 1954.

———. *Rousseau, Kant, Goethe: Two Essays.* Translated by James Gutmann, Paul Oskar Kristeller, and John Herman Randall, Jr. Princeton, NJ: Princeton University Press, 1947.

Cohen, Joshua. "Deliberation and Democratic Legitimacy." In *The Good Polity: Normative Analysis of the State,* edited by Alan Hamlin and Philip Pettit, 17–34. Oxford: Blackwell, 1989.

———. *Philosophy, Politics, Democracy.* Cambridge, MA: Harvard University Press, 2009.

———. "Procedure and Substance in Deliberative Democracy." In *Deliberative Democracy: Essays on Reason and Politics,* edited by James Bohman and William Rehg, 407–37. Cambridge, MA: MIT Press, 1997.

Cole, G. D. H. Introduction to *The Social Contract and Discourses by Jean-Jacques Rousseau.* Translated with an Introduction by G. D. H. Cole, 2–19. Toronto: J.M. Dent and Sons, 1923.

Dahl, Robert. *Democracy and Its Critics.* New Haven, CT: Yale University Press, 1989.

d'Entreves, M. Passerin. "Aristotle or Burke? Some Comments on H. Schnaedelbach's 'What Is Neo-Aristotelianism?'" *Praxis International* 7, nos. 3–4 (1987): 238–45.

Di Cesare, Donatella. *Gadamer: A Philosophical Portrait.* Translated by Niall Keane. Bloomington: Indiana University Press, 2013.

Dickey, Lawrence, and H. B. Nisbet. "General Introduction." In *G. W. F. Hegel: Political Writings,* edited by Lawrence Dickey and H. B. Nisbet, vii–xli. New York: Cambridge University Press, 1999.

Dostal, Robert J. "The Experience of Truth for Gadamer and Heidegger: Taking Time and Sudden Lightning." In *Hermeneutics and Truth,* edited by Brice R. Wachterhauser, 47–67. Evanston, IL: Northwestern University Press, 1994.

———. "Gadamer, Kant, and the Enlightenment." *Research in Phenomenology* 46, no. 3 (2016): 337–48.

Douglass, Robin. *Rousseau and Hobbes: Nature, Free Will, and the Passions*. Oxford: University of Oxford Press, 2015.

Dryzek, John. *Deliberative Democracy and Beyond: Liberals, Critics, Contestations*. New York: Oxford University Press, 2009.

———. *Discursive Democracy: Politics, Policy, and Political Science*. New York: Cambridge University Press, 1990.

———. "The Forum, the System, and the Polity: Three Varieties of Democratic Theory." *Political Theory* 45, no. 5 (2017): 610–36.

Estlund, David M. "Who's Afraid of Deliberative Democracy? On the Strategic/Deliberative Dichotomy in Recent Constitutional Jurisprudence." *Texas Law Review* 71 (June 1993): 1437–77.

Finlayson, James Gordon. "Habermas' Discourse Ethics and Hegel's Critique of Kant's Moral Theory." In *Habermas: A Critical Reader*, edited by Peter Dews, 29–52. Oxford: Blackwell, 1999.

———. "Modernity and Morality in Habermas' Discourse Ethics." *Inquiry* 43, no. 3 (2000): 319–40.

Fishkin, James M., and Jane Mansbridge, eds. "The Prospects and Limits of Deliberative Democracy." Special issue, *Daedalus* 146, no. 3 (2017).

Fortin, Ernest. "Gadamer on Strauss: An Interview." *Interpretation* 12 no. 1 (1984): 1–13.

Foster, Matthew. *Gadamer and Practical Philosophy: The Hermeneutics of Moral Confidence*. Atlanta: Scholars Press, 1991.

Gadamer, Hans-Georg. "Aristotle and Imperative Ethics." In Gadamer, *Hermeneutics, Religion, and Ethics*, 142–61.

———. "Citizens of Two Worlds." In Gadamer, *Hans-Georg Gadamer on Education, Poetry, and History*, edited by Dieter Misgeld and Graeme Nicholson, 209–20. Albany: State University of New York Press, 1992.

———. *Dialogue and Dialectic: Eight Hermeneutical Studies on Plato*. Translated by P. Christopher Smith. New Haven, CT: Yale University Press, 1980.

———. "Dialectic and Sophism in Plato's Seventh Letter." In Gadamer, *Dialogue and Dialectic*, 93–123.

———. "The Ethics of Value and Practical Philosophy." In Gadamer, *Hermeneutics, Religion, and Ethics*, 103–18.

———. "Friendship and Self-Knowledge: Reflections on the Role of Friendship in Greek Ethics." In Gadamer, *Hermeneutics, Religion and Ethics*, 128–41.

———. *The Gadamer Reader: A Bouquet of the Later Writings*. Edited and translated by Richard E. Palmer. Evanston, IL: Northwestern University Press, 2007.

———. "Greek Philosophy and Modern Thinking." In *The Gadamer Reader*, 266–73.

———. "Hermeneutics as a Theoretical and Practical Task." In *The Gadamer Reader*, 246–65.

———. "Hermeneutics as Practical Philosophy." In *The Gadamer Reader*, 227–45.

———. *Hermeneutics, Religion, and Ethics.* Translated by Joel Weinsheimer. New Haven, CT: Yale University Press, 1999.

———. *The Idea of the Good in Platonic-Aristotelian Philosophy.* Translated by P. Christopher Smith. New Haven, CT: Yale University Press, 1986.

———. "Logos and Ergon in Plato's Lysis." In Gadamer, *Dialogue and Dialectic*, 1–20.

———. "On the Possibility of a Philosophical Ethics." In Gadamer, *The Gadamer Reader*, 274–92.

———. *Philosophical Hermeneutics.* Edited and translated by David E. Linge. Berkeley: University of California Press, 2008.

———. *Plato's Dialectical Ethics: Phenomenological Interpretations Relating to the Philebus.* Translated by Robert M. Wallace. New Haven, CT: Yale University Press, 2009.

———. *Reason in the Age of Science.* Translated by Frederick G. Lawrence. Cambridge, MA: MIT Press, 1982.

———. *The Relevance of the Beautiful and Other Essays.* Translated by N. Walker and edited by R. Bernasconi. Cambridge: Cambridge University Press, 1986.

———. *Truth and Method.* Translated by Joel Weinsheimer and Donald G. Marshall. 2nd rev. ed. New York: Continuum, 2004.

Galston, William. *Kant and the Problem of History.* Chicago: University of Chicago Press, 1975.

Gordon, Jill. "John Stuart Mill and the Marketplace of Ideas." *Social Theory and Practice* 23, no. 2 (1997): 235–49.

Gourevitch, Victor. "Recent Work on Rousseau." *Political Theory* 26, no. 4 (1998): 536–56.

Grondin, Jean. *Hans-Georg Gadamer: A Biography.* New Haven, CT: Yale University Press, 2003.

———. "The Metaphysical Dimension of Hermeneutics." In *Hermeneutics and Phenomenology: Figures and Themes*, edited by Saulius Geniusas and Paul Fairfield, 125–37. New York: Bloomsbury Academic, 2018.

Günther, Klaus. *The Sense of Appropriateness: Application Discourses in Morality and Law.* Translated by John Ferrell. Albany: State University of New York Press, 1993.

Guthrie, W. K. C. *The Sophists.* New York: Cambridge University Press, 1971.

Gutmann, Amy, and Dennis Thompson. *Democracy and Disagreement.* Cambridge, MA: Harvard University Press, 1996.

———. "Moral Conflict and Political Consensus." *Ethics* 101, no. 1 (1990): 64–88.

———. *Why Deliberative Democracy?* Princeton, NJ: Princeton University Press, 2004.

Habermas, Jürgen. *Between Facts and Norms: Contributions to a Discourse Theory of Law and Democracy.* Translated by William Rehg. Cambridge, MA: MIT Press, 1996.

———. *Communication and the Evolution of Society.* Translated by Thomas McCarthy. Boston: Beacon, 1979.

———. "Discourse Ethics." In *Moral Consciousness and Communicative Action*, 43–115.

———. *Habermas and the Unfinished Project of Modernity.* Edited by Maurizio Passerin d'Entrèves and Seyla Benhabib. Cambridge, MA: MIT Press, 1997.

———. *Justification and Application: Remarks on Discourse Ethics.* Translated by Ciaran Cronin. Cambridge, MA: MIT Press, 1993.

———. "Lawrence Kohlberg and Neo-Aristotelianism." In *Justification and Application*, 113–32.

———. *Moral Consciousness and Communicative Action.* Translated by Christian Lenhardt and Shierry Weber Nicholsen. Cambridge, MA: MIT Press, 1990.

———. "On the Cognitive Content of Morality." *Proceedings of the Aristotelian Society* 96 (1996): 335–58.

———. *On the Pragmatics of Social Interaction.* Translated by Barbara Fultner. Cambridge, MA: MIT Press, 2001.

———. *The Philosophical Discourse of Modernity.* Translated by Frederick Lawrence. Cambridge, MA: MIT Press, 1987.

———. *The Postnational Constellation: Political Essays.* Translated and edited by Max Pensky. Cambridge, MA: MIT Press, 2001.

———. "Reconciliation through the Public Use of Reason: Remarks on John Rawls's Political Liberalism." *Journal of Philosophy* 92, no. 3 (1995): 109–31.

———. *Theory of Communicative Action.* 2 vols. Boston: Beacon, 1984 and 1987.

———. "Toward a Theory of Communicative Competence." *Inquiry* 13, nos. 1–4 (1970): 360–75.

Hendel, Charles. *Jean-Jacques Rousseau: Moralist.* New York: Bobbs-Merrill, 1962.

Hinman, Lawrence. "Quid Facti or Quid Juris? The Fundamental Ambiguity of Gadamer's Understanding of Hermeneutics." *Philosophy and Phenomenological Research* 40, no. 4 (1980): 512–35.

Hittinger, Russell. "John Rawls, *Political Liberalism.*" *Review of Metaphysics* 47, no. 3 (1994): 585–602.

Hobbes, Thomas. *Leviathan.* Edited by Richard E. Flathman and David Johnston. New York: Norton, 1997.

Holston, Ryan. "Anti-Rationalism, Relativism, and the Metaphysical Tradition: Situating Gadamer's Philosophical Hermeneutics." In *Critics of Enlightenment Rationalism*, edited by Gene Callahan and Kenneth B. McIntyre, 193–209. Cham, Switzerland: Palgrave Macmillan, 2020.

———. "Deliberation in Context: Reexamining the Confrontation between the Discourse Ethics and Neo-Aristotelianism." *Telos* 181 (2017): 151–75.

———. "The Poverty of Antihistoricism: Strauss and Gadamer in Dialogue." *Modern Age* 58, no. 2 (2016): 41–53.

———. "Two Concepts of Prejudice." *History of Political Thought* 35, no. 1 (2014): 174–203.

James, David. "Rousseau on Needs, Language, and Pity: The Limits of 'Public Reason.'" *European Journal of Political Theory* 10, no. 3 (2011): 372–93.

Kant, Immanuel. *Critique of Practical Reason.* Translated by Werner S. Pluhar. Indianapolis: Hackett, 2002.

———. *The Critique of Pure Reason*. Translated by Werner S. Pluhar. Indianapolis: Hackett, 1996.

———. *Grounding for the Metaphysics of Morals*. Translated by James W. Ellington. Indianapolis: Hackett, 1993.

———. *Metaphysics of Morals*. Translated by James W. Ellington. Indianapolis: Hackett, 1983.

———. *Perpetual Peace and Other Essays*. Translated by Ted Humphrey. Indianapolis: Hackett, 1982.

Kelly, George Armstrong. *Idealism, Politics, and History: Sources of Hegelian Thought*. New York: Cambridge University Press, 1969.

———. "Rousseau, Kant, and History." *Journal of the History of Ideas* 29, no. 3 (1968): 347–64.

Kuhn, Thomas. *The Structure of Scientific Revolutions*. 3rd ed. Chicago: University of Chicago Press, 1996.

Larmore, Charles. *Patterns of Moral Complexity*. Cambridge: Cambridge University Press, 1987.

Lawrence, Frederick G. "Gadamer, the Hermeneutic Revolution, and Theology." In *The Cambridge Companion to Gadamer*, edited by Robert J. Dostal, 167–200. Cambridge: Cambridge University Press, 2006.

———. "Hans-Georg Gadamer: Philosopher of Practical Wisdom." *Theoforum* 40, no. 3 (2009): 257–90.

Locke, John. *Two Treatises of Government*. Edited by Lee Ward. Indianapolis: Hackett, 2016.

MacIntyre, Alasdair. *After Virtue*. Notre Dame, IN: University of Notre Dame Press, 1981.

———. "Contexts of Interpretation: Reflections on Hans-Georg Gadamer's *Truth and Method*." *Boston University Journal* 24, no. 1 (1976): 41–46.

———. "Does Applied Ethics Rest on a Mistake?" *Monist* 67, no. 4 (1984): 498–513.

———. "A Partial Response to My Critics." In *After MacIntyre: Critical Perspectives on the Work of Alasdair MacIntyre*, edited by John Horton and Susan Mendus, 283–304. Cambridge: Polity, 1994.

———. *Three Rival Versions of Moral Enquiry*. Notre Dame, IN: University of Notre Dame Press, 1994.

———. *Whose Justice? Which Rationality?* Notre Dame, IN: University of Notre Dame Press, 1988.

MacLean, Lee. *The Free Animal: Rousseau on Free Will and Human Nature*. Toronto: University of Toronto Press, 2013.

Markel, Patchen. "Contesting Consensus: Rereading Habermas on the Public Sphere." *Constellations* 3, no. 3 (1997): 377–400.

Masters, Roger. *The Political Philosophy of Rousseau*. Princeton, NJ: Princeton University Press, 2016.

McCarthy, Thomas. *The Critical Theory of Jürgen Habermas*. Cambridge, MA: MIT Press, 1985.

————. "Kantian Constructivism and Reconstructivism: Rawls and Habermas in Dialogue." *Ethics* 105, no. 1 (1994): 44–63.

Meier, Heinrich. *On the Happiness of the Philosophic Life: Reflections on Rousseau's Reveries in Two Books.* Chicago: University of Chicago Press, 2017.

Melzer, Arthur. *The Natural Goodness of Man: On the System of Rousseau's Thought.* Chicago: University of Chicago Press, 2016.

Müller, Jan-Werner. "Rawls, Historian: Remarks on Political Liberalism's 'Historicism.'" *Revue internationale de philosophie* 3, no. 237 (2006): 327–39.

Neal, Patrick. "In the Shadow of the General Will: Rawls, Kant and Rousseau on the Problem of Political Right." *Review of Politics* 49, no. 3 (1987): 389–409.

O'Hagan, Timothy. "Taking Rousseau Seriously." *History of Political Thought* 25, no. 1 (2004): 73–85.

O'Neill, Onora. "Kantian Ethics." In *A Companion to Ethics*, edited by Peter Singer, 179–85. Oxford: Blackwell, 2003.

Ormiston, Gayle L., and Alan D. Schrift, eds. *The Hermeneutic Tradition: From Ast to Ricoeur.* Albany: State University of New York Press, 1990.

Plato. *Gorgias.* Translated by Walter Hamilton and Chris Emlyn-Jones. London: Penguin, 2004.

————. *Meno.* Translated by G. M. A. Grube. Indianapolis: Hackett, 1985.

————. *Phaedo.* Translated by David Gallop. New York: Oxford University Press, 2009.

————. *Philebus.* Translated by Dorothea Frede. Indianapolis: Hackett, 1993.

————. *Protagoras.* Translated by Stanley Lombardo and Karen Bell. Indianapolis: Hackett, 1992.

————. *The Republic.* Translated by Desmond Lee. New York: Penguin, 2007.

————. *Timaeus and Critias.* Translated by Desmond Lee. London: Penguin, 2008.

Poblet, Marta, Pompeu Casanovas, and Víctor Rodríguez-Doncel. *Deliberative and Epistemic Approaches to Democracy.* Cham, Switzerland: Palgrave Macmillan, 2020.

Rawls, John. "The Idea of an Overlapping Consensus." *Oxford Journal of Legal Studies* 7, no. 1 (1987): 1–25.

————. "Justice as Fairness: Political Not Metaphysical." *Philosophy and Public Affairs* 14, no. 3 (1985): 223–51.

————. *The Law of Peoples.* Cambridge, MA: Harvard University Press, 1999.

————. *Lectures on the History of Political Philosophy.* Edited by Samuel Freeman. Cambridge, MA: Harvard University Press, 2007.

————. *Political Liberalism.* New York: Columbia University Press, 1993.

————. *A Theory of Justice.* Cambridge, MA: Harvard University Press, 2009.

Riker, William. *Liberalism against Populism: A Confrontation between the Theory of Democracy and the Theory of Social Choice.* San Francisco: Freeman, 1982.

Rorty, Richard. *Philosophy and the Mirror of Nature.* Princeton, NJ: Princeton University Press, 1979.

Rousseau, Jean-Jacques. *Discourse on the Origin of Inequality*. Translated by Donald A. Cress. Introduced by James Miller. Indianapolis: Hackett, 1992.

———. *Emile, or On Education*. Translated by Barbara Foxley. Waiheke Island, NZ: Floating Press, 2009.

———. *Reveries of the Solitary Walker*. London: Penguin, 1980.

———. *Rousseau's Political Writings*. Translated by Julia Conaway Bondanella. Edited by Alan Ritter. New York: Norton, 1988.

Ryn, Claes G. *A Common Human Ground: Universality and Particularity in a Multicultural World*. Columbia: University of Missouri Press, 2003.

———. *Democracy and the Ethical Life: A Philosophy of Politics and Community*. 2nd ed. Baton Rouge: Louisiana State University Press, 2001.

———. "Philosophical Reason: Historical, Systematic, and Humble." *Humanitas* 6, no. 2 (1993): 81–90.

———. "The Politics of Transcendence: The Pretentious Passivity of Platonic Idealism." *Humanitas* 12, no. 2 (1999): 4–26.

———. "Universality and History." *Humanitas* 6, no. 1 (1992): 10–39.

Sandel, Michael. *Liberalism and the Limits of Justice*. 2nd ed. Cambridge: Cambridge University Press, 1998.

Shell, Susan. *The Embodiment of Reason: Kant on Spirit, Generation, and Community*. Chicago: University of Chicago Press, 1996.

———. *The Rights of Reason: A Study of Kant's Philosophy and Politics*. Buffalo: University of Toronto Press, 1980.

Siep, Ludwig. "Rousseau's Normative Idea of Nature." *Redescriptions: Political Thought, Conceptual History and Feminist Theory* 4, no. 1 (2000): 53–72. http://doi.org/10.7227/R.4.1.5.

Smith, P. Christopher. "The Ethical Dimensions of Gadamer's Hermeneutical Theory." *Research in Phenomenology* 18 (1988): 75–91.

———. *Hermeneutics and Human Finitude: Toward a Theory of Ethical Understanding*. New York: Fordham University Press, 1991.

———. "The I-Thou Encounter (*Begegnung*) in Gadamer's Reception of Heidegger." In *The Philosophy of Hans-Georg Gadamer*, edited by Lewis Hahn, 509–25. Chicago: Open Court, 1997.

———. "Not Doctrine but 'Placing in Question': The 'Thrasymachus' (Rep. I) as an *Erotesis* of Commercialization." In *Who Speaks for Plato? Studies in Platonic Anonymity*, edited by Gerald A. Press, 113–26. Lanham, MD: Rowman and Littlefield, 2000.

———. "*Phronesis*, the Individual, and the Community: Divergent Appropriations of Aristotle's Ethical Discernment in Heidegger's and Gadamer's Hermeneutics." In *Gadamer verstehen = Understanding Gadamer*, edited by Mirko Wischke and Michael Hofer, 169–85. Darmstadt: Wissenschaftliche Buchgesellschaft, 2003.

———. "Plato as Impulse and Obstacle in Gadamer's Development of a Hermeneutical Theory." In *Gadamer and Hermeneutics: Science, Culture, Literature*, edited by Hugh Silverman, 23–41. New York: Routledge, 1991.

———. "Toward a Discursive Logic: Gadamer and Toulmin on Inquiry and Argument." In *The Specter of Relativism: Truth, Dialogue, and "Phronesis" in Philosophical Argument*, edited by Lawrence K. Schmidt, 159–77. Evanston, IL: Northwestern University Press, 1995.

———. "The Uses of Aristotle in Gadamer's Recovery of Consultative Reasoning: *Sunesis, Sungnome, Epieikeia*, and *Sumbouleuesthai*." *Chicago-Kent Law Review* 76 (2000): 731–50.

Strauss, Leo. *What Is Political Philosophy?* Chicago: University of Chicago Press, 1959.

Strauss, Leo, and Hans-Georg Gadamer. "Correspondence concerning *Wahrheit und Methode*." *Independent Journal of Philosophy* 2 (1978): 5–12.

Sunstein, Cass. "Free Speech Now." *University of Chicago Law Review* 59, no. 1 (1992): 255–316.

———. *The Partial Constitution*. Cambridge, MA: Harvard University Press, 1993.

Taylor, Charles. "The Motivation behind a Procedural Ethics." In *Kant and Political Philosophy*, edited by Ronald Beiner and William James Booth, 337–59. New Haven, CT: Yale University Press, 1993.

———. *Sources of the Self: The Making of the Modern Identity*. Cambridge, MA: Harvard University Press, 1989.

Thompson, Dennis. "Deliberative Democratic Theory and Empirical Political Science." *Annual Review of Political Science* 11 (2008): 497–520.

Vattimo, Gianni. *The End of Modernity: Nihilism and Hermeneutics in Postmodern Culture*. Baltimore: Johns Hopkins University Press, 1988.

Velkley, Richard. *Freedom and the End of Reason: On the Moral Foundation of Kant's Critical Philosophy*. Chicago: University of Chicago Press, 1989.

Wachterhauser, Brice R. *Beyond Being: Gadamer's Post-Platonic Hermeneutical Ontology*. Chicago: Northwestern University Press, 1999.

———. "Gadamer's Realism: The 'Belongingness' of Word and Reality." In *Hermeneutics and Truth*, edited by Brice R. Wachterhauser, 148–71. Evanston, IL: Northwestern University Press, 1994.

———. "Getting It Right: Relativism, Realism, and Truth." In *The Cambridge Companion to Gadamer*, edited by Robert J. Dostal, 52–78. Cambridge: Cambridge University Press, 2002.

Walhof, Darren. *The Democratic Theory of Hans-Georg Gadamer*. Cham, Switzerland: Palgrave Macmillan, 2017.

Warner, John M., and James R. Zink. "Therapeutic Politics: Rawls' Respect for Rousseau." *Review of Politics* 78 no. 1 (2016): 117–40.

White, Stephen K. "Reason and Authority in Habermas: A Critique of the Critics." *American Political Science Review* 74, no. 4 (1980): 1007–17.

Wiggins, David. *Needs, Values, Truth*. Oxford: Oxford University Press, 1987.

Williams, Bernard. *Ethics and the Limits of Philosophy*. Cambridge, MA: Harvard University Press, 1985.

Williams, David Lay. *Rousseau's Platonic Enlightenment*. University Park: Pennsylvania State University Press, 2007.

Wilson, James Lindley. "Deliberation, Democracy, and the Rule of Reason in Aristotle's *Politics*." *American Political Science Review* 105, no. 2 (2011): 259–74.

Wittgenstein, Ludwig. *On Certainty*. Edited by G. E. M. Anscombe and G. H. von Wright. Translated by Denis Paul and G. E. M. Anscombe. New York: Harper and Row, 1972.

———. *Philosophical Investigations*. Translated by G. E. M. Anscombe. Upper Saddle River, NJ: Blackwell, 1958.

Index

abstract community, 155–63
abstract individualism, 150–55
abstraction, problem of, 4–5, 27–33,
    40n45, 45, 47–48, 59n22, 60n24,
    81–82, 84, 94n73, 95n86, 105–6,
    117n38, 122, 132, 143n46,
    144n70, 175n28, 177n38
anamnesis (recollection), 9, 108–11,
    118n51, 130
anti-historical, 5, 18, 26, 31, 33,
    40n45, 41n53, 44, 53–55, 60n34,
    61n41, 80, 162
Apel, Karl-Otto, 66
arête (virtue), 108, 124, 135, 137
Aristotelian, 8, 11, 54, 106–7, 135,
    138, 140n1, 164, 167, 170,
    179n75
Aristotle, 4, 11, 62n54, 118n51, 137,
    145n72, 145n81, 147n99
    critiquing Plato, 105–6, 116n36–44,
    117n39–40
    deliberation. See *bouleuesthai*
    ethical principles, 11, 104–5
    eudaimonia (flourishing), 116n31,
    116n36
    Gadamer drawing heavily from,
    103–8, 118n46
    Heidegger's reading of, 117n45, 140n1
    and imperative ethics, 11, 122–29,
    140n2, 141n7–8, 142n34

Nicomachean Ethics, 1, 108, 117n45,
    125–26, 129, 140n1
phronesis, 107–11, 116n38, 118n46,
    142n34
Politics, 1, 12n4
    on problem of natural law, 103–6,
    116n37
    teleology, 119n55
autonomy, 5–6, 20, 27–28, 41n58, 46,
    50–52, 54, 60n29, 61n34, 64,
    83, 85, 93, 123, 143n34, 163,
    170
    beyond, 181–84
    individual, 2, 18, 23, 40n43, 44–45,
    83, 150, 157, 170
autonomy tradition, 6, 10–12, 18,
    26, 32–35, 35n1, 40n42, 43–44,
    47–48, 57, 58n5, 58n7, 63–65,
    77–79, 83, 91n57, 97, 150, 156,
    160–62, 176n37
    deliberation and, 72–77
    negative liberty in, 71, 92n65, 93n65

Babbitt, Irving, 38n34, 118n53
Beck, Lewis White, 50–51
Beiner, Ronald, 124–25, 132, 142n25,
    142n29, 142n32, 149, 176n37
being (*Dasein*), 101
Bertram, Christopher, 73, 92n58–62,
    94n75

201

www.ingramcontent.com/pod-product-compliance
Lightning Source LLC
Chambersburg PA
CBHW020351270326
41926CB00007B/390